E.J. Rudsdale's
Journals of
WARTIME COLCHESTER

E.J. Rudsdale's
Journals of
WARTIME COLCHESTER

Edited by CATHERINE PEARSON

First published 2010

The History Press
The Mill, Brimscombe Port
Stroud, Gloucestershire, GL5 2QG
www.thehistorypress.co.uk

British Library Cataloguing in Publication Data.
A catalogue record for this book is available from the British Library.

ISBN 978 0 7524 5821 2

Typesetting and origination by The History Press
Printed in Great Britain
Manufacturing managed by Jellyfish Print Solutions Ltd

Contents

Acknowledgements

Many people have contributed to this research project and I am greatly indebted to Ronald Bond, retired Archivist from Essex Record Office, who first introduced me to Rudsdale's journals. I have also been most fortunate in the encouragement I have received from Eric Rudsdale's family and my sincere thanks go to Catherine Goldfinch, Professor Roger Plumb and Ann Plumb for giving their permission for this publication, as well as to Essex Record Office as the holder of the Rudsdale archive.

The majority of my research was undertaken at the Colchester branch of Essex Record Office and I owe a debt of gratitude to Jane Bass, Jane Bedford and Paul Coverley who gave me so much of their time and expertise. Subsequently, the records were transferred to Essex Record Office in Chelmsford and I have benefited from the help of Jennifer Butler, Sarah Dickie, Stephen Dixon, Deborah Peers and the ERO Reprographics Team, as well as Caroline Adlem at Essex County Council and Mark Lees.

In September 2009, I launched a blog posting extracts from Rudsdale's wartime journals (www.wwar2homefront.blogspot.com) and I am most grateful to followers of the blog for their support and comments. This experience has led to the publication of this book and my sincere thanks go to Nicola Guy, David Lewis, Beth Amphlett and the design team at The History Press for seeing the potential in Rudsdale's journals and for the valuable help and advice they have given me in the preparation of this publication. It is particularly fitting that Rudsdale's journals are being published in the year that marks the centenary of his birth and when the events of the Second World War are being remembered seventy years after they occurred.

My special thanks go to Douglas Carter for sharing his memories of E.J. Rudsdale with me and to Olive Laudrum for her recollections of wartime Colchester. The late Joanna Down also kindly shared her memories with me. I am further grateful to Andrew Derrick, Gavin Freeguard, Roger Kennell, Bill Lamin, Tom Parkes, Andrew Phillips, Karen Taylor Burge and Dr Chris Thornton for sharing their knowledge with me. I have also received invaluable assistance from Mei Boatman, Theresa Calver, Ciara Canning and Tom Hodgson of Colchester Museums, Robert Bell of Wisbech and Fenland Museum, Becky Wash of Essex Police Museum and Daragh Kenny of the National Gallery Picture Library. Above all, my heartfelt thanks go to my family for their constant support and encouragement, without whom this book would not have been possible.

Finally, I am greatly indebted to the Trustees of Essex Heritage Trust and The Hervey Benham Charitable Trust for their support for this research project and their awards of grants which enabled the inclusion of the archive images in this book.

Introduction

The journals kept by E.J. Rudsdale provide a remarkable insight into life on the Home Front during the Second World War. Rudsdale lived in Colchester, Essex, which, owing to its proximity to the East Coast, was threatened by both invasion and regular bombing raids. Rudsdale's account explores the impact of these wartime events on the people of Colchester and gives a vivid portrayal of his experiences as a superintendent of the air-raid shelter at Colchester Castle and later as an observer for the Royal Observer Corps during the VI flying-bomb attacks. As a curator at Colchester Castle Museum, Rudsdale chronicled the effects of the war on museum work and archaeology. He was later seconded to the Essex War Agricultural Committee and recorded the impact of state intervention on farming in Essex. Rudsdale's journals, therefore, provide a broad perspective on life in wartime Britain and highlight the changes in society that were provoked by the war. *[See Images 1, 2 and 3]*

Eric John Rudsdale was born in Colchester on 14 February 1910 to schoolteacher parents, John and Agnes Rudsdale (née Webb). His father was from Whitby, North Yorkshire, where the family had owned a coach-building business and this inspired Rudsdale's love of horses and horse-drawn transport. His mother's family originated from North Wales and Rudsdale maintained a close allegiance to his Welsh heritage. His father was from Whitby, North Yorkshire, where the family had owned a coach-building business and this inspired Rudsdale's love of horses and horse-drawn transport. *[See Images 4 and 5]*

Rudsdale gained a place at Colchester Royal Grammar School and with the encouragement of his schoolmaster, Richard Poskitt, developed a great interest in the history of Colchester and its Roman archaeology. Rudsdale regularly visited Colchester Castle Museum, assisting the then curator, A.G. Wright, and shortly after leaving school in 1928 he was appointed as the Castle Museum's first assistant to the curator and renowned archaeologist, M.R. Hull, who had succeeded Wright in 1926.

The inter-war years were a time of great expansion for the museum service, with the opening of Hollytrees Museum as a museum of later antiquities in 1929 and the appointment of H.W. Poulter as curator of this branch museum. The re-roofing of Colchester Castle in 1935 created an enlarged Castle Museum and the collections benefited from a series of important archaeological excavations conducted in this period. Rudsdale himself began a collecting initiative to preserve the traditional agricultural heritage of Essex, which was under threat from changes to farming methods. This led to an invitation to install an annual museum exhibition depicting farming in the past at the Essex Agricultural Show from 1932 to 1939. As a member of the newly formed Colchester Civic Society, Rudsdale also campaigned to protect Colchester's historic buildings and took a particular interest in the conservation of Bourne Mill, a sixteenth-century fishing lodge where he stabled his horse and acted as custodian for the National Trust. *[See Images 6, 7 and 8]*

Rudsdale had kept a diary from the age of ten, which evolved into the 'Colchester Journal' as his interest in history and archaeology grew. He was influenced by the diaries of William Wire, who had recorded archaeological finds and daily life in Colchester in the nineteenth century. Rudsdale sought to emulate this record for the twentieth century, as he declared on 1 January 1929:

> It is my ambition to become a diarist and I think that a successful journal should contain the domestic and social interest of Pepys, the travellings of Evelyn, and in my case the careful observations of buildings and drains of William Wire. That then is my aim in this and future volumes. If I succeed or not, it will at least be my best. I must, of course, crave pardon for suggesting that they might be of interest but I think perhaps one day someone may be interested in the social life of the 20th century.

The outbreak of the Second World War in September 1939 provided the opportunity to capture an era of living history and marked Rudsdale's most prolific period of journal keeping.

Rudsdale's writing is characterised by his wry observations of wartime officialdom and his nonconformity with the prevailing views of the time. He was a supporter of pacifism and his journals shed light on the diversity of views that existed. His reluctance to participate in the war also stemmed from his poor physical health – the result of a serious illness in childhood – which led him to doubt his fitness for armed service. However, even as a civilian, Rudsdale was unable to avoid the consequences of the conflict because Colchester was a garrison town and a military target. His journals, therefore, reveal periods of intense fear, anxiety and personal tragedy but throughout it all his sense of humour is never diminished for long.

The experience of war, therefore, enabled Rudsdale to fulfil his ambition to become a journalist. From his vantage point at the Castle Museum he had the perfect opportunity to observe the changes inflicted on his home town by the conflict. In his journals he brings to life a vivid array of characters and conveys the turmoil of events, thus transmitting a powerful sense of what it was like to live on the Home Front.

My aim in editing these journals has been to retain Rudsdale's individual style of interweaving events, observations of contemporary life and his own opinions within the broader context of the war. I hope that by doing so, I have done justice to Rudsdale's record and presented it in a way that he would have chosen himself. The short extracts he edited for inclusion in Hervey Benham's book *Essex at War* (1945) have proved a valuable guide to his own intentions, although the extracts selected in this volume remain entirely my own responsibility. For the sake of consistency some corrections to grammar, spelling and punctuation have been made and additions to the text, included for the purposes of clarity, are given in square brackets. Short commentaries providing a context for the journal entries are given in italics.

Catherine Pearson, 2010

Chapter 1

❧ 1939 ❧

E.J. Rudsdale's wartime journals begin on 3 September 1939, the day that war was declared. Immediately prior to the outbreak of war, evacuees from London had begun arriving at Colchester's St Botolph's Station from 1 September and were despatched to villages in the surrounding area. At Colchester Castle Museum, the curators were packing away the museum's prized exhibits to ensure their safety in the event of bomb damage. Colchester Castle's Roman Vaults, which form the foundations of the Norman castle, had been requisitioned for use as an air-raid shelter [See Image 9]. The castle was believed to be one of the safest buildings in Colchester because its walls measured up to 30ft in depth. By 3 September people waited in anxious anticipation for the declaration of war and E.J. Rudsdale was poised to record these momentous events in his 'Colchester Journal'.

September 3 Sunday

Woke up at 7. Beautiful summer day, hot and sunny. Heard on radio across the way that an important announcement would be made at 10am. Sounded very ominous. Went to feed Bob [Rudsdale's horse] and decided to go down to the Fire Station to see if I could do anything in the AFS, thinking that if anything is going to happen in Colchester, I might as well be in a front seat to see it. On the way down I saw placards 'Italian Peace Hopes'.

The Fire Brigade now take themselves very seriously and the general appearance of the station is that of a besieged fortress. Great masses of sandbags block every window and door, so that you have to crawl through tunnels to get into the watch-room. I offered my services but found to my amazement that there are now no volunteers – all AFS men are full-time and are paid! Apart from the fact that I was gently told that I was not suitable physically, this of course put a very different view on the whole matter, as I have no intention of leaving the Museum. While I was there the 10 o'clock announcement came through, which was to the effect that an ultimatum had been delivered to Germany which expires at 11 o'clock, and that the Prime Minister would speak at 11.15. I felt I could not hear this, so I went off on my bike but as I came along Mile End Road, I could hear radio booming from many houses and could not but stop. A man saw me from his window and called out 'It's come matey'.

I went back to town. Lots of cars on the By-Pass, mostly people rushing back from the coast, with bundles of bedding tied all round. Very few going the other way but some cyclists were.

Went down to Bourne Mill and rowed out in the boat, trying to think. Twenty-five years rolled back to the last war, 'the war to end war', they told us there could never be another and we believed it. Think of the millions of lives lost in the last war, all wasted. Think of the misery now of relatives, who have believed that their dear ones died 'to save civilisation'. Now they want another million to die. What rubbish. What rotten, sinful rubbish! Now the first to go will actually be the sons of those who died 25 years ago.

This afternoon went to tea with Rose [Browne, Rudsdale's girlfriend], who was rather distressed – so was I. Much talk about pacifism and should she close up the café? I said no, people will always eat.

Later: When I went to bed last night, I somehow felt that we should have a raid. Bright moon and stars, 'lovely night for a raid', as they used to say 25 years ago. I was dozing when every siren in the town leapt into life at half past 3. I jumped up and pulled the curtains to see out. The moon shone brightly and the air was filled with the most incredible wailing noises, while all over the town dogs were barking.

I went along to the old folk's room and heard Father stirring. He said, 'Is it a raid?' I said, 'Yes, are you going to get up?' He and Mother began to dress. I put on gum boots and a Mac and went out into the front garden. Bugles were sounding in the barracks and the big siren sounded again. The moon shone beautifully and I thought 'How incredible that people we didn't know were coming away from the east to kill us'. I thought, 'God, they said 7 minutes warning at the most. Am I really going to be dead 7 minutes from now?' I caught a whiff of a funny smell and thought, 'My God, is that gas?' But it was only our dustbin. I kept thinking, 'Well, this is it, it's come at last, just like they all said, though no one believed it would.' Father came out in the road. We could hear voices at several front doors down the street. He looked at the sky and said that there did not seem to be much to see. The noise of 'planes could be heard flying east, very fast and high. We talked stars for a few minutes and argued mildly about names of planets. Our local warden came by, quite unhurried and fully dressed, even to his collar and tie. Suddenly the 'all clear', sounded, a long, wailing cry, which went on and on. I went in and started to make tea.

Are we to be scared like this every night for years to come? What a terrible time for people with children. When the wailing stopped we could hear bugles blowing up in the barracks and people talking all up and down the road. I locked up, we all drank tea. Back to bed. Looked out of the window and could hear the trains shunting. The Co-op Bakery, over the back, started up again. Time, 4am.

September 4 Monday

All talk today about the alarm. Curious how many people never heard a sound. Neither George Farmer nor Mary Tovell heard it, perhaps because the siren at the Horse Show Ground did not sound because the key was mislaid, so they could not get in to start it.

Men working all day moving the Roman tombstones [in the Castle Museum, as a precaution against bomb damage].

September 5 Tuesday

Both the tombstones and the Sphinx are now safely downstairs, after an immense amount of labour, but by a miracle unbroken. They have been placed on the floor, against the west wall of the Castle, towards the north end, and have been covered with two layers of sand bags.

Hull [the Curator] is now taking his annual holiday. Today in his absence, the Attendant, Waters, went quite mad in a most alarming way and stormed about the building, raving and shouting. He was wearing jodhpurs which he claimed to have worn in the Air Force in the last war, his police steel-helmet and carried a gas mask stolen out of the barracks and a loaded revolver. Mary Tovell rang Holly Trees [Museum] as soon as this performance started, so I went into the Castle and found the man walking up and down the gallery, shouting out loud that Colchester would be bombed to hell in a very short time. Every now and then he sat down at a form, loading and unloading the revolver with trembling hands. I was scared stiff, although Tovell seemed to be quite calm. Waters wanted Chapman to go into the dungeons with him and watch him shoot flies off the wall. Chapman said that would not do, as the noise would be heard and they would get into trouble. Waters shouted, 'That doesn't matter! There's a war on. Nobody will notice a few more bangs!' He said to Tovell before I came 'I've never been so happy for years.'

However, before anything worse happened Mrs Waters came in. Apparently she guessed something was very wrong today and had decided to call in at the Castle when up town. She at once saw how bad he was and insisted on his going home with her, which, thank heavens, he did. What is to happen now I don't know. While Hull is away Poulter [the Curator at Holly Trees Museum] refuses to take any responsibility in the Castle, as he does not feel he is called upon to do so.

September 6 Wednesday

I woke early today (sleeping badly), and lay reading 'Pickwick Papers', when at about 6.50am the sirens sounded. Oddly enough I did not feel frightened as I did on Sunday but I thought 'O God, are they going to do this every morning?' I could hear a lot of talking outside but no 'planes came across the blue, sunny sky. I heard a man's voice say 'Well, I'm off to work.' There was no sound of traffic but I could hear trains in the distance.

Mother got up about 7.30 and I heard her go downstairs, open the front door, and make a little exclamation of annoyance on finding no milk there. I went down and she mentioned the fact. I said, 'Well, what do you expect in an air raid?' She was quite unaware there was an alarm on. I said I would go for the milk, so went off on my cycle. There was hardly a soul about except a few wardens, wearing helmets and armlets. One said to me 'Go back, you'll be stopped' but I took no notice. The AFS men at the steamroller depot were in full regalia, gas clothing and all, but looking very bored. The sky was clear, dark blue, not a 'plane in sight. Watts was very fed up. All his horses [and milk carts] were stranded all over the town. The police and 'Specials' had even stopped the men with barrows. I collected a pint of milk and went back to breakfast, by this time convinced that nothing would happen. Father was down now and quite uninterested. At half past 8, the 'all clear' sounded and one could hear a distant murmur as traffic got started again.

Interesting find [came into the Museum] today [found] when digging an air raid shelter in Mercer's Way – some pieces of coarse Roman wares, apparently the remains of a burial, and about a third of a Late Celtic polished bowl, with pierced base.

Although the general feeling of alarm still remains, people are not quite so anxious, now that the promised giant air raids have not materialised. If the Germans really did have 70,000 'planes, as we were told, it is odd that they have not sent them over. They are winning easily in Poland, however.

In spite of the lack of raids, all picture-houses are closed by order of the Government, so the wretched soldiers have nowhere to go at night except the pubs. All the same, there is no drunkenness in the streets at night but everywhere soldiers going back to billets and barracks singing 'Roll out the barrel'.

September 8 Friday

Shelters were begun today at St Helena School but they are not being sunk very deep, only about 2 feet. The top part of the shelter is covered with earth and the whole looks rather like a long-barrow. One only hopes they will not indeed become tombs for their occupants.

September 9 Saturday

Heard today that when Waters left the Museum on Tuesday he became quite unmanageable and was sent to Severalls Asylum yesterday for the third time and will not come back to the Castle.

September 18 Monday

It has been suggested that in view of the fact that Chapman is now the sole Special Constable at the Castle shelters, I and Harding should also be sworn in to assist him.

[As a Special Constable, Rudsdale was to be responsible for opening the Castle Vaults to the public in the event of air raids.]

October 5 Thursday

Wrote to Maitland [Underhill] today, telling him that this Museum was still at work in spite of the war. From the 'Museums Journal' this month I gather that at least 75 per cent of the museums in this country are shut and I fear that many of them may never reopen. The hasty packing of exhibits must have resulted in a terrible amount of damage being done.

[Despite Rudsdale's fears, two-thirds of the UK's museums did reopen during the war and continued to provide a service.]

October 17 Tuesday

Air raid alarm at 1.35pm today. I had the Vaults open in a second and 156 people came in. They were mostly women and did not seem very alarmed. The 'all clear' was at 2.05pm. No 'planes came over. I went up on the roof twice but there was nothing to be seen.

    Museum Committee this afternoon. The ancient house in Culver Street is finally doomed – no further efforts are to be made and it is to be demolished forthwith. Our fight for 6 years has been lost.

[Colchester Civic Society had campaigned to save this fifteenth-century timber-framed hall from destruction. Rudsdale was Acting Secretary of the Civic Society during the war.]

October 20 Friday

Mother's birthday today. She was a little gloomy, as she always is at such times, due I suppose to her Welsh ancestry. Gave her handkerchiefs and a new bag.

October 22 Sunday

To tea at Rose's flat this afternoon. I love these Sunday teas, they are the best thing in the whole week.

October 27 Friday

Work began yesterday taking down the old house in Culver Street. At first they allowed the ARP Demolition men to go at it like mad bulls, smashing and crashing with axes and hammers. I went to see Orchard [of the Borough Engineer's Department] and told him that this would not do, so he agreed, with bad grace, to employ carpenters when it comes to taking down the actual hall.

November 7 Tuesday

Took Rose to see the film of the 'Mikado' at the Regal Cinema tonight. It was really very good, although a little slow at first. The colours and music were excellent.

[The government order which had closed cinemas at the start of the war had been lifted in full by November 1939.]

November 8 Wednesday

It has now been agreed that Vaughan the builder, who has considerable experience with old timber-framed buildings, shall dismantle the hall, so I went to see him tonight and arranged that he should inspect the place.

I heard today that both I and Harding are definitely to be Special Constables and are to be sworn in on Saturday.

November 9 Thursday

Vaughan came along this morning and we made a thorough examination of the whole structure as it stands. It suddenly occurred to me that, while there is little hope that the whole place would ever be re-erected in its present form, there is no reason why one bay should not be re-erected forthwith in the Castle Main Hall. There is only one hammer beam actually complete, and that lacks one of the curved braces, and many of the smaller timbers are very rotten and would have to be replaced. In my opinion it would therefore be a much more sensible thing to re-erect only one end bay, using all the best timbers in that section. The whole thing could stand over the Easthorpe fireplace like a great wooden canopy.

[See Images 10 and 11]

November 10 Friday

The more I think of yesterday's idea the more attractive it seems. Vaughan says he would be prepared to do the whole job for £60, very reasonable I think.

I told Poulter and this afternoon we both told Doctor [Laver, the Honorary Curator], who received the scheme so mildly that I am sure he is in favour. We all went over to the Castle and surveyed the proposed site, after which the Doctor went home very thoughtfully.

November 11 Saturday

If this was this day 21 years ago the war would be over. As it is, it has not begun.

This morning Harding and I were sworn in as 'Specials' before old General Towsey. We all swore to obey our King etc. The General said, 'Jolly good luck, men' and that was all. We each received a warrant card but no helmets or other equipment.

Little Tovell is now determined to leave us and has given notice she will go next Friday. I shall miss her.

November 13 Monday

The Doctor fully agrees to the re-erection scheme and has told the Chairman [Sir W. Gurney Benham] of the proposal today. Vaughan will make a start next week. I hear Orchard is very alarmed lest the whole structure topples into the street.

November 17 Friday

Tovell left today. I really believe she was quite sorry to go. She is such a bright, intelligent little thing she will be quite a loss to us. She is going to be a nurse at Erith in Kent.

November 21 Tuesday

Museum Committee. The Doctor got the old house scheme put through without any bother at all. They seemed glad to have such a simple solution to the matter.

I admit this is a very poor second to preserving the house on the site but what else could I do? I don't know what Penrose [Secretary of Colchester Civic Society] will say, but I do not expect he will ever come back from Canada.

December 3 Sunday

The moon is dying now and the nights are black as ink [owing to the blackout regulations]. I am very nearly blind at night and make my way through the streets full of pushing, jostling soldiers at considerable peril. I wonder if, as the years roll on, people will come to accept these ghastly nights as being quite normal?

December 15 Friday

Nothing to note nowadays. Vaughan is bringing the timbers in as fast as he can but there are no other museum activities at the moment. The weather is dark and gloomy and everybody appears very depressed. There seems not the slightest chance that the war will ever stop.

December 18 Monday

Went to London in dull, wet weather. All the museums shut, most of the shops shut at half past 4. Went to Foyles and bought a few books and Christmas cards and walked about in the wet, damp streets. I have never felt so miserable before.

December 25 Monday

Dear old Mother produced the usual huge Christmas dinner, which we ate with the usual difficulty. All the relatives and friends sent the usual Christmas cards (now showing guns and ARP wardens as well as robins and mail-coaches) and of course all these have to be displayed all over the mantelpiece and sideboard. The one I got from Sir Gurney and Lady Benham is given special prominence.

December 29 Friday

Still bitterly cold and snow fell last night, with more to come by the look of the sky.

[This was the onset of the severest winter for forty-five years]

December 31 Sunday

And so this year ends, a year which began so well and ended in such tragedy. However, whatever happens, nothing can take away the joy and pleasure I had at the Royal Show [when Rudsdale staged an 'Old English Farm' exhibition at Windsor Great Park in July 1939]. I don't suppose I shall ever have such a chance again but I have had it once. *[See Images 12 and 13]*

What will be the outcome of the present terrible state of affairs I cannot imagine. Some people think the Germans will attack in France at any moment, although considering that this is the worst winter for a quarter of a century I should not think it very likely. Meanwhile we carry on with our ordinary work as if our lives still stretched before us. There are no air raids, as we were so faithfully promised by the Government. The ARP workers are very despondent.

My only personal worry is that I shall be taken for the Army. If that should happen I really don't know what I shall do. However, it seems that only men under 25 are really wanted and at any rate I am still in a reserved occupation as a local government official. I think I shall never again see the word 'reserved' without the most peculiar feelings.

The general atmosphere is gloomy. Most people hope the war will be over next year, although they don't really believe that it will be. A few think it will go on for ten years and will involve every country in Europe. Some hope that the Russians will join with the Germans in a military sense, as they believe the Russians to be so incredibly incompetent that their aid would be a liability rather than an asset but I cannot see why an additional 170,000,000 enemies should be an asset to this country. At the moment the Russians are pilloried in every paper for their attack on Finland and there is a great agitation for an expedition to help Finland.

The weather is quite amazing. I have never seen such snow since 1916. What must it be like in France? Many villages round Colchester have been quite cut off.

[The National Service (Armed Forces) Act 1939 had imposed a liability to conscription on all men aged eighteen to forty-one. However, the call-up proceeded slowly at the start of the war with conscription mainly being confined to men under twenty-five. Local government officers, such as Rudsdale, were classified as being in reserved occupations at first, although they often undertook Civil Defence duties in addition to their work. However, by 1942 all men between eighteen and fifty-one and women between twenty and thirty became liable to call-up.]

Chapter 2

❧ 1940 ❧

January 1 Monday

Never during my lifetime have I viewed a New Year with more unrelieved gloomy prospects than 1940. I have never been much of a one to look into the future and although I always, at these times, wonder whether each successive New Year's Day is the last I shall see, I have never before felt so sure that it may really be the last. If I see New Year's Day 1941, still in the place I am now, I shall regard it as no less than a miracle. As for myself, were it not for the war, I should be considerably prosperous. I have about £200 in cash, £90 in superannuation fund, books etc. worth at least another £50. Taking everything into account I may be worth £400, with a steady job. The joke is that within 6 months it is not improbable that I shall have lost my job and be coughing my life out in some remote barracks, while my £200 rusts in the bank.

My Mother and Father are quite well, considering their ages, although Mother I believe worries a good deal about the war and its probable effect on me. I worry about most things now so that my sleep is haunted by the most dreadful nightmares.

Hull is away ill. The Museum is dreadfully cold, as we are unable to get enough coke. The weather is very bad.

Announcements today of a new Royal Proclamation calling up men from 21-27 inclusive. Grim forebodings.

January 2 Tuesday

Greatly to my surprise and joy, Vaughan came to the Castle today and began work re-erecting the old house. There are four men on it and they laid out one side on the floor today. Nice to see such work going on.

January 6 Saturday

Today went off on a journey to Braintree and Chelmsford by bus. At Braintree there are many soldiers – all the big pub yards seem to be in Army hands. Braintree doesn't bother about gas masks or air raid shelters, although in the last war a bomb fell on a house here and killed 7 people. The biggest joke, the Air Raid Precaution to end all Air Raid Precautions, is that they have stopped the Town Hall clock and covered it in sacking, so that the enemy cannot see it or hear it strike! The idea of a man in a bombing 'plane, 20,000 feet up, hearing a clock strike, seems to me to be distinctly funny. The Town Hall is almost buried in sandbags but apart from that only one or two shops have boarded up their fronts. The town looked very busy. I had a good look round and found that the beautiful Courtauld Fountain has been boarded round 8 feet high, with printed notices on the boarding to say that this precaution is necessary owing to the wilful damage done to the fountains and figures by school-children evacuated from London 'over whom there is no control'.

Caught a bus to Chelmsford. Had a look at the Market. Very poor horse-sale. Good cobs for £6! Cart-horses, 8 years old, only £20, perfectly sound in every way. Instead of the war bringing back horses, it would appear to be the cause of their extinction.

January 10 Wednesday

Went up to London this morning to attend the first Royal Archaeological Institute Council since the war began [Rudsdale served on the Council of the RAI from 1939-1942].

The first thing you notice is that barrage balloons are up and very beautiful they look too. The next is that the tremendous works for extending the Central London Tube are still going ahead, with many hundreds of men working on them, especially round Stratford way.

In London all the police now wear 'tin-helmets' all the time, though why is difficult to see. The traffic looks, to me, quite normal, in the City at least. Sandbags are everywhere. Some big banks are actually having brick and concrete buttresses put over their basement windows as if they expect the war to last for a century. Perhaps it will.

Walked down to London Bridge, always a favourite spot of mine. Several Dutch and Belgian boats in, unloading bananas of all things. The usual crowd, nearly all workmen and office girls, feeding the sea-gulls. To see the British workman feeding gulls with part of his dinner is a pretty good sign that there is no food shortage in this country. While I was there a little Dutch boat slipped down the river, tooting her siren, the crew nonchalantly leaning over the rails, a brand new lifeboat ready on the davits. I uttered a prayer that she would get across the other side safely.

Had lunch in a milk bar and then went to Burlington House. Dr [Mortimer] Wheeler was there in a Colonel's uniform and one man actually turned up as an AFS man, complete with tin-hat and axe, which made it very awkward for him to sit down. Apart from these our august assembly looked and behaved normally. I noticed that the President never spoke of the war, he occasionally mentioned 'the present circumstances' or 'the international situation' but nothing more outspoken than that.

After all was over I went to a News Cinema for an hour and came home on the 7.30. A dreadful journey, with only dim blue lights, the train packed full of soldiers going on leave, singing because they were happy, soldiers going back from leave, singing to cheer themselves up and new young conscripts, too miserable to sing at all.

January 12 Friday

German 'planes in the district this morning. Heavy gunfire heard from the direction of Clacton but no alarm.

January 14 Sunday

Went to tea with Rose and stayed all evening. This kind of life seems to me to be the same as being married only rather better. In her cosy little room, with the fire burning bright, her old furniture, beautifully polished, the prints I gave her on the walls, the wireless I helped her buy playing softly. It really is an ideal way of spending the evening.

Terribly cold and very dark tonight. I find my eyes are getting very bad at night. I cannot see a thing and have had several narrow escapes.

January 16 Tuesday

This evening a tremendous fall of snow began. Never in my life have I seen such a fall. It started about teatime and fell in huge, soft flakes, hour after hour, with a north wind piling it up into drifts. By 10pm there was over a foot deep and still snowing hard. I think it must be more than the great fall of 1916, which I remember so clearly. To this day I remember the roar of snow sliding off the roofs which so terrified me.

Everything that could have been said about the beauty of snow has been said but it is a chance we may never have again of seeing heavy snow as they saw it in olden times, silent, white, still, with no street lights to give any touch of modernity. Tonight Bourne Mill and the Pond were transformed in an hour from the 20th century to the 16th, without a single thing visible to connect the scene with the present day. If I were 20 years younger, how I would revel in all this. As it is, while I make the most of its beauty, I wonder how I am going to get hay and fodder down to Bourne Mill, as the hill is now just a sheet of ice.

January 17 Wednesday

Woke this morning to find it still snowing. I decided that tonight Bob and the donkey must be shut in the Bourne Mill stable but I must let them out during the day to drink. This morning the donkey was rolling joyously in the snow, while Bob trotted round and kicked up his heels. The Pond has been mostly frozen over about 6 inches deep for a week or more now. The stream side never freezes and the horses can always drink out of the stream lower down.

In the Castle Park the white carpet lay undisturbed at a depth of about 18 inches. It was almost impossible to get into the Castle. I had to wear top-boots.

January 19 Friday

Vaughan got all one side of the old house up today and Sisson [the architectural adviser] came in to inspect it. It looks even more impressive than I thought it would but the interior of the Castle Main Hall is so high that the thing will not, I feel sure, look out of place. Sisson is taking a great deal of trouble over this and we must be grateful to him.

January 21 Sunday

More heavy snow today. The whole countryside is now absolutely impassable. Several cars have been abandoned by the roadside and quite lost to view, while all round Colchester there are snow drifts right over the hedges.

January 22 Monday

More heavy snow all day. This is absolutely incredible! The general opinion is that this sort of winter occurs every 25 years and that this is as severe as the 1890-91 spell and considerably worse than 1916.

January 26 Friday

Another tremendous snowstorm today from 4.30 to 6pm so that a further 6 inches fell. I am told that at places only a couple of miles out of the town, people have been snow-bound for more than a week.

January 31 Wednesday

Chapman came to work today, looking most unwell, to find the whole place like an ice-house as we have no coke. Why we stick this sort of thing for the blasted Museum, God alone knows. I believe everybody who has ever had anything to do with this place have put themselves in an earlier grave than they need on account of conditions here.

February 4 Sunday

Signs of a thaw beginning. One of the swans at Bourne Pond has been frozen to death. It is a curious thing that although the ice on the pond is 6 inches thick and people are continuously sliding on it, neither Bob nor the donkey have ever made the slightest effort to walk on it, as can be clearly seen from their footmarks in the snow.

February 7 Wednesday

Went up to London today to the Royal Archaeological Institute meeting to hear Stuart Piggott talk on Stonehenge and similar monuments. He wore his own clothes, although he is a private in the Territorials and is strictly forbidden to appear without his uniform. Peggy Piggott told me he was very depressed and had been trying hard to get out of the Army into a Ministry job but nothing had yet been done. So we see England's leading palaeontologist acting as office boy to an anti-aircraft battery, which is about what one would expect in England.

The RAI Council now have tea before the Council meeting, with sugar almost ad lib, from great bowls of it, so I took a few away with me to use in a café, where you only get 3 lumps!

[Stuart Piggott was an archaeologist who had undertaken excavations with Rudsdale in the 1930s. His wife Peggy was also an archaeologist. Later in the war, Stuart Piggott became an air photo interpreter and was posted to India.]

February 10 Saturday

Tonight I went down to Bourne Mill about 6 o'clock. It was very dark but many search-lights were out and almost as soon as I got there anti-aircraft guns began firing over in the direction of Mersea. I could neither see nor hear any 'planes but the firing kept up for nearly an hour. You could see the double flashes of gun and shell and then hear the double, coughing explosion.

A good many people were walking about at the time but seemed quite unperturbed by it. No sign of any yellow [preliminary] warning being given to the ARP people but I stood by at the Castle until about 8.30pm and moved on several cars which tried to obstruct the gates.

February 12 Monday

Vaughan finished the old house today and I think it can be clearly said that he has made a very good job of it. It looks very well in the Castle and is quite the most impressive thing we have ever had.

February 14 Wednesday

My 30th Birthday. A year ago how depressed I felt at the prospect of becoming middle-aged. Now how cheerful I feel at the idea that I am now in a more senior age-group and much more likely to be in a reserved job. Went down to Rose's tonight and had a specially nice supper for my birthday and she gave me a lot of chocolates and a fountain pen, a thing I have wanted for years.

February 16 Friday

Weather improving now but still no coke for the Museum. I am told it is only available for essential purposes, ARP or AFS stations.

February 25 Sunday

The Government brought in summer time today, so it was light this evening until about 7.30. Thaw complete, so I went down to Bourne Mill and baled out the boat.

I went to the Castle at 1pm as they tested the sirens and I thought people might run to the shelters but no one did.

March 1 Friday

St David's Day – Y Ddraig Goch [the Welsh flag] flew on the Town Hall this morning and the Welsh Guards walked about the town with leeks in their caps, while over in Wales the War Office are evicting hundreds of peasant farmers from the holdings they have held for generations, in order to make artillery ranges. It should be observed that England is only concerned to preserve the rights of small nations outside the British Isles.

[Rudsdale refers to the removal of the farming community of Mynydd Epynt, near Brecon, by the War Office in 1940.]

March 13 Wednesday

Lovely warm spring day today. From the general news, it looks as if the Finn-Russian war is now about to end, so Thank God there's one place in the world where killing is stopping instead of starting.

March 16 Saturday

Hervey Benham told me today he was trying to join the Navy for coastal patrol work.

March 23 Saturday

My Father's birthday, 68 years old. Still keeping as well as he can and seems to take a bright interest in things. Gave him the usual tobacco, etc. and a silly little box of fancy matches. He knew more or less what was coming but was just as quietly satisfied as always, dear old man. I do so hope he can see this war out.

March 25 Easter Monday

Great crowds in the Museum – 1,508 in the Castle. Stayed open until 5pm although still only in March.

April 5 Friday

Went over to Chelmsford this afternoon and went across to see the Horse Sale, which was a very fair entry and a good attendance. It is noticeable at all these sales that farming folk do not carry gas masks – I don't believe there was one in the whole market. It is so nice to see a large crowd of men, not one in uniform, and to know that their whole efforts are engaged in growing food and raising stock and not in slaughtering Germans.

April 8 Monday

Today I had one whole, complete day off. I went up to London [and met] little Mary Tovell and we strolled off to see whatever was showing. Across London Bridge we saw Rawle's harness shop with all the men busy sewing Army draft harness (this is supposed to be a great military secret but anybody looking through the shop windows can see them working on the stuff), then we saw an accident, admired the river, admired the horses coming over the Bridge, strolled through the City, along the Embankment, to Charing Cross, then, quite on the spur of the moment, decided to go to Hampstead.

The Heath was bare and cold but we wandered arm-in-arm by the ponds and up back by the paddock where the deer are kept. Near the 'Old Bull and Bush' there is a warden's post and there are new above-ground shelters at the top of Heath Street. 'Jack Straw's Castle' seems to be full of soldiers.

Quite a lot of houses are empty, which seems funny, as the war seems to be very far away. We had lunch at a cafeteria in Heath Street and a very good lunch it was for only 1/6 each – as much as you could eat. Then we went down to Pond Street to see the picture house there and spent the rest of the afternoon in cosy darkness. After that we set off back to London Bridge, where I left her, I think having had a happy day.

She is a dear little kid. I enjoyed myself immensely and spent a whole day without tin-hat, identity card, warrant and gas mask or park keys, absolutely free.

Tonight's newspaper placards announced that the German fleet is moving in Norwegian waters.

April 9 Tuesday

On the news this morning that the Germans have invaded Denmark and Norway, apparently without any appreciable resistance. Great excitement everywhere. I had another day's leave today and went over to Ipswich.

Went along to the Museum and saw both Maynard [the Curator] and Spencer [Assistant Curator]. All very busy there, doing much educational work among the school children evacuated into the town. Ipswich Museum always seems so much more alive than we do – next week they are even having Gilbert & Sullivan played in the Museum lecture hall. Spencer showed me his model of the Sutton Hoo burial and of the general scenery in which it was found, two lovely pieces of work. At 4 o'clock we heard a special news bulletin about the latest invasion but it did not tell much. It seems that vast numbers of troops have been landed by 'planes and parachutes.

[The Ipswich Museum staff had assisted in the discovery of the Anglo-Saxon burial ship at Sutton Hoo in the summer of 1939.]

April 13 Saturday

When I was down at Rose's tonight we heard a special announcement on the radio that the British Fleet had had a great action at Narvik in Norway and had sunk a large number of German ships of all kinds.

April 22 Monday

Fine day, warmer. Hull away all day. He is away so often now, presumably on Observer Corps duty, that sometimes we only see him for 2 half days in the week.

[Hull served part-time with the Royal Observer Corps throughout the war and also spent time away from the Museum preparing archaeological research.]

April 25 Thursday

Bad news from Norway. English losing all along.

April 27 Saturday

Men of 26 registered for military service today. The ginger-headed conscientious pacifist stood outside the Labour Exchange all day, holding up a pacifist placard. He is a brave man.

April 30 Tuesday

At about 11.15 tonight the whole town was shaken by a tremendous explosion. Doors and windows rattled, china jumped about. We were all sitting in the dining room, round the fire. Mother and Father were considerably startled. I looked outside but all was black as pitch and nothing more could be heard. I expect it must be an explosion in a munitions works.

May 1 Wednesday

Heard at the railway station that the bang last night was a German bomber which crashed at Clacton, so that its whole carcase exploded. Besides the crew, at least two people are dead and several houses have been demolished.

[These were the first civilian deaths of the Second World War on mainland Britain. A Heinkel He 111E bomber, which had been on coastal mine-laying operations, was hit by anti-aircraft fire from a Harwich battery and crashed on Victoria Road, Clacton. One of the mines that it was carrying then detonated, causing a huge explosion.]

May 7 Tuesday

Terrible accident in Barrack Street today. An Army lorry was travelling at a tremendous speed when the driver, a boy of 19, completely lost control. He swerved across the road and crashed into a house, rushed on to the corner, killed a girl there, rushed across the road, killed a woman on the other corner and brought down a lamp-post, finally crashing into a garden fence. These lorries are a terrible menace.

May 9 Thursday

Went off this afternoon on my cycle to see Clacton. It is a long time since I went so far on a bicycle. It took about 2 hours. You have to go to within a few hundred yards of the smash before you see anything, then every house has a few windows gone and as you get nearer the scene, tiles are missing and gardens full of wreckage. The actual house that was hit is just a pile of bricks and the two next ones are very badly damaged, having one wall quite gone. Thousands of windows are missing in the adjoining streets. Everywhere are lorries and even horse-drawn pantechnicons loading up furniture. It is a sad scene of desolation and made me think of the days when I drove through these very roads in the yellow gig, Bob arching his neck and tittupping along. *[See Image 14]*

    Clacton is, I should think, about half empty now. There are quite a lot of soldiers about and most of the houses on the front seem to be taken over by the Army. The beach is quite open, no signs of fortifications like in the last war. The pavilion advertises band concerts by the Cavalry Band from Colchester.

May 10 Friday

Announced on the radio, 8 o'clock news, that the Germans have invaded Holland and Belgium this morning. Great excitement. General opinion is that the BEF will now smash them entirely and the war will certainly end this year. Personally I am not so optimistic. I see nothing cheering in having the war coming nearer and nearer to Essex. There was considerable anti-aircraft fire at half past 11 tonight and the garrison seem to have some sort of wind-up. Guards are posted on the roads, I saw them at Old Heath and Blackheath.

May 11 Saturday

Special Notice appeared in Benham's [Press Office] tonight from the Regional Commissioner, saying that all ARP organisations should now be ready for instant action and warning people of the necessity of taking great care about lights. I started carrying my police helmet again. Most of the soldiers were confined to barracks all day and were only allowed out for a couple of hours this evening. By order of the new Government, the Whit Monday Bank Holiday is cancelled.

May 12 Sunday

We could hear AA firing this morning. At 1 o'clock, 11 'planes flew over, going east and about 3pm, eight came back, so I suppose they had been over to Holland or Belgium bombing. Soldiers seem to have been allowed out again today.

May 13 Whit Monday

This evening I cycled to Dedham to see Sisson. He told me about the ARP arrangements there, how each is perfect in its kind – Ambulance, Wardens and AFS – but each loathes all the others so much that all exercises are done separately. It is hoped that it will be alright on the night. Had a most pleasant evening in his lovely house.

There is a guard on East Bridge now and all persons are stopped after dark. I came back at midnight, in glorious moonlight, and as I was carrying a plan of the Roman streets on the Colchester library site, I hoped that I should not be searched. I was not, as besides soldiers, there were several policemen who I knew.

[Sisson lived at Sherman's, a Georgian town house in Dedham High Street, which he later bequeathed to the National Trust. Sisson was the architect of the new Colchester public library building at this time.]

May 14 Tuesday

German Army running very fast through Holland. The defences about which we heard so much seem to be non-existent. Our troops were confined to barracks all day, poor devils. A great deal of chatter in the Press about forming 'Local Defence Volunteers'. People seem to be a little nervous war is getting so close. Beautiful weather today.

May 15 Wednesday

Holland very wisely gave up fighting today to stop further slaughter and destruction. Weather continues wonderful.

May 16 Thursday

The papers seem more optimistic today and claim that the advance in Belgium is halted.

May 17 Friday

Papers as pessimistic today as they were optimistic yesterday. German Army irresistible.

After nearly 9 months, the old 'spy' scares, for which Colchester was famous in the last war, have been revived. This time the main attack is against [the landlord] who keeps the 'Albert' pub near North Station. His father was a Czech or Slovak but he himself, (a man of 60 at least) was born in this country. Without any rhyme or reason some persons have spent this week spreading tales to the effect that [he] was a German, that he had Germans at the 'Albert', that the bar-maids were spies, that he had radio apparatus on the premises, etc. all of which was pure invention. He has had to go to the trouble and bother of inserting a denial of these rumours in the local paper tonight.

May 18 Saturday

German advance continues unchecked. The weather is so beautiful it seems incredible that war is advancing upon us such a comparatively short distance away. The town looks busy and perfectly normal. Hundreds of cars about. We have even had a few holiday people in the Museum this week and today quite a number of young lads and girls with cycles have been in. It is sad to see them, all of military age. I wonder where they will be this time next year?

May 19 Sunday

The war is getting closer, as the Germans advance irresistibly into France. At the barracks they were standing-to all day but I don't think they were really expecting anything to happen.

May 20 Monday

Germans still advancing, heading for Cambrai.

May 21 Tuesday

Germans advancing very fast. The radio news gets more and more gloomy every hour.

May 22 Wednesday

The news in the papers today seemed a little better but was followed almost at once with the startling intelligence that the Germans were in Abbeville, miles from where they were expected to be. It is obvious that the BEF are in a very tight corner and that the French Army is very badly beaten. There is great consternation everywhere.

In view of the greatly increased danger of air raids and the possibility that the country will soon be invaded, I told Father that he and Mother must move.

May 23 Thursday

We had a disturbed night last night, with 'planes flying over all the time. I think Father is getting a little nervous. Germans are now in Boulogne and advance quite unchecked, only 30 miles from the English coast.

May 26 Sunday

Packing up to take Father and Mother to [stay with Aunt Het Underhill in] Maidenhead. Went to Seymour's tonight [a schoolteacher at Colchester Royal Grammar School]. Quite a lot there, everybody aggressively pro-British, on-to-victory, etc. Germans advance into Channel ports.

May 27 Monday

Took Father and Mother up to London. Had a taxi from Liverpool Street to Paddington. In Trafalgar Square, Admiralty Arch, Horse Guards, etc. there are masses of barbed wire, sandbags, gun-emplacements and all the accoutrements of a siege. At the Palace we were just in time to see the Changing of the Guard – all khaki, gas masks and steel helmets now. Father was very thrilled. I got them to Paddington and put them on the train.

Then went back to Tottenham Court Road and on to the Museums Association and had a chat with Wignall [the Secretary]. I'm afraid we were both rather gloomy about museums and the general future.

Leaving him, I wandered through the streets for a while. London University's great new building [Senate House] is now used by the Ministry of Information and is thickly surrounded by barbed wire. Perhaps this is what keeps the information in, for precious little leaks out in either press or radio.

From Bloomsbury to Paddington again and met Mauna Benham outside St Mary's Hospital [where she works]. Went along to her garret near Cambridge Terrace and had a fine high tea. It was lovely up there, a beautiful summer evening, with the sun shining on the backs of the mews and the noises of them floating up, radio, gramophones, children laughing, and ponies coming in and out, where greengrocers had their stables.

I was sorry to go in order to catch the last train home. The journey was (as usual) bad, the train crammed with soldiers and sailors and hardly any light at all. It was a wonderful relief to get home to an empty house and know that I can do exactly what I please. Free as a bird!

May 28 Tuesday

News very bad today. Belgians suddenly make an unconditional surrender. Great outcry against King Leopold. Typical comments: 'How could he be such a traitor? And he had such a nice face!' And 'Can't understand it. Why, dammit, the man was at Eton!' Naturally any man who tries to save his country from useless slaughter and ruin for the second time in a quarter of a century must be a traitor.

They are now talking about the evacuation of the East and South Coast towns. I fear Colchester will be included in this. Children are being moved from Harwich, Clacton and Southend.

May 30 Thursday

Rose's brother Archie is safe back from France. He had a very bad time but is now safely housed near Dorchester. I don't think Rose knew how narrow an escape he had this last few days.

May 31 Friday

There is a great scare now – we are going to be invaded by Germans landing by parachutes, so in order to confuse them every place-name in the whole of Britain is to be obliterated. I can see that this would have some value in rural districts but I really cannot believe that it is possible for the Germans to reach Colchester without knowing where they were. It doesn't seem to occur to anybody that the Germans have maps. Corporation men were running round tonight taking down all signposts or boards with the name 'Colchester' on them.

June 1 Saturday

Great excitement today – all Museum notice boards bearing the name 'Colchester' hastily removed. The name is also to be obliterated from all trade vehicles. The Curator solemnly considers as to whether or not he should advise the authorities to remove all tombstones in churchyards and the cemetery which say '… late of Colchester'. I believe great damage has been done in some parts by the destruction of ancient milestones.

June 3 Monday

News today that all the BEF are out of France, it is believed with very little loss. This is the most staggering defeat that the British Army has ever had.

June 4 Tuesday

The Premier [Winston Churchill] spoke on the retreat of the BEF today. It has undoubtedly been a most successful withdrawal and has been brought about with the minimum loss of life. About 330,000 men have come home. Some have been landed at Harwich – I saw them on the station.

June 10 Monday

At Rose's tonight we heard on the 9 o'clock news that Italy had declared war on England. A terrible tragedy it should be Italy. Now I shall never see the wonders of Rome, Pompeii and Naples. The Germans are only 30 miles from Paris, still advancing very fast.

June 11 Tuesday

News today that the Germans are advancing over the Marne.

June 13 Thursday

Germans now only 17 miles from Paris. The city is undoubtedly lost but it is believed that the French will have the good sense to abandon it to save it from bombardment.

June 14 Friday

Germans entered Paris today and the city is safe from destruction.

June 15 Saturday

Went down to Maidenhead for the weekend. The aged parents seemed very well. I had a long talk with my cousin, Maitland. He is somewhat gloomy and considers that the future is very black. If there is an invasion he believes the financial system of this country will collapse. I was not surprised to hear that he holds the opinion held by most people, that the Army is no good, is badly trained and badly organised and that the whole safety of the country depends upon the Navy and the Air Force.

Maitland is hardly more happy about the future than I am. He tells me there are (or were) large numbers of Austrians and Germans working at Slough Trading Estate. Sixteen of his bank's customers are now interned, some for no reason whatever.

June 17 Monday

News that the French have called for an Armistice. I wish the English had.

June 18 Tuesday

Raid alarm tonight. I was just about to put away my cycle, when a dull distant explosion shook the garden gate and rattled windows. It was a glorious night, the moon riding huge and high in the heavens. Almost at once the sirens sounded, so I put on my helmet and pedalled away, dodging as best I could the numerous wardens, ambulance men and others who were hurrying to their posts.

As I went up to the Castle, I could hear 'planes behind me, away to the east and there was the dull thump of distant bombs. A few people were coming into the Park and put on the [Vault] lights. The sky was a blaze of searchlights by now and at least 2 'planes were going across the town, apparently Germans.

I went up onto the Castle roof. Several 'planes moved across, going westwards and at last one was picked up in the searchlights. He seemed to be very low and went immediately over the top of the Castle. Just as he was over us, an English 'plane in the darkness above the searchlight opened fire with machine-guns. The German replied and I could clearly see the tracer bullets streaking off into the blackness. It was all over in a flash but I was quite scared at the time. After that very little happened and I was very tired by the time 'all clear' went, at nearly 4am. As I cycled home it was just getting light, coming up in a pinky, bluish wash from the north-east.

June 21 Friday

I was interested to see that, after all the panic to remove the name 'Colchester' the place can still be identified from the Park gates, where it is cut in stone, and the war memorial, where it is cast in bronze.

There was another alarm tonight at 11 o'clock, which lasted until 2.30am. We had 9 people come in. Nothing much happened but we could see AA fire in the direction of Harwich and distant bombs could be heard.

June 22 Saturday

Today I had to register under the National Service Act. I thanked God I was over 30, although I had to register as being 29 last year. The reserved age for local government staff is to go up to 30 in August so I am still covered. The registration was very short, because being a local government officer they did not require any particulars. It was a great relief to get it over as the prospect has been worrying me for months.

June 25 Tuesday

The Army are making a 'strong point' in the Park, close to the bandstand, it seems to resist an attack from the north.

June 26 Wednesday

Alarm this morning from half past 12 until 4am. 16 people came in. They are all folks who live in nearby houses and feel better for having a few feet of concrete over their heads. I don't blame them. These nights are very tiring but the dawns are exceptionally beautiful and it is indeed a glorious thing to see the moonlight fade and the pink of the day come up.

June 28 Friday

There were more 'planes over tonight but no siren was blown and I hear that it is not intended that the siren shall be sounded unless it is obvious that a direct attack is being made on Colchester by a number of 'planes. Single 'planes, or odd 'planes flying singly, will be ignored. The decision is causing a certain amount of anxiety in the town. After all, it only takes one bomb to kill you.

June 29 Saturday

Heard some dull explosions late last night or early this morning and I now learn that nearly 20 bombs were dropped just outside the Borough at Ardleigh. Nobody was hurt but one bomb fell in the garden of a cottage and seriously damaged the place. All the rest were in fields and some did not explode. Incendiary bombs were also dropped but did little damage except to set fire to hedges. I saw part of one when I called at the Fire Station this morning, to see if I could get any appliances for the Castle.

There is quite a lot of talk now about an invasion. Capt Ellis of the Fire Brigade has two shotguns ready in his office and is prepared to use them.

There was a lot of blasting down by North Bridge and at East Bridge today, where tree stumps are being removed. Apparently all the bridges are to be mined at once.

June 30 Sunday

Poulter and I took duty at the Castle from 2.30 till 5pm. This is the second Sunday afternoon we have been open and 519 people came in, mostly soldiers.

July 1 Monday

The Town Clerk rang up today to say that Barclays Bank were preparing to move all their valuables from Colchester in event of an invasion and that he had agreed that the Museum's gold coins should be taken out of the town. Hull got in a great panic and began talking about having a great pit dug in the Vaults in which he would bury the entire collection.

It is becoming more and more clear to me that I must get out. It is farming I want yet that seems quite hopeless.

[See Image 15]

July 2 Tuesday

Our Castle Vaults were inspected today by an official from the Ministry of Home Security. When I told him that they must be the most ancient shelters in use, he pointed out that the Royston Cave [in Hertfordshire] was being used as a shelter.

July 4 Thursday

At teatime the news placards (now handwritten on odd sheets or blackboards) announced that the Navy had taken the French fleet, or at least a good part of it.

July 6 Saturday

Concrete pill boxes, for machine-guns, have been built at Middleborough, on the corner of St Peter's Street and on the site of the Town Wall at the bottom of Maidenburgh Street.

July 9 Tuesday

A German 'plane came over at 1am. By the news tonight it seems that 22 German 'planes have been shot down today.

[These air battles marked the opening days of the Battle of Britain.]

July 10 Wednesday

It has been obvious for some time that we are in danger of having daylight raids in this area, in which case some provision must be made for horses. The obvious scheme would be to list all stables, on the assumption that as almost every horse is working during the day, his stable would be available for any horse passing nearby during a raid. In those parts of the town where no horses are kept, disused stables and empty garages could be used. This matter is serious, not only on account of public safety but on account of the horses themselves and their drivers. Obviously, most drivers would remain with their horses during an alarm but they would feel much freer to look after themselves, if the horses could be kept tied up under cover.

I had already approached Councillor Pye, Chairman of the ARP Committee but obtained no sympathy from him and was recommended to see Mr Murphy [the local vet], who is in sole charge of the National Air Raid Precautions for Animals.

When I called [tonight] he cheerfully admitted that nothing had been done of the slightest use. He had made out a provisional list of 12 'standings' in the town and when I pointed out this was quite inadequate for 300 horses, he merely smiled and said he did not think such a number existed in the town. At any rate, I got two notices from him and shall open Port Lane and Bourne Mill stables at once.

July 11 Thursday

There was a raid alarm at 1am, which lasted until 3.40am. Half a dozen people came in. I got back home, had a couple of hours in bed and then there was another alarm at 5am, which lasted until 7. Not a 'plane was to be seen or heard.

When I got home I went to bed until 10am and got back to the Castle at 11. As this was my half day I was only there for an hour and a half. Hull was very annoyed. However, I did not get the half day, because at 3pm, when I was dozing on my bed, there was another alarm, so back I had to go. Seventy-two people came into the Vaults but only a few 'planes near the town.

Tonight the Cavalry Band played in the Park, a most pleasant diversion.

July 13 Saturday

This morning old Mr Rose, our wealthy next door neighbour, stopped me at the gate and said, 'I suppose you have to go out at night when there's an alarm?' I replied, 'yes, I did.' 'Well,' he said, 'would you mind not banging your doors as much as it wakes up my wife!'

In the evening papers tonight I read that little Betty Mason* in the Telephone Office has been arrested under the Defence Regulations. She is a little, mild looking girl and what she has done I cannot imagine. The charge involves talking peace to soldiers.

[*Name has been changed]

July 14 Sunday

The Prime Minister spoke on the radio today, promising nothing but death and destruction for years to come until the final victory which will give us FREEDOM and so on.

July 16 Tuesday

[Heard] today about Betty Mason. It is very sad. She was tricked and trapped into saying doubtful things by a man of the Field Security Police disguised as a Tommy. The whole case stinks. Apparently she was driven to an outburst in the first place by the fact that some soldiers deliberately broke into her beach-hut and smashed up the place. I [said] I would give money towards her defence if necessary. It seems that some of the other girls at the [Telephone Office] are contributing.

July 17 Wednesday

Went over to Dedham tonight to Sisson's. A lot of talk about invasion. Harwich, Clacton, Walton, Frinton, etc. are being rapidly emptied. Yet only 3 months ago Clacton was still hoping for a 'season' of sorts. There is perturbation too about arming the Home Guard with petrol bombs made out of beer-bottles, a very simple weapon to make, yet most dangerous. Some people doubt the wisdom of spreading such things about so widely. Many Communists in the country urge that the whole population should be armed, men and women, a scheme which might well call forth numerous 'German atrocities' if a landing were ever made.

July 18 Thursday

[Heard about Betty Mason's] case again. Apparently no money is needed, as her brother is paying. Poor girl, she has lost her job and her pension.

Got 'Horse Shelter' notices up at Bourne Mill and Port Lane, the first in the town.

July 20 Saturday

When I saw Sisson on Wednesday, I told him of my difficulties in getting any form of land work, so he promised to mention it to a friend. This morning the friend arrived, none other than Mr Parrington of Sherbourne Mill, Lawford, who came to see us years ago about an [archaeological] discovery on his land. He was very kind and said he could certainly give me work for the harvest, for which I was very grateful. It depends on how things turn out but if the opportunity offers I should stay on with him and never come back to the Castle. I am to go over to Lawford in the first week in August and shall stay at the Sissons' part of the time.

A very busy market today, the town very full. All the 'pillboxes' and gun posts are manned all day long now. This morning I saw a very young soldier in the one on the Town Wall trying to get some milk off one of Watt's roundsmen but he was too lazy to go back, so I went and bought the poor lad half a pint, for which he was most grateful.

July 23 Tuesday

Raid alarm at 11.45pm tonight. Half a dozen or so people came into the Vaults, including a soldier, who walked in about midnight. He spoke with a very broad Lancashire accent and was apparently on leave. However, Forsett [who was also on duty] thought it very suspicious and took it upon himself to report it to the officer in charge of the patrol in the Park, who promptly arrived with a revolver and accompanied by a soldier, rifle, fixed bayonet and all. They made an impressive entry, except that the soldier, who was leading, misjudged the height of the low archway and became wedged, finally emerging into the Vaults backwards. The poor solider was 'put through it' and after searching questions and much investigation of papers, was admitted to be on leave. He wore rubber shoes and carried his Army boots round his neck because he said they hurt his feet. The soldier and officer retreated up the stairs, unfortunately without noticing the small step out of the Well-Room, over which they both stumbled, while the words 'Blast!' and 'Bugger!' rang out in the darkness.

About 1am on Wednesday morning Richardson [from the ARP headquarters] came in, doing a round of shelters. I took the chance to tell him of our complaints, emphasising that we still have no fire-fighting appliances of any sort.

Had a letter from Mother, threatening that they must come home. What a fantastic absurdity, when an invasion is certain within a month or two.

July 25 Thursday

Went down to Maidenhead today and after long talks I persuaded [Mother and Father] that they must stop away at least until the end of August, as an invasion was practically certain. At last, after a lot of argument, they are agreed and I made a run for the train to Paddington.

July 29 Monday

There was a raid alarm this afternoon at 5.30 when 166 people came in, nearly all of them women, mostly with babies. Nothing happened.

July 31 Wednesday

Raid alarm tonight from 9.30 to 10pm. Only 17 people came in. It is surprising how few people bother to take cover at night.

August 3 Saturday

Clearing up today, doing all books and seeing that the cash was right. Alarm at 11.30pm, until 12.30am. My last for a time!

August 4 Sunday

Twenty-six years ago today England embarked on a disastrous war. Who knows but what this one will be even more disastrous? Some have thought that Hitler would begin an invasion today, as he has a weakness for commemorating dates.

I packed up today and after a lot of bother got away at 4pm. 'Sherman's' [the Sissons' house], Dedham, is really lovely and I am going to enjoy this. There is no siren at Dedham at all.

August 5 Monday

Began work at Sherbourne Mill today. There did not seem very much to do but I amused myself successfully. I had lunch and tea at the Mill, all the butter and cream you could eat, and home made bread, made from corn grown on the farm and ground in a little hand mill.

August 7 Wednesday

While we were having supper at 'Sherman's' this evening, a friend of Sisson's rang up from Thorington Hall (Penrose's old house) to say she could hear church bells ringing and asked if it was at Dedham? It certainly was not, and it was obvious that she was imagining things, but although we all went on calmly eating our food, I think every mind was beginning to wonder if there really was anything in it. However, the matter was not mentioned again.

[The ringing of church bells was to be used as a warning of an invasion.]

August 9 Friday

This is a very charming life. Out on the farm all day. Good food and plenty of it. Back to this lovely house. Supper by candlelight, then talking in the drawing room, Sisson playing his spinet, Mrs Sisson with the recorder, reading or sometimes sketching each other.

The weather continues very fine, good for the harvest.

August 12 Monday

Fred, the youngest of the four men on the farm, sometimes talks of the futility of the war. He said today how mad it was that we should have to kill Germans who we didn't know and that they would kill us if they could. Talking of the German air force, he said how some of the men in the Home Guard (to which he belongs) would kill any German they captured but he would not, 'For' he said, 'the poor buggers are just like us really.' He is a typical farm labourer of about 24 and such sentiments are rather unusual. Fisher, a man of about 45 (stockman), is also in the HG, and says he is prepared to kill any German he can get and is not particular how he does it either. The two old men on the farm, the horseman and an odd job man, never mention the war, except to say if a 'plane or a bomb has come down near at hand.

News on the radio today of German attacks on the South Coast, several towns bombed.

August 14 Wednesday

The Sissons have decided to go for a fortnight in Yorkshire tomorrow, so I shall have to go up to Sherbourne Mill for the rest of my time. There has been so much talk about invasion recently I rather think they would like a change of air.

Carting wheat today. Not such tiring work as I thought. I get on the cart and load and Fred pitches.

Tonight we were told that news had been given at 9 o'clock that German parachutes had been found in some parts of the country but that there was no sign of the owners. To me this smells like a plant. If spies or saboteurs had really descended they would naturally destroy their parachutes, not wishing to advertise their arrival. As it is, if the 'chutes were sent down empty, naturally nobody will be found and the Germans can use it as showing the ease with which agents can be landed of whom there is no trace!

August 15 Thursday

I moved my kit up to Sherbourne Mill when I went this morning. I now have a pleasant room in front of the Mill house. The Parringtons sleep downstairs, after bombs fell a quarter of a mile away about a month ago, and I must admit that one does get a very extraordinary impression when a 'plane flies over that it will drop one bomb which must hit your house, although it may be the only one for miles.

It seems from today's papers that the parachutes found yesterday were bluff – some of them had not even been opened.

August 16 Friday

Most alarming experience today. We all went to tea at Mrs Belfield's at Dedham. It was a dull afternoon and Agatha Belfield, a somewhat intense young lady, was explaining to me various aspects of hand-weaving, a subject on which she is most enthusiastic. Through the conversation I heard the obvious thuds of bombs and an ever-increasing roar of aircraft. At last, being unable to stand it any longer, I remarked that there must be a very large number of 'planes about, so the whole company tramped outside, where we could at once hear machine-guns firing among the roar of engines, all high above the clouds. Suddenly I heard a horrible whining shriek and said, 'Isn't that falling bombs?' We all scuttled back indoors, expecting to hear a tremendous explosion at once but only a dull reverberation came. The noise of the aerial battle died away towards the coast. We left shortly after and when calling at a house in Lawford, Mrs Parrington was shown a bomb splinter picked up on Brantham marshes, still warm, but our biggest surprise was when we got back to Sherbourne to be told by Fisher that seven bombs had fallen on the other side of the railway line, towards Manningtree, about a quarter of a mile away. These were the ones we heard fall. Fisher and everybody else nearby threw themselves down, thinking the bombs must be right on top of them. Fisher insisted on showing everybody the exact spot among the cabbages where he performed this act.

Later we got news that a large body of German 'planes was being chased away from London and in their headlong flight scattered bombs all over the district. Almost 100 fell in fields round Langham and Boxted, some perilously close to houses. Not a single person was injured, though tiles were knocked off and many windows broken. This is nothing short of a miracle.

Mrs Parrington is very anxious that I should stop all next week in order to finish the barley, so I shall go into Colchester tomorrow and see Hull about it. I don't see how he can refuse, especially as harvesting ranks as being of 'national importance'.

August 18 Sunday

This afternoon I drove Mrs Parrington over to Dedham and Langham [where] we were stopped by the Home Guard, which was rather awkward as I had no identity card. Mrs Parrington had hers in her garter, which was also awkward. However, they let us through after a short lecture, and we drove away keeping a careful eye open as there were a number of 'planes about but apparently all British.

August 20 Tuesday

We all went to supper at Mr and Mrs Stuart Rose's, who live in a nice little thatched cottage at Dedham. While we were having supper there was a tremendous explosion and the windows blew open. This was apparently a delayed action bomb at Langham going off. [Before the war] Mrs Rose was something to do with the League of Nations and Mr Rose was an artist. She is now a proof-reader at a printing works in Brantham, while he is a cowman on a farm.

August 21 Wednesday

Carting all day. I stayed to get the harvest finished, which we did, carting the whole of the barley in one day.

August 22 Thursday

German 'planes over this afternoon. The old horseman was ploughing in the big field and he did not even bother to look up at them.

I now realise that there is no hope of my getting permanent work here. It is a very small farm and farming is now in such a terribly depressed state that it is unreasonable to expect farmers to take on any more men. Wages [have been] put up from 32 to 48 shillings a week and it is obvious that many men must be stood off by winter time. Parrington is a most humane man and I am sure he will not put any of the men off if he can possibly help it.

August 24 Saturday

Came back from Lawford today. This afternoon there was a raid at 3 o'clock, so I went straight back to the Castle. There was an enormous crowd in the Vaults, so it was lucky I did. A lot of German 'planes were chased over the town and we could hear the rattle of machine-guns and then the awful screaming of a 'plane coming down out of control. It crashed in flames at Abberton.

This evening had supper at Rose's. It was nice to be back again.

August 26 Monday

Tremendous air battle this afternoon. The sirens sounded and we had a full crowd in the Vaults. I went up on the roof and very soon the air seemed full of the screaming of falling 'planes. We have all heard the sound so often on films that it really seems quite natural and one tends to forget that this is real and that you are watching young men go down to a particularly unpleasant death. We could see burning 'planes to the east, west, and south and I saw one of our fighters make a forced landing in the east. All this took place in brilliant sunshine.

August 27 Tuesday

Heard today that the parents are determined to come home at the end of this week, so I must bow to the inevitable.

August 30 Friday

Alarm today at 4.15pm when more than 200 people came into the Vaults. Hot day.

August 31 Saturday

My day to go to Maidenhead. Awakened by sirens at 8am, so I rushed up to the Castle unwashed and unfed. While I was on the roof a big flock of 'planes came over from the west at a great height and I could hear machine-gun fire and suddenly, in the midst of it, the scream of falling bombs. They seemed right overhead and I fled down the stairs at top speed. Rather as an anti-climax there were no explosions, only 'plops'. As the noise of 'planes died away I went back aloft but could see no sign of damage or smoke anywhere. Scores of incendiary bombs also fell, doing little damage, although one fell into a room where there was a mother and a new-born child without injuring either.

As soon as we got an 'all clear', I went off to see if the stables were damaged but no sooner had I got there then the sirens went again, so back to the Castle. Nearly 200 people came into the Vaults this time. However, nothing happened. I went back home but before I could get anything to eat there was another alarm at 1.15pm. This lasted until 2pm.

I decided to catch the 5.35 to London but found it had been cancelled. The next was the 6.13 but at 6 o'clock there was another alarm and all passengers were made to shelter in the new subways. The London train came in and crawled along at 15mph as far as Ingatestone, where an 'all clear' was given and finally got to Liverpool Street at 8.30pm. Got to Paddington to find no train before 10.05pm. I tried to ring Aunt's next door neighbour to explain this but could not get through and, almost at once, a dreadful amplifier arrangement in the roof announced another raid.

Instantly every light was extinguished. The darkness was intense. People began to hurry backwards and forwards buying tickets and looking for trains. I was very nervous and walked slowly towards the tube entrance, together with many others. The tube station was instantly shut, thereby excluding the public from hundreds of yards of very safe shelters and we had to stand in the short length between the tube station gates and the bottom of the stairs. I heard the loudspeaker say, 'Will persons standing beneath the glass roof kindly refrain from striking matches?'

At 10 o'clock I went to the booking-hall and could hear sirens wailing all round the station, a much worse noise in the intense darkness of Paddington than at home. I got a ticket and in great anxiety found the train. Once or twice I nearly fell off the edge of the platform. The train was so black it was impossible to see if the carriages were full or not but I found one with only 2 people in it. The train left sharp on time. Westbourne Grove, Acton etc.

were dark as hell, the only gleam being the beams of far off searchlights above the houses. At Ealing, we could hear 'all clear' sounding and to my joy the lights came on in the carriages, revealing my travelling companions were RAF men. We chatted a bit and when they mentioned Maidenhead I knew they were going to the aerodrome at White Waltham but none of us said so, although we knew what was meant. At Taplow we could see searchlights wandering all over the sky and leaving Maidenhead Station I heard with a sinking heart the familiar hum of a German 'plane. Even here there was no escape from them.

All were in bed except Aunt, so after a brief greeting to the parents, I went to bed in the dining room and lay listening to the German 'plane until at last he dropped 9 bombs and made off into the distance.

September 1 Sunday

Seeing that there was no possible hope of extending the parents' stay at Maidenhead, I determined to bring them back today. It was a glorious evening and as we crossed Brunel's bridge I could see the gleaming river bearing processions of boats up to the lock, while away to the south the tower of Windsor Castle shone pink in the evening sun. It was a slow train but reached London eventually and I was relieved to find no warning on. A taxi from Paddington to Liverpool Street went through the Park, where we saw hundreds of people sitting on seats, chairs, or on the grass, under the shadow of AA guns, apparently without a care in the world.

At Liverpool Street we found a notice to say that all passengers beyond Brentwood must change there as there was an unexploded bomb on the main line. Apparently it was there last night when I came through but had not been noticed. This meant that after travelling in acute discomfort we were compelled to take buses from Brentwood to Shenfield station. Only three double-decker buses were provided for at least 500 people. The scrum was terrific and we all got separated, each on a different bus. Father seemed to stand up to the battle very well and fairly fought his way onto a bus.

I noticed that a German 'plane was brought down right across the railway line near Shenfield. There were still bits lying about. The train to Colchester was packed, mostly with soldiers, but the parents fortunately got seats as soldiers gave them up, most kindly. We did not reach Colchester until 9.30pm. Called at Rose's and had some tea. So home to bed. What a day.

September 4 Wednesday

An alarm at 9.30pm. Tremendous firing in the direction of Harwich. A dozen people came into the Vaults. This is the 50th raid since the war began. Made a lot of tea for all and sundry to celebrate the fact.

September 5 Thursday

A whole day without any alarms. A big flight of German 'planes flew over the town about 11am, going towards London but no sirens sounded, it is alleged on account of a failure in the electric current. They made a great roar as they crossed the crowded streets, fortunately without dropping any bombs.

September 7 Saturday

There was an alarm on this afternoon at 5.30. 126 people went into the Castle Vaults.

Had supper with Rose and was much disturbed by the number of 'planes going over about 10pm. The radio news tonight says there have been severe raids on London today. There was some excitement in the town during the evening and apparently an invasion scare is in progress. All soldiers were fetched out of the pubs by the Military Police and the Home Guard was called out. I saw several lorry loads of soldiers going into the Park about 10.30pm to man the strong points there. It seemed to me a most unlikely night for an invasion, as the weather is cold and windy.

[The London raids marked the beginning of the Blitz that continued until 10 May 1941.]

September 8 Sunday

News today confirms that there were tremendous raids in London yesterday and at least 400 were killed. Terrific damage done, especially in the Docks areas. News tonight of further great attacks on London and several hundred more killed.

Invasion scare seems to have died down. No soldiers on duty tonight and a good many were allowed out of barracks this evening for the first time for several days.

September 10 Tuesday

Alarm this morning from 2am to 5am. 'Planes were coming in very fast on their way to London. Terribly cold on the Castle roof.

At 10am came what I had expected all the summer, and had half begun to hope we should escape – notices for the evacuation of Colchester. Old or infirm people, retired persons, women and children are urged to leave immediately. How I cursed and raved at having the old parents here, after all the trouble I had in getting them away. I felt sick with anxiety. I went up the street and saw a crowd outside the Town Hall, reading larger bills about the same thing.

As soon as these notices were received, all schools shut immediately and everybody in offices and shops that were responsible for old parents were sent home at once to see after them. As I thought, when I got home the parents resolutely refused to leave again under any circumstances. Mother dismisses the whole thing as 'a piece of nonsense'.

More terrible raids in London. Two or three hundred dead and much damage done. I do hope both Mauna Benham and Mary Tovell are safe. Several hospitals have been hit.

Tonight I took all available blankets and rugs to the Castle which was as well I did, for there was an alarm at 9.30pm, which lasted until 5am on Wednesday. Many 'planes came over and I could hear a lot of bombs falling but nothing very close. The blankets made all the difference.

[The evacuation notice, pasted into Rudsdale's journal, at this point states:

Urgent Notice: Temporary Transfer of Population
The public throughout the Country has been asked to 'stay put' and that it will do, but special considerations apply to this town. Some reduction in its population will make it easier for the Army

to operate. For this reason we ask, as a patriotic duty, all those whose work does not require them to remain, to leave the town temporarily as soon as possible.]

September 12 Thursday

An announcer van was going round the streets today, urging all who could to leave at once. Another notice was published today, warning inhabitants that in the event of an invasion this town was liable to heavy bombing.

It is said AA guns are being brought here. Of course, their presence makes bombing very probable but I think it is better to have them about, for at least you feel that something is being done. Everybody asking, 'Well, what do you think of things now?'

The weather is overcast and gloomy. The wind has been getting up a bit this last day or two, so perhaps gales will stop them. Poulter and my Father profess to disbelieve in any real invasion.

Anxious about the future of the Museum. Strong possibility that I shall lose my job. I would give anything to be settled down in a farm in Wales.

September 14 Saturday

Two alarms this afternoon, one at 4.15, when we had a couple of hundred in and the other at 6. 'All clear' by 7.15. The atmosphere in the Vaults gets very bad after a big crowd has been in.

Had a card from Mauna Benham to say she is alright and little damage has so far been done in Paddington.

September 17 Tuesday

Papers still talking invasion. Churchill spoke again today. He said that although wind, waves and bombs had severely damaged the Germans, we must expect invasion in the enemy's good time.

Heard that the police raided the pacifists' home at Langham Oaks, where Max Plowman [the writer and pacifist] lives, on August 16 but with little result. Simply malicious persecution.

September 20 Friday

Rose had a letter from her brother John today, to whom she had written about a job for me. He cannot suggest anything. He says 'we are nearing the end of our busy season and as wages have been raised there are a great many farm workers round here going to be out of their jobs this winter. So far, since the spring, we have lost 9 men and when we need extra labour for fruit or hop-picking we import some of the Land Army people who are prepared to camp in buildings for a month or so at a time. We are reducing pigs from nearly 1,000 to somewhere about 300, owing to shortage of feeding stuffs, which means less labour will be needed and again, crops will probably be lighter another year after going without manure and so they will not take so much harvest labour.'

Could one have a gloomier picture of the future of agriculture in this country? This man is in charge of a big farm and if this is typical of the rest of England I really believe there will be a great deal of hunger in the land before the end of next year.

September 21 Saturday

This evening there was an alarm at 8pm. A lot of 'planes were coming and going across moving apparently slowly, each at the apex of a mass of searchlights. At about quarter to 10 there was an immense flash towards the north, beyond the station and a dull explosion. Within a few minutes we could see the red flickering of a fire, while the searchlights followed a 'plane away towards the coast.

September 22 Sunday

Heard from Poulter that the fire to the north, which we saw last night, was at Horkesley, where the church and a public house had been totally destroyed. I decided to investigate and was very sceptical. However, on reaching Horkesley I found the disaster had been entirely understated. It is Little Horkesley Church that has gone and the 'Beehive' [pub] nearby. Two parachute-mines fell, one scoring a direct hit on the church and the other falling in the yard at the back of the 'Beehive'. Alas, there is no exaggeration – the church has been totally destroyed, not a fragment of wall standing more than 3 or 4 feet high. What of the wooden effigies, the Swynborne brasses and all the rest [of the church artefacts]? I felt urged to instant action. The whole parish was closed off, every road was being guarded, as it was suspected there might be a further bomb, unexploded. I went to the Police Station and after a bit of argument with the Sergeant, I got permission to see the Vicar.

Back I went in teeming rain and went through the barrier to the Vicarage. The Vicar, the Revd Lawrence, is a New Zealander and has only been there since May. I offered him all the help we could give him and suggested that we should make an immediate start on salvage work tomorrow, as whatever remains of the effigies would obviously suffer severely in such weather as we have had today. He more or less agreed to accept our help and then pushed me off hurriedly as he had people coming to tea. Apparently even such a disaster as this cannot interfere with a Vicarage tea.

If the whole contents of the church have been lost, it is indeed a terrible disaster. But how much there is to be thankful for, that nobody was killed and only one person seriously injured (Mrs Patten, wife of the landlord of the 'Beehive').

I phoned Duncan Clark and Dr Laver and heard they had been over this morning. Duncan Clark promised full help and cooperation, although he, as diocesan architect, is only responsible for parsonage houses and not the churches themselves, I discover to my amazement.

September 23 Monday

This afternoon Laver, Poulter, me and George Farmer all went over to Horkesley.

The church is a terrible complete wreck. There is no shape or form. It is just a vast pile of rubble, with beams and planks sticking out of it like a porcupine's quills. Timbers at least 9 x 9 inches have been shattered and split in the most extraordinary way. Lengths of 4 x 2 inches have been driven into the ground like giant arrows. The whole district, it seems, is covered with dust, rubble and bits of lead. Some lead sheets were blown 300 yards into a field full of horses and cows and never hit one of them.

Even the bells are shattered to fragments, some pieces and parts of bell ropes being in the east end of the churchyard. The east wall and east window have completely vanished and huge fragments of the window stones landed on a lawn 100 yards away, making dents several inches deep. The scene is one of incredible desolation. The nearby 'Priory' has every window blown out and all the tiles off, yet the occupier, Mrs Denham, and her young daughter were untouched. She was at her front door when the church was hit and actually saw the building dissolve before her eyes. At Little Horkesley Hall, every window has gone, some ceilings are down, and lumps of timber and lead were found on the roof. Great sheets of lead are all over the lawn in front. Over everywhere is a smell of dust and powdered mortar.

In the Hall stables were several pieces of the female oak figure which Duncan Clark and the Doctor had picked up in the churchyard yesterday morning. Heaven knows where the rest of them may be. We quickly located the great Swynborne brass and uncovered the lower part of it. Its stone bed is utterly shattered and the brass in dozens of fragments but we were careful to save every piece.

[Little Horkesley Church contained three wooden effigies of two knights and a lady, dating from the thirteenth century, and two medieval brasses for the Swynborne family and the Marney family, all of which were located and salvaged by the Museum staff and restored to the church when it was rebuilt in 1958.]

[See Images 16, 17 and 18]

September 25 Wednesday

To Horkesley all day. We got the whole Swynborne brass out and transported into the stables. It looks in a terrible mess, the great marble slab being broken into eight or nine pieces.

While searching round the site at lunchtime I was lucky enough to find part of one of the oak knights. Poulter came over this afternoon and photographed the Swynbornes before removal.

September 27 Friday

Today is the 80th Anniversary of the opening of the Colchester Museum in the Castle Crypt, 1860 and yesterday was the 11th anniversary of the opening of Holly Trees in 1929. How nice it would be to be back in either year, preferably 1860. Only one alarm today.

September 29 Sunday

[These air raid alarms] make me think how our glorious system works in a time like this – the really rich got a sure tip and went [abroad] before the war began; the next wealthiest go to Welsh resorts and the Lakes. The middle classes go to stay with relatives in the country. The lower middle classes make do with the Anderson shelters and weird contraptions which they invent for themselves and the really poor, the classes who always suffer in any war, win or lose, just continue to suffer. Thank God they still had enough guts to get into the [Underground] tubes and stay there, defying all efforts to move them.

September 30 Monday

Most surprised to have a letter from Hervey Benham at Southampton, begging that I shall keep a careful record of Colchester matters during the war and expressing the hope (with which I fervently concur) that I may escape the Army.

October 2 Wednesday

A day of considerable excitement. I was cycling up Queen Street this morning, when I heard a 'plane and looking up saw him flying very low, towards the north. I was just thinking 'I wonder if that's a German?' when he opened fire with machine-guns. I did not wait to think further. I went up on the [Castle] Tower and saw several Spitfires rushing about, obviously hunting the intruder. No alarm was sounded although he dropped four or five bombs. One fell in the gateway to the back premises of the Borough's Maternity Hospital and another dropped in Vint Crescent, breaking windows and blowing off tiles. A little girl in one of the houses was cut by broken glass but the only other casualty of the whole affair was a proof-reader at the 'Essex County Telegraph' office, who received a bullet in his back. He is not badly hurt. [Later] I heard that our 'plane was shot down at Earl Soham in Suffolk, all the crew escaping alive by parachute.

October 3 Thursday

Dreadful tragedy. It was a dull, rainy morning, with low cloud. As I walked across the Park I heard a 'plane right overhead, appallingly threatening and quite invisible. It died away and I went home, just before 1 o'clock. At a few minutes past, as I stood in the dining room reading the paper, there were three big explosions, rattling doors and windows. I called to Mother and Father to keep away from the windows and get down the cellar but they would not. I ran out into the road and could hear a 'plane receding. It was still raining. I sensed that something must be wrong and got on my bike just in time to see the AFS unit dash off down Old Heath Road. I followed. Over the brow of the hill a cloud of yellow smoke drifted away in the rain. The road was full of people and about half way down, on the left side, was a great pit, with brown clay sent right across the road. The path had vanished and the railings of two front gardens had gone. George [Farmer]'s wife, rather white, was standing there holding George's helmet and gas mask. She begged me to find him and give them to him. The bomb was about 20 yards from George's house. George was coming up the hill from Scarletts Road. 'There's a house down, round the corner,' he said, 'with some people under it.' We hurried down. It was a house on the east side, right on the corner where the road bends. The whole house was down and there was an awful smell of lime and mortar in the air. [See Image 20]

We went right into the garden. There were Rescue Parties on top of the stuff. Somebody had just been put into a car, which was driven off at great speed, ambulance men standing on the running board, horn blowing loudly. Two wardens just in front of me suddenly dragged out what appeared to be an old woman, thickly covered with dust and mortar. They carried her down the road. Her skirt was torn and you could see the red flannel drawers underneath. Her eyes were open and she stared hard ahead of her. On the wreckage was a man with a bloody bandage round his head. There seemed to be great confusion all around, some cars and cycles were trying to get up the road, two buses trying to get down. I heard a cry of 'escaping gas', 'no smoking', 'don't light any matches'. I thought 'God! Now I suppose the whole thing will blow up again'.

A warden came up to me and said, 'Why the hell don't you stop the traffic?' so I went down to the bottom of the hill and did so. I heard somebody mention the Laundry and several ambulance cars went off in a hurry down Distillery Lane. A warden came past, so I asked him what happened at the Laundry. He said three girls were dead.

It was still raining. A man came out of a house nearby and lent me a raincoat, for which I was grateful, as I was wet through. After some hours, about 3 o'clock I suppose, I left my post for a few minutes to go down to rescue my cycle. I found the hill roped off, as they had discovered an unexploded bomb in a house on the west side. It had gone through the roof and buried itself in the kitchen floor, while a boy of twelve, who was actually in the room, was uninjured. He was alone in the house and, after a time, very shyly told a Warden what had happened. Everybody had to move for 50 yards on either side. A Royal Engineer Sergeant nearby said it might be days before the bomb went off, so I thought I might safely fetch my cycle, which was standing half-way up the hill.

Back on my 'point', I had to deal with several people in cars that were looking for rela- tives in Scarletts Road. It was lucky that I knew the name of the people in the bombed house – Strong – so I could relieve their fears. About 5 o'clock another Special came up and told me I could go, as Scarletts Road was now clear. I took back the raincoat and went. George was still hanging around, very smart in his official police mackintosh [but] wet and worn out like me. It was only then that I heard what had happened at the Strongs' house. Strong himself, a boot maker at Scheregate Steps, had just come home to dinner and was in the act of putting his cycle away, when the bomb fell onto his house. In an instant, his wife, child and sister were buried. It was the sister I saw brought out and the child who was taken away in a car. He is not expected to live.

It seems incredible that at 1 o'clock this man had a wife and family and a home. At 5 past he had nothing. His wife was in the kitchen. Did he see her for the last time as he went past the window? Was he intending to say something special to her when he got home? What had he hoped his boy would become when he grew up? This seems to me a most appalling tragedy.

I went down and had a look at the Laundry, which was a complete wreck. A bomb had just hit one corner and the whole place had collapsed in ruins, killing three girls and an elderly woman, who were having lunch there. If the bombs had fallen a little later, 150 girls would have been in the place. The girls were killed instantly. They were only 18 and 19 years old.

Then I went back and saw George and told him he and his wife could sleep at ours if he wished as they had to move because of the unexploded bomb but they had already made arrangements. He told me Mrs Strong's legs could now be seen deep in the bomb crater. As I stood there an ambulance drew up, apparently by mistake, for a Rescue party man said, 'It isn't an ambulance we want,' but after some muttered conversation a stretcher and some waterproof covers were taken into the wreckage.

By this time I had had enough, so I decided to cycle over to Dedham to get a quiet evening [and had] 4 hours quiet enjoyment, good company and food. It seemed very strange to relate this afternoon's scenes, sitting in that 18th century drawing room. The strange thing was that I hardly ever felt really frightened, not even when, on point duty,

I could hear a 'plane hovering overhead. Two women, passing by, asked if it was one of ours, I said I didn't know but advised them, if they heard anything whistle, to lie down at once. 'Oh,' said one, 'we couldn't, on a wet day like this.'

[See Image 19]

October 5 Saturday

Hardly got to bed last night before I was turned out to an alarm at 2.45am. I am beginning to think I should do very much better if I slept at the Castle every night. Getting up and dressing there would be much less trouble and harmful to my health than these mad rushes through inky black streets.

Quite unexpectedly, little Tovell came in today. She looks remarkably well, although she has had some unpleasantly narrow escapes.

Alarm at 9.10pm lasting all night. A good number of 'planes over but no bombs.

October 8 Tuesday

George Farmer went to Uxbridge today to see about a job as a ground-staff wireless operator in the RAF.

October 9 Wednesday

There were two alarms in the early hours of this morning but I was so tired that I did not hear either of them. Mother and Father both went downstairs (as they invariably do) but never woke me. In the evening an alarm began at 7.45pm and went on all night. I settled down to sleep in the Castle's 'Oven' or Guardroom.

[The 'Oven' is a cell in the castle entrance where the Quaker martyr James Parnell was imprisoned and died in 1656.]

October 12 Saturday

Advance party of Australian troops [arrived in the town] today, looking very tough, capable and untidy. Another alarm tonight. Only two people came in. Nobody bothers any more now. Few 'planes.

October 14 Monday

This evening a large body of Australians arrived, marching down the High Street behind their band, which was playing the great Australian march, 'Waltzing Matilda'. They marched oddly, carrying their rifles as they pleased, looking like some strange Army of bygone ages as they straggled along the street, laughing and shouting, their great cowboy hats looking strange in the moonlight. There must be many thousands of them. Some say 10,000. All the while German 'planes were passing over. Big crowds lined the streets to see them go by. It was a most amazing sight.

October 16 Wednesday

Today I bought two volumes of Kilvert's Diary [a record of rural life in the Welsh Marches in the 1870s], which I so much admire. Went to the pictures tonight but had to come out for an alarm soon after 7 o'clock. Lot of bombs falling round about, in heavy rain. One thing, every bomb that falls in our fields is one less in London.

October 20 Sunday

My dear Mother's birthday. I do not know her age but I fancy she must be about 70.

October 21 Monday

A whole day without any alarms at all! Spent a peaceful evening with Rose. The first for a fortnight. Went to bed at home tonight, reluctantly.

October 22 Tuesday

My reluctance to sleep at home justified. Alarm at 3am. Not worth coming home for this.

October 23 Wednesday

Being unable to borrow a horse anywhere to go to Little Horkesley, I took old Bob up, with nothing in him but hay and grass, and drove him over there with the van, taking him very steady. It was cold and rather wet but he went very well. I loaded up all the effigies and the brasses, which I had already packed. Old Bob came back wonderfully, hardly a sweat mark on him, yet we must have had half a ton on board.

Decided that for the time being I will always stay in the Castle at nights.

October 30 Wednesday

Coming back down Lexden Road [this afternoon] I saw a small crowd opposite the house which the Australians have taken for HQ offices, outside which was a large maroon-coloured Daimler which I recognised to be the King's. Sure enough, in a few minutes he came out, with half a dozen officers and walked slowly down the drive towards his car. The crowd gave a cheer and he got in and drove away towards London, with several staff cars and an escort of Army motorcyclists. Nobody had any idea that the King was coming today, he was in the town and district all day, inspecting the Australians.

October 31 Thursday

The King was here again today. He spent last night near Bishop's Stortford and came into the town again today to inspect the headquarters of the Observer Corps.

Very lonely in the Castle tonight, All Hallows' Eve. Went on the roof for a long time, more than half expecting to see horrible shapes flying through the air. After 11 o'clock

I could hear strange little creakings and patterings in the distant parts of the building, caused I suppose by rats. Any rate, I hope so.

November 5 Tuesday

I finished cleaning the Horkesley effigies today and the pieces are all ready to be joined together.

Heard today that young Tim Smith, George Farmer's brother-in-law, has been killed in Malta. He was a very pleasant young man, only about 22. My Father used to teach him at Hamilton Road School. Poor lad, I so often saw him in the Town Clerk's Office. Who would have thought he would die in an island far away in the Mediterranean?

November 12 Tuesday

This morning Poulter, Laver, old Mailar and I were examining the [Little Horkesley] figures on the floor of the Holly Trees drawing room, when I heard a 'plane approach, then a whistle and the thud of bombs. There was, of course, no warning. They were all discussing details of the repairs, so I said, 'Excuse me a minute' and rushed out. I went up onto the Castle roof with binoculars and could see a hazy cloud of smoke drifting over Ipswich Road. When I went back to Holly Trees the old gentlemen were still discussing the figures, so I said the bombs appeared to have fallen somewhere near Ipswich Road. They replied, 'What bombs?' and admitted that they had heard neither the 'plane nor the explosion. I only wish I could be as gloriously detached as that.

November 15 Friday

I notice how charming women's clothes are becoming – the pretty little hats, the hooded cloaks, the fur-lined boots. Most women, providing they are reasonably slim and under 40, contrive to look very charming in trousers or 'slacks' as they generally call them.

Alarm at a quarter to 6 tonight until 7 o'clock the following morning. 'Planes seemed to be going over in hundreds and after midnight there was a steady roar, hour by hour, as they flew back towards the sea. Searchlights flickered about but there was not the slightest opposition, in this area at any rate. When the afternoon papers came out, we learnt that there had been a terrible devastating raid on Coventry. Although not more than 250 people have been killed, not so many as a London raid, the damage appears to have been terrific. The Cathedral and almost the whole centre of the city has gone. As I listened to the 'planes last night I wondered why they were flying to the north-west instead of west or south-west. Apparently there were little or no defences at Coventry, so that the Germans were able to send hundreds of 'planes with no more damage than if on peacetime manoeuvres.

November 21 Thursday

Short alarm during the afternoon and the usual evening alarm at 7.45pm. Shortly after midnight 'planes began to come over and I heard bomb explosions in the distance. Becket, the architect, and three other wardens had come in to see the Horkesley figures by the light of torches. I was describing the work of restoration when another warden ran in to say there were fires to the north. We all went up to the roof and stood on the central lantern from which we could see dozens of incendiary bombs around the station. In one place a shed or chicken house was burning but no other buildings were alight. One of the wardens almost walked off the lantern roof being unable to see the edge in the dark. I must have a white line painted on it. The fires gradually died away. Trains were stopped outside the station for a time but soon moved on. After that nothing more happened.

November 30 Saturday

Big crowds about the town today. Everybody seems very gloomy about Christmas. Next year is promised to be far worse than this. I don't know what I shall do. I do so wish I could get settled.

December 1 Sunday

Lay late in bed, felt ill. Mauna Benham came to Port Lane this morning and we went carting hay. She takes a very gloomy view about the war. London hospital authorities are convinced that the Germans will shortly begin great gas attacks.

December 3 Tuesday

The 200th alarm came tonight, from 9.35 to 10.35pm. A few 'planes were about but nothing happened.

December 9 Monday

Another alarm this morning at 12.30am lasting until 5am. I heard that a 'plane let go a mass of incendiary bombs over the west end of the town. One went through the roof of 'Westfields', the Benhams' house, right into the bedroom of Lady Benham's sister but did not ignite, while several others fell in the garden.

I went up to Sir Gurney Benham's office to congratulate him on a narrow escape and found the old gentleman calm and nonchalant. He said they all got up, all of them quite old people, and he advised the cook not to rush outside in case there were high explosives nearby. Of course, this business happened when there was no alarm on, so that there was some difficulty in getting the fire service people to react quickly, as they were nearly all asleep.

December 11 Wednesday

Short alarm in the middle of the morning. Very few bother to come into the shelters now, either in daytime or night time. In spite of the terrible raids that go on in London and big cities in the north very few people seem to have any fear of the bombers and you find the streets full of the usual strollers, men and girls laughing and talking, while the great bombers sail over the town at a tremendous height.

December 12 Thursday

Went down to Rose's tonight. There was a sergeant of the Tank Corps there, named Brotherton. She met him at a 'musical evening' recently and suggested he should come down to the flat. Can't imagine why. He is stationed in Wivenhoe Park. Stayed until half past 11 in order to 'sit him out'.

December 16 Monday

Expected to get a letter from Leslie, the Executive Officer [of the Essex War Agricultural Executive] at Chelmsford. I wrote to him last week, asking if there was any opening for me, as I feel time is getting short. There are rumours that great changes will take place next year and that there will be a tremendous 'comb-out' to get men into the Army. I want to make sure of something as soon as I can.

Went down to Rose's for supper and was very glad to find that the sergeant was not there.

[J.C. Leslie had been the Principal of the Essex Agricultural Institute at Writtle, near Chelmsford. At the outbreak of war, the Institute became the headquarters of the Essex War Agricultural Executive Committee and Leslie was appointed as the Committee's Executive Officer. Rudsdale had known Leslie through collaborations with the Institute on agricultural exhibitions in the 1930s.

The role of the County War Agricultural Executive Committees was to oversee and maximise agricultural production in wartime on behalf of the Ministry of Agriculture and Fisheries. The Committees proved controversial, however, because of the powers vested in them to serve orders on farmers, forcing them to plough up land or grow particular crops, for example. Failure to comply could result in a Committee taking possession of land in order to bring it into cultivation under the direct control of the Executive Committee or by letting the land to approved farmers.]

December 17 Tuesday

Received a most extraordinary Christmas present from Sir Gurney Benham – a large tin of ox-tongue! However, it is really very acceptable in these days.

December 18 Wednesday

The papers are talking about the chance of immediate invasion. Personally I don't think anything is likely to happen before the spring, say April or May.

Still no letter from Leslie. Felt very worried and finally decided to telephone him. Had a little trouble to get through but spoke to him eventually and he promised to call and see me tomorrow. I was overjoyed and felt as if some great anxiety had been removed. Actually nothing whatever has been promised but I have great hopes. Leslie said he had never had my letter so I suppose some other official sidetracked it.

December 19 Thursday

Leslie came this afternoon. He was most pleasant and I think genuinely helpful. He promised nothing definite but says there will be no difficulty in finding me a post in the New Year. Apparently they are taking on any number of people during the next few months.

December 21 Saturday

Three alarms today, morning, afternoon and night, the last of which is still going on now. Nothing about.

All the shops are making a pathetic attempt to keep up Christmas, with paper decorations, bits of holly etc. Buying presents is almost impossible, as there is so little to buy. Only books seem to be fairly plentiful and the bookshops are crowded with buyers, mostly soldiers.

Children still sing carols and one often hears the shrill little voices singing 'Nowell' while the German bombers drone over towards London. I suppose the German children, in their blackout, are singing 'Stille Nacht, Heilige Nacht'.

December 24 Tuesday

The usual last minute rush to get cards and gifts for people who had been forgotten. No chocolates or sweets to be had at all. I miss them a good deal. Pathetic to see how empty the provision shops are compared with normal times. Went down to Rose's tonight. Took her a few little gifts. No alarm.

December 25 Wednesday

The second Christmas of this disastrous war. How many more shall we see before the end? No Christmas bells owing to the fantastic order by which bells may only be used as an invasion warning. This was put on last June and has never been rescinded.

Lay very late this morning and ate breakfast in bed. About 10 o'clock I heard shouting and screaming in High Street, the sound of a motor engine and then what seemed to be shots. I thought at first that a 'plane must be shooting at the town and rushed onto the roof, when I found it was two Australians on a motorcycle, the one on the pillion firing a revolver into the air, both shouting and screaming.

Home to lunch. Mother managed to make a plum-pudding as usual and had a small turkey. Rose was in London today. Had an early supper by myself in the 'Oven' [at the Castle], listening to the shouts and screams of soldiers in the streets. Lots of drunks about tonight.

December 26 Thursday

Rose back from London. The Tank Corps Sergeant came in and we both stayed there until nearly midnight. Then I had to lend him my bike to get back to Wivenhoe Park, as he would otherwise have had to walk. He is quite a nice young chap but I wish he would keep away from Rose.

Heard rumours today that there is another invasion scare on and that all schools have been warned but I don't suppose there is anything in it.

December 27 Friday

Rumours today that a number of men on leave have been hurriedly recalled. Rose says Sergeant Brotherton is leaving shortly. I shan't miss him. Short alarm tonight. Few 'planes.

December 30 Monday

Rumoured that there have been great fires in London and enormous damage done. The Australians are leaving. Hundreds in the town tonight, mad drunk. Our local police keep well out of the way.

December 31 Tuesday

The end of 1940, a year of unparalleled disasters for England. To what can we look forward in 1941? Some poor deluded fools think that the war will end during the next twelve months. We shall be very lucky if it ends within the next twelve years.

Chapter 3

❧❦ 1941 ❧❦

January 1 Wednesday

A year ago today I wrote of a prospect of unrelieved gloom. I said it would be a miracle if New Year's Day 1941 found me alive and at Colchester Castle. That miracle has come about. I am alive, if not exactly well, and am more in the Castle than ever, as I suppose I must be spending about 16 hours a day in it. Since my gloomy writings a year ago, bombs have fallen within a few hundred yards of me but I have been in no ways affected. I am not worried by the fate of friends, because even now, after 16 months of war, I have only three friends in the Forces – Stanley Hills and Hervey Benham in the Navy and George Farmer in the RAF. It is terrible to think of girls of 20 to 25, with every male friend in some dangerous job.

My cash affairs remain about the same but the cost of horse-keep has gone up a lot – hay nearly £10 a ton, oats 18/3 per hundredweight, bran 11/6 per hundredweight. Dreadful prices and not going to the poor farmers either.

My parents are still well and as happy as possible. I am no worse, still coughing, with pains in several parts, bad exhaustion at times, eyesight rather weaker and a recurrence of my old sleepwalking-amnesia trouble (I have done it once at the Castle).

Enemy action in Colchester has not yet had very much effect. The great dangers are now (a) bombing or machine-gunning by solitary 'planes in daylight (b) bombs dropped by 'planes returning from London and (c) an invasion. This last is always in our minds, although hardly anyone ever mentions it, except in joke. At any moment during the next few weeks we may find it is no joke but a terrible reality. I firmly believe (and so do many others) that if the Germans once get a landing in England nothing will stop them. The defences erected look ridiculously inadequate.

Today I was much cheered to have a visit from Mr Sadler and Capt Folkard of the Essex Agricultural Executive, offering me a job as Clerk to the District Committee which is to sit at Colchester. I expressed willingness to take it and sincerely hope I shall get the job, although I shall find it a fearful wrench to break away from the Castle. I told Poulter tonight and he did not express much opinion either way.

Poulter suggests that they ought to take Holly Trees Museum Library as an office, which I must admit would be rather ideal. One thing I should miss here more than anything would be Parnell's Cell which I now find most cosy and (I hope) comparatively safe. As I write in it now (quarter to midnight) 'planes are flying east and 3 or 4 bombs have just dropped. I suppose this is another London attack.

January 2 Thursday

I telephoned to Capt Folkard first thing this morning and suggested the use of the Holly Trees Library. He was pleased with the idea and promised to let me know about my own position early next week. I still can't make up my mind what I ought to do.

At 6pm it began to snow hard and soon 2 or 3 inches lay on the ground. It came over in great clouds and I was surprised to hear 'planes coming over. At one time there were at least six on all sides of the town and I began to fear that there was going to be an attack but they all passed over. A good many searchlights were out and twice the whole heavens were lit by curious green flashes, rather like magnesium flares, which I believe is a dodge to try to locate 'planes. Naturally, being a British idea it doesn't work.

It was most amazing to me to hear these 'planes flying about in thick snow. We have been told that even a thin ground mist will make flying very dangerous and almost impossible, yet on an awful night like this they are all over us, unhindered and quite unperturbed.

January 3 Friday

At last got the third volume of Kilvert's Diary, which seems to me to be just as good as the other two, although I think the Clyro period in the first was the best of all. Kilvert's question of himself (November 3, 1874) 'Why do I keep this voluminous journal?' I too might ask and his answer seems to me to give the best reason that any journalist can hope for – 'Partly because life appears to me to be such a curious and wonderful thing that it almost seems a pity that even such a humble and uneventful life as mine should pass altogether away without some such record as this, and partly because I think the record may amuse and interest some who come after me.' How true this is. Certainly I cannot see any other justification for writing, except that in my case I consider it my duty to record as faithfully as possible the archaeological matters which come to my notice (and how badly I do it!).

January 4 Saturday

Today I had the most incredible luck. If only it holds good I ought to be the luckiest man in Colchester. When I got home I found a form from the Ministry of Labour – fill in exact details of your employment. This did not look too good and I determined to write to Capt Folkard, emphasising my desire to work under him but before I could do so he came into the Castle to see me. He seemed to presume that my appointment was almost fixed! 'When could I begin? At once?' I told him I ought to give a week's notice. 'Could I be "temporarily transferred" from the Museum?' I thought this over, wrestling with my conscience. Finally I thought I might. 'Would I see the Chairman today?' I would. 'Would Capt Folkard like to see the Holly Trees room?' He would, and was charmed with it. 'Would I also mention this to the Chairman?'

After lunch I telephoned Sir Gurney Benham and told him the whole thing. First he did not want me to go – Museum could not manage without me. I talked to him a bit, pointed out the advantages of letting the Library, of transferring me and so saving my salary and yet still having me about the place. At last he agreed and said I might tell

Folkard that the matter would receive favourable consideration but that the Committee would be the final authority.

After tea I phoned to Capt Folkard, who seemed very pleased at what I had done. If this all comes off, my luck is incredible. I shall have a good job, a safe job and still keep my little cubby-hole in the Castle. I don't believe I could bear to sleep at home now.

The last of the Australians went today, so the town is fairly quiet. Nobody knows where they have gone. Scotch soldiers are now in the Mersea Road barracks.

January 5 Sunday

This afternoon went over to Dedham to Sisson's for tea. Sisson had been to London last Thursday and says the scenes of ruin and desolation are indescribable. He reckons that the best of the Wren churches are gone but points out that only 8 may be said to be destroyed, whereas a few years ago the Ecclesiastical Commissioners and the Bishop of London wanted to destroy 19, so the Germans have a good deal to do before they reach an English standard of destruction. Came home on sheets of ice, in bleak cold, with German 'planes coming over very low every few minutes, accompanied by heavy gunfire to the east. I felt pretty scared but no bombs were dropped.

January 6 Monday

Met Capt Folkard at half past 9 and went out to Birch Hall [to attend my first meeting of the Lexden & Winstree District War Agricultural Committee]. We met in the main hall before a roaring log fire, the mantel above which was carved with the Borough Arms, and sat on uncomfortable chairs having the Round crest of a lion couchant in high relief on their backs. Capt Round [Chairman of the District Committee] came in, looking every inch the country squire and was very nice to me. I sat at the table with Capt Folkard and took notice of how the meeting was run.

On the Committee were Col Furneaux from Fingringhoe Hall and Frank Warren the Suffolk breeder from Godbolts, also Councillor Alec Craig from Moat Farm who spoke to me and was pleased I was coming in with them. I soon found it was presumed by all present that I have now taken up this work. The meeting was very long, lasting from 9.45am to 1.15pm and a big agenda was dealt with. I felt quite at home with the whole affair and even made a suggestion about acquiring Hall Barn and the stables at West Mersea, which was well received.

Folkard brought me back and I said I would see Sir Gurney Benham again, [so that] we could begin without delay. As it happened, I saw Hull first and was told Sir Gurney had arranged to hold a Special Committee Meeting on Wednesday. This is wonderful, as it will hardly give Laver enough time to work up a successful opposition. Tonight rang Folkard and told him what progress had been made. He was very pleased.

[The Round family had previously owned Colchester Castle and Hollytrees before they were bought for the Borough of Colchester with money donated by Viscount Cowdray (formerly MP for Colchester) in the 1920s. Capt Round's great uncle, Charles Gray Round, had first given permission for part of the castle to be used as the town museum in 1855.]

January 7 Tuesday

Busy clearing up matters at the Castle. Laver came over, quiet as a lamb, enquiring as to exact details of the whole scheme. No opposition at all. Anyway, I told him exactly what had happened so far.

Three alarms this afternoon but the rest of the evening quite quiet and went down to Rose's. She is overjoyed about the new job.

January 8 Wednesday

Well, it is all settled. The Museum Committee agreed to the proposals. Sir Gurney Benham came out at the end and told me it was settled and the Doctor threatened me with the rigours of working under Capt Round but I don't feel very nervous about that.

I can't yet believe that it is really true. This afternoon I went to the Ministry of Labour and enquired in what way I should fill in the form which I received last Saturday. I gathered (without asking directly) that I am definitely 'reserved' and that local government staffs are also still 'reserved', both at 30. To be in a 'reserved' job and still with my connections at the Museum undisturbed, what could possibly be better? What have I done to deserve all this, when so many men are ruined?

When I went to the Ministry of Labour I had to go to the department which has taken over [the old timber-framed] house in East Stockwell Street. When I agitated to save that house, all those years ago, little did I think to what use it would be put in 1940. The rooms are filled with men working out the fates of thousands of others, while all round stand filing-cabinets labelled 'Army', 'Navy', 'Air Force', 'Medical', etc.

January 9 Thursday

About a quarter to 6 tonight, while I was at Bourne Mill, German 'planes started to come over and although it was still broad daylight, there was no opposition whatsoever. No sirens sounded, although they continued to come over every five minutes or so. At last, just as I was about to go to Rose's, the sirens went at 8 o'clock.

The whole system of alarms is perfectly farcical. Any one of the 'planes could have bombed or machine-gunned us. It is almost the truth to say that when an alarm is sounded we may anticipate no danger. Most of the bombs dropped in this Borough have fallen at times when no alarm is in operation. About 9.30pm 'planes began to go back, quite unhindered, of course, and just as the Town Hall clock struck 11pm, six or seven heavy bombs fell. I rushed up to the Tower and saw a big glare to the south-east, perhaps at Brightlingsea or beyond. Sincerely hope nobody was killed or hurt.

It was in the press yesterday that one night recently a bomb exploded at the BBC in Portland Place, just as the 9 o'clock news was being read. The bang was heard over the air, quite distinctly. I heard it myself at Rose's and than a voice said 'It's alright', after which the announcer went on reading the news. At that moment seven people were killed in the building, five of them girls.

January 10 Friday

Learnt this morning that the bombs which fell at 11 o'clock last night demolished 3 houses at Brightlingsea and severely damaged two others. Although people were sleeping in them upstairs, by a miracle nobody was injured.

January 13 Monday

I began with the Essex War Agricultural Executive today and went down to Wivenhoe with Capt Folkard this morning. I have long known that the British Army is 'organised chaos' but the EWAE is not even organised. Never have I seen such a mess. Masses of papers, files, chits, more files, without order, without system. Everybody connected with the organisation claims to have only just begun or to have been transferred from another area or at all events to be quite ignorant of whatever matter is brought up. For the Lexden and Winstree District there will be drainage and implement men, myself and one typist.

[The Essex War Agricultural Committee office in north-east Essex had been based at Wivenhoe but was now split into two district offices, one covering the Tendring district and one covering the Lexden and Winstree district, for which Rudsdale was Secretary. The role of the District Committees was to maintain close contact with farmers in that district in order to maximise food production and to make recommendations to the County Executive Committee to serve directions on the farmers concerned as necessary.]

January 15 Wednesday

It is interesting to see what a hatred of farming and farmers and country people exists among townspeople, as shown by various letters in the daily press. There is a great outcry now about the Government's proposals to take men off the land by increasing the reserved age – some say 100,000 men will be taken and that the age will be put up to 30. Some newspaper correspondents write bitter hatred against all men who have taken up agricultural work since the war began and urge that they should be conscripted at once. Others sneer at the alleged value of any agricultural worker and claim that any labourer could easily be replaced by women. The curious thing is that nobody ever indicts the hundreds of thousands of young men who have gone into engineering, mostly at very high wages. Even learners can get £3.5 a week.

Another aspect of the hatred of the urban dweller for the countryman is shown in the letters complaining about the conditions in which town evacuees live in rural parts. In these farmers are referred to as 'uncouth', 'turnip eaters', 'hay seeds' and other similar terms.

January 16 Thursday

Very busy all morning in my new office, having a hard time with the weekly wage sheets. Ida Hughes-Stanton came in and asked me to go out to lunch, which I did and afterwards to the Regal to see 'Gaslight' [based on Patrick Hamilton's 1938 play]. As a film it was most enjoyable, that strange, mysterious period, the 1880s, being brought out so well. I enjoyed myself enormously. Took Ida to tea as well and then went to feed Bob.

[Rudsdale was a friend of the artist Blair Hughes-Stanton and his partner Ida.]

January 17 Friday

Today the Cultivation Officer [Stanley Nott] reported that a man at East Mersea had nearly cut his foot off in a grass mower. 'Who is it?' asked Folkard, 'one of the Conchies?' 'No,' said Nott, 'a pity it wasn't'. There are half a dozen conscientious objectors working on the land in East Mersea, mostly for ridiculously small wages.

January 18 Saturday

Got a fair amount of stationery in from Writtle today and feel we are really making a start now. Very odd that there is no register or list of the land of which the Committee has actually taken possession, so I have got to make one myself. So far as I can see, the whole job is being left very much in my hands.

Began snowing hard this morning and kept on all day. Surprised to hear the sirens at 1.45pm and the noise of a 'plane receding. It appears that a German 'plane, flying in a thick snowstorm, dropped 4 bombs near the London–Yarmouth train as it passed Chitt's Hill [on the approach to Colchester's North station]. All missed but he opened fire and broke many windows, hitting six people. Two, I believe, are rather seriously hurt. It seems most amazing that the Germans can operate at such times as this, when our fighters cannot possibly go after them.

Mr and Mrs Stuart Rose from Dedham came in this afternoon. They are moving to another cottage at Boxted, so I suppose he is still on land work. Good luck to him. She looked very pretty in the driving snow, in fur coat, fur lined boots and a little cap.

January 19 Sunday

The Scots soldiers went to All Saints Church this morning, each company led by a piper. They marched up through the snow, the wailing of the pipes drifting over the town on the breeze. Poulter said, 'What an outrage to let them make that hideous din on a Sunday!'

January 20 Monday

Committee meeting of the War Agricultural Executive at Birch Hall. Went very well. I made no mistakes. Lasted from 9.45am until almost 1.30pm. A good deal more land taken over. This system seems to be a sort of reverse Socialism. Instead of the people getting possession of their own land, when they have got it they will probably lose it to some big farmer nearby. A return to feudalism? Terribly hard on those who have bought small farms on which they intended to live. I notice that the members of the Committee are very antagonistic against women farmers – not one has any chance of a fair hearing.

January 21 Tuesday

Very busy all day. Four or five raid alarms during the day but none at night. Clacton, Walton and Harwich were machine-gunned during the morning but I believe only one casualty was caused. Two of the people hit in the train on Saturday are dead – the guard and a woman. A young man, a professional pianist, lost all the fingers on one hand.

Museum Committee today, the first since April 1928 which I had not prepared. Laver seems to be ill. I have not seen him for some days now and today a postcard arrived to say he would be unable to attend the Committee.

January 22 Wednesday

All day we could hear the firing of the guns at Harwich. A good deal of nervousness about, as some of the papers are running an 'invasion scare', prophesying 'a tremendous attack within 7 days'.

January 24 Friday

Laver is dead. He died in the Nursing Home about 10 o'clock. I at once went over to the Castle. Met Coucillor Blomfield on the way and he suggested we should fly the flag at half-mast, which I set about doing.

So the old man has gone at last. All these years we have talked of 'when the Doctor goes …'. Now he has gone. Never again shall we see him, battered soft hat, carefully trimmed beard, long brown overcoat, big brown, highly polished shoes, gloved hands behind his back, walking slowly and rather splay-footed across the street and into the Holly Trees. Never again to hear him say 'Where are my other eyes?' as he gets out his glasses to see some object for his inspection. Never again to hear him creak down the basement stairs to talk to Poulter. He was an eminent citizen of the Borough, as was his father before him and Essex archaeology will be greatly the poorer by his loss.

It must be about a week since I saw him last. He came into my new office, made some remarks about a book and walked out. I little thought then that I should never see him again. Sometime yesterday he was removed into the Nursing Home. I wonder what thoughts passed through his mind as he lay there in those last hours? His old father, 'The Guvnor', his brother Edward, cut off so soon in the midst of his great work on the Lexden Tumulus, old A G Wright [Curator of Colchester Museum 1902-1926], the good old days of the Museum and the [Essex Archaeological] Society, days of harmony, research and quiet achievements.

What will happen to his collections now? His sister, Mrs Lyon Campbell, would have no compunction about destroying all his records and papers if she so thought. Incidentally, there must be many things in the house which are not his property – he has had Wire's 'Diary' for nearly two years.

[The antiquarian, William Wire, had kept a diary of archaeological finds in Colchester in the nineteenth century which had inspired Rudsdale to keep a journal.]

January 25 Saturday

Lot of talk about 'fire watching'. Many people doing turns of duty in the shops, with the result that almost every place in High Street shows lights leaking out of cracks and crevasses.

As I walked across the Park tonight the half-masted flag flapped out black against the grey sky. Poor old Laver. I think he must have liked me sometimes. When I was a boy he often used to take me out in his car, as I well remember.

January 29 Wednesday

[Met] Margery Frost of the Post Office. She said that Betty Mason, the girl who was charged with sedition last year, has been reinstated in the Post Office and has a job at Guildford. Only a fortnight ago her father died after a long illness and just after that her house at Clacton was damaged by a bomb. Who could wonder if the girl is embittered for life.

January 30 Thursday

Sub-Committee on implements at the office this morning. Matter mentioned regarding Bond, the new Drainage Officer, who is only 19, so Capt Folkard wanted the Committee to try to get him exempt. The Committee refused point blank, told Folkard that in their opinion there were far too many young men on this job, that the Executive at Writtle had no business to put them on and that they should all be in the Army. Of course, the Drainage and Cultivation Officers, the Tendring staff and myself are all under 35. I wondered when something of this sort was coming. The job as I first saw it seemed too good to be true. Well, whatever happens, if the war lasts three years I shall have escaped half of it!

February 3 Monday

Committee meeting at Birch Hall this afternoon. Old Round blew off about young men in administrative posts [and] insisted that any administrative or even drainage work could be done by women.

The Committee refused to recommend that a man of 36 should be retained for agricultural work (he has been a gardener). Folkard told me that the attack on administrative staff was not intended to apply to me, as Capt Round does not consider me fit for military service, or to Nott, who is regarded as a valuable man.

February 6 Thursday

An incredible piece of luck today. A phone message from Craske, the auctioneer, revealed that he was now putting in a valuation of [Laver's] estate. When Poulter explained the position about [Wire's] 'Diary', Craske came down at once and we had a long interview. He was most helpful and the upshot is that he arranged for me to go to the house with him on Saturday morning to see Mrs Lyon-Campbell, who will then let me find the 'Diary'.

February 7 Friday

To Rose this evening. She was very tired, as she is up all Thursday nights now, on fire watching.

February 8 Saturday

I hear that either yesterday or the day before, Winston Churchill was in the town, inspecting troops. All kept very quiet.

Went up to Doctor Laver's this morning with Mr Craske. Mrs Lyon-Campbell said she was sure I would do right with her brother's things. It always seems to me slightly indecent to pull out a dead man's books and I felt particularly embarrassed in his little room, where he would so have hated to see me. Poor old man, I will treat his stuff as fairly as I can, as I believe he would have liked to have seen it done. It was sad to see his desk, with rough notes on it that he will never use again. His books, some open on the table, that he will never close. Parcels tied up in the peculiar way in which he always did them. Dear old man. The end of nearly 100 years of local research and now nobody to take his place.

Alarm tonight 7-10pm. Went down to Rose's and found the Tank Corps Sergeant was back and was 'well dug in'. I stayed until midnight but he stayed me out.

February 10 Monday

Big manoeuvres on tonight, Tuesday and Wednesday and much excitement in the town today when military police were searching for German spies. None found.

February 11 Tuesday

Action at last. Special meeting called last night of an Emergency Committee to deal with compulsory fire watching. Hull attended with other chief officers. When asked by the Mayor what precautions had been taken at the Castle and Holly Trees, he had to admit – none! The Mayor was furious and ordered him to procure at once stirrup pumps, buckets and more sand, and instructed that two night watchmen should at once be appointed one in each place. Butcher, Chapman, Hull and myself are expected to man the Castle so that it is never left at any moment of the day or night.

There is great excitement all over the town and 'fire-parties' are being formed everywhere, even in private streets. All offices and shops must by law have some person sleeping in them. It is expected that this night-watching will lead to a certain amount of immorality, in fact the Post Office and some other big concerns which employ both men and women have decreed that two girls may watch with one man but never two men with one girl.

February 12 Wednesday

Had an unpleasant job today. I was instructed to give a week's notice to a one of the conscientious objectors working on Mersea. The authorities believe he is a ring leader, stirring up the others to insubordination, slowing down work, etc. The only point I feel is that he has probably suffered a good deal already and he may be desperately in need of this job. Anyway, I sent a brisk, business-like letter. All I could do. (Ought I to rebel against this inhuman system? I am now part of it but if I acted according to my conscience I should walk out tomorrow. To what – the Army?)

February 14 Friday

My birthday, 31 years old. Mother gave me a new pair of shoes, Father a new cycle lamp. Rose gave me some sweets and a book token for 10/6. So sweet of her. She is so very good to me. How glad I am now to be a year older and still alive. There is so much to see and do.

March 1 Saturday

This evening I was looking over some of poor old Laver's stuff, when I found a number of old appointment books, going back to 1909. I was idly flipping over the pages when I chanced to see my own name and to my amazement saw 'Rudsdale, 1 Har' meaning No. 1 Harsnett Road, where I was born, and sure enough the date of the entry was February 14 1910. I sat and looked at that simple note and to think I was actually staring at my own beginning. What an extraordinary coincidence. Never could Laver have thought, as he made a note to call on Mrs Rudsdale, that 31 years later the little scrap he helped into the world that day would read that very note.

March 2 Sunday

Called at Sisson's and he told me about his appointment as liaison officer with the ARP Controllers as regards bomb damage to ancient buildings. Between us we have worked out a pretty comprehensive list [of historic buildings]. Had tea there, and then had to rush back as I had to be at the Castle by 8pm to relieve Butcher. Few 'planes over tonight and an alarm just before 9pm.

March 6 Thursday

This evening I moved two wood chests containing all my journals and notebooks into the Castle, where they may be safer and where I can work on them freely.

March 13 Thursday

Full moon but only a short alarm tonight. Few 'planes over. Probably wet weather on the Continent keeps them down. The ideal weather is gloriously fine days, so the RAF can see 'em, and filthy nights, so they can't see us.

March 16 Sunday

Went along to Brick House, Mr Filer's place, to get two horses out on his marsh. When I was there last it was all grass and sheep but practically every acre has been ploughed by our Government Tractors. They are now starting cultivating for him, as he has no means of doing anything. The farm is about 200 acres and besides Filer there is only one old age pensioner, who is at present ill. The stock consists of 5 cows and a pet lamb. Incredible state of affairs.

March 17 Monday

Message from the Waterworks today to say that a [Roman] lead coffin had been found in their new trench in Mersea Road, quite close to where Roman burials were found in 1937. I went up as soon as I knocked off and saw it lying, north-south, right on the edge of the trench. A small grey flask was found by the north end but was broken. Made arrangements to get it out tomorrow and arranged transport by Wick's cart. Much disappointed not to be able to use Bob for a third lead coffin.

March 18 Tuesday

Coffin taken out this morning. I got an hour off to help in the removal. It was necessary to break up part of the road but the Waterworks people gave every help and by great good luck the contractor's foreman had once unearthed several lead coffins at York.

At the very moment the coffin was raised from the grave, a motor hearse rushed by taking a shining new coffin to the cemetery. How one could moralise on that moment! What an example of continuity, what an illustration of the one same permanent unalterable thing – death.

I believe Hull is going to empty it tomorrow but there will doubtless be nothing in it.

March 19 Wednesday

The coffin was empty, nothing but a faint smear of thighs and pelvis on the bottom.

Tremendous number of 'planes over tonight, flying right over the town. There must have been a dreadful raid somewhere in London. I hope to goodness they are not changing their route – previously they always fly either north or south of Colchester.

March 20 Thursday

The raid last night was on London Docks and I believe enormous damage was done 300 or 400 killed. It seems incredible that in a few hours they can kill a number equal to the population of an average village.

March 22 Saturday

New 'invasion' notices suddenly appeared this afternoon, much the same as last September, but no specific arrangements have been made to get people away. Old people, children, women, etc. are urged to go 'at once' to anywhere except East Anglia or the Southern Counties. It is so strange, as there is nothing in the press lately to indicate any immediate likelihood of attack. Very worrying. However, did not tell the old parents, as they will refuse to move in any case.

Reports in the press today of raids on Plymouth, where there have been enormous numbers killed. Most ports have been raided this week. Alarms here on and off all day but no 'planes came, for which we were very thankful. Nobody worries about night raids now, not even bothering to go into shelters. All our regular customers of last autumn have deserted us. I believe a few families still sleep in their own shelters, or else underneath a heavy table, which is fairly safe. My old people often come downstairs and sleep in armchairs.

Spoke to Folkard today about my reserved position, as changes in the schedule seem very probable. He said that he would at any rate wish to retain me until after harvest, as that would be essential.

March 23 Sunday

Father's birthday, 69. Dear old man. Gave him some tobacco and he was just as quietly pleased as he always is.

When I got into the Castle [tonight], Poulter came over to tell me (a) that one of the coin drawers had been broken open and some coins stolen and (b) this afternoon a small boy was caught breaking open one of the lavatory locks with a jemmy. Poulter caught him and took him off to the Police Station. If any persons can walk in and out of the Castle and break open coin drawers, entirely undetected, our sad condition cannot be hid from the most undiscerning eye.

March 25 Tuesday

Heavy rain again, especially at night. Everything soaking. Drilling and ploughing stopped. It is obvious we shall never get the full quota of ploughing done by March 31.

March 27 Thursday

George Farmer came home yesterday and called at my office this morning, wearing an Air Force uniform and looking thinner and younger. He did not seem very happy and is no longer being trained for wireless work. He has been 4 months in Blackpool and never a raid or an alarm.

This afternoon a conference was held at the office to consider a protest from neighbours against our taking King's Farm, Fordham, from old Mrs Playle. Leslie attended. Capt Round came in to preside. Young Playle was there and was given a thorough dressing down by Leslie and was told that possession would not be relinquished.

March 31 Monday

Went to Rose's tonight but she was in a very bad mood and would hardly speak to me. I believe she is tired of me and would like to take up with this Tank Corps man.

April 3 Thursday

Rose still the same, obviously anxious to be rid of me in order to devote all her time to Peter, who is soon going away.

April 7 Monday

Rose rang up and asked me not to see her tonight. Went to Seymour's instead. He tells me there is as yet no talk of closing the schools here but the final evacuation plans entail the complete removal of the population, mostly to Leicester, leaving only 1,500 men to work electricity, pumping station, gas-works, railway etc. He does not think anything else will be done unless a real emergency arises, although considerable pressure is likely to be brought to bear upon old or sick people. I think my aged couple ought to go.

April 8 Tuesday

German Army is now well into Greece and Yugoslavia, carrying all before it, completely victorious. There is a tiny British force in one corner of Greece but they will have to evacuate before the end of this month.

Hull went down the Park today with two Army officers and Inspector Barricoat of the police, to examine Duncan's Gate [also known as the North-East Postern – a gateway in the Roman town wall in Castle Park] to see if a safe, secret hiding place can be found for Army purposes, I suspect for a secret wireless transmitter to be used in case the town falls into enemy hands.

I went round to Rose's tonight and by 8 o'clock it was all over. She reproached me for not offering to marry her. We had more words and I asked her if she had ever loved me. She did not answer and I walked out, never to go there again.

April 9 Wednesday

Awoke to the realisation that 'my dear acquaintance' was gone. How can I hope to effect a reconciliation? Is it wise to do so? In our real fundamentals, two people could hardly be more different than we are.

German advance into Greece continues. Allied armies in full retreat in Libya as well.

April 10 Thursday

The evening paper placards tonight read 'Raid on Berlin. State Library and Opera House on Fire'. The English press has at last descended to openly gloating over the destruction of cultural institutions.

April 13 Sunday

There have been Sundays when, for one reason or another, I knew I should not be having tea at Rose's but this is the first Sunday when I knew I could not and never could again.

April 16 Wednesday

No less than five raid alarms during the day but no 'planes were seen or heard. It seems a miracle that we are preserved so often.

Many 'planes over tonight. Beautiful, clear starlight, pierced by the wandering beams of searchlights.

April 17 Thursday

Papers very late. Tremendous raid on London last night. Reports of 'heavy casualties' – may be hundreds, may be thousands, no one knows. Last month there was a big raid on the Clydeside. At first reports said 'Very light casualties'. Then figures were given – 500 dead, 1,300 injured.

April 19 Saturday

Alarms soon after dark tonight and many dozen 'planes passed over towards London, I fear another big attack. It seems so extraordinary to sit in this cell, where James Parnell died so many years ago, listening to the 'planes and knowing that in a few minutes hundreds of people now alive and well will be blown to pieces. One feels there ought to be something one could do about it. How long can this go on?

April 20 Sunday

On a sudden decision, went over to Boxted this afternoon, to find Mr and Mrs Stuart Rose's new cottage. I found it easily, in a lovely little lane near Rivers Hall. They were both there, working in the garden, she as pretty as ever, he big and strong and yet wholly the artist.

The cottage is charming. They gave £120 for the cottage, which was practically condemned. What luck for them to get such a beauty at such a price! He is still working on the land. I do hope he can keep his job.

Three alarms today, the last at 11.30 tonight. About 2 o'clock this morning I was awakened from a doze by banging on the Castle door. I called out 'Who's there?' and a voice answered, 'George'. To my surprise it was George Farmer home again, a very scared, shaken George. Since he was home only 3 weeks ago he has been sent to Tangmere aerodrome, near Chichester, and has already been through one attack. It shook poor George badly, although not much harm was done. Anyway, he was so worked up he could not spend the night in the [family's cutlery] shop, fire watching with Maisie [his wife], as he felt he could not bear to listen to the 'planes going over, so he came into the ancient castle, liking the feel of many feet of solid stonework all round him. I woke myself up and we sat and talked all the rest of the night, eating some chocolate which I managed to get last week. He told me some curious things about the RAF. Many men in his unit are Communists. Everybody is so scared of night attacks that all the men sleep in Chichester, in billets, or else in ditches, or under the stands at Goodwood Racecourse. Anywhere but barracks.

George is a very disappointed man, besides a scared one. He intended to be a wireless operator but could not do the work, so he is now an 'AC2', a person who fills in bomb holes and does other menial work. Poor George. This time two years ago he was a business man, running his own car. What can his future be?

George said that when he was coming down by train last night, they passed through hundreds of incendiary bombs about 5 miles the other side of Chelmsford. There is no doubt that there has been a dreadful raid on London.

April 21 Monday

Mother and Father really determined to go away. Aunt Het has sent a most pressing letter and both are getting very weary of these continual night raids.

Hear tremendous damage was done on Saturday at Ilford, Stratford, Chadwell Heath, etc. The whole line is completely blocked and London trains were yesterday being sent round by Braintree and Bishop's Stortford. Railway emergency posters announced 'indefinite delay to London'. Shall we ever hear the true story of these nights?

Work began today on the 'secret' dug out at the North-East Postern. This has been arranged in a blaze of 'secrecy'. First, Hull walked up and down the field on several days with Inspector Barricoat and Army officers. Then it was decided that the men doing the actual work should be disguised. The result is that four men arrived today 'disguised' in blue ARP dungarees but, unfortunately, they were brought into the Park in a large Army lorry, which rather gave the game away.

April 27 Sunday

To Maidenhead today by car, driven by a member of the Women's Voluntary Services (WVS). The Watford By-Pass looks just the same, except for occasional tank blocks and barricades. Really, the so-called 'defences' of this country are absurd! They wouldn't stop Boy Scouts on bicycles. Watford looks amazingly undamaged and was packed with people. There was a 'War Weapons Week' in progress, with guns and aeroplanes outside the Town Hall.

Into Maidenhead, all unchanged, even the aged cab-horse still on the rank by the bridge. Then through the maze of one-way streets and so up to Aunt's house in Grenfell Road. We all had a hurried lunch before I started back.

April 29 Tuesday

Shock today to find that in future there will be no oat or bran ration for trap or riding horses. This is terribly hard luck on those persons who now depend entirely on horse transport.

May 1 Thursday

Went into the little café in Culver Street tonight. There were several lots of Canadian soldiers there and rather to my surprise, an English 'Tommy' and a captain sitting at the same table. There is now a certain amount of so-called 'democracy' in the Army but I was surprised to see a captain and a private together in such a place as this. When the radio came on at 9 o'clock, the captain talked rather loudly and laughed a good deal, and when the announcer stated that the bulk of the troops had left Greece for Egypt where they would immediately be re-armed, he said loudly, 'Like hell they will!', so that the Canadians all looked at him somewhat strangely. At last he got up to go and I could then clearly see that he was quite drunk. He stumbled over a chair, laughed a good deal and finally went out holding the private's arm. I looked at the café proprietress, Winnie, and said how class distinction appeared to be abolished, in some sections of the Army at any rate. She replied, 'You know, I'm tired of that chap. He's in here two or three nights a week, and he's always drunk'. I asked if he always had a soldier with him. 'Oh, yes,' she said, 'he has him to take him home!'

May 3 Saturday

Weather turned bitterly cold. There was no heat of any description at the Holly Trees. Capt Folkard was very annoyed and, on finding that Poulter had removed the electric fuses to prevent us from using a stove, he sent a complaint to the Town Clerk. Poulter is incredibly mean over heat, as he is over most things. He insists that no matter what the weather is like, there shall be no artificial heat after April 30.

May 4 Sunday

Went down to Bourne Mill and met Mauna Benham. She told me that in all probability Hervey could have a permanently stiff leg and would be invalided out of the Navy.

The clocks were advanced another hour today, so that we are now two hours ahead of natural time. This makes a wonderful difference. It will mean that soon we may have daylight until 10pm.

[Hervey Benham had been injured in the leg whilst on coastal patrol work. Henceforward he resumed his career in Colchester as a journalist and editor on his father's newspapers.]

May 5 Monday

On Saturday night 16 German 'planes were shot down. Still, as they probably sent 500 over it is not a very appreciable loss.

Tonight the news came that the British have invaded Iraq.

May 6 Tuesday

I noticed this evening that a little shop, which used to be a sweet shop when I was at school has now opened as a 'Sex Shop'. A large board outside says 'Lady Herbalist; advice free to ladies; consult at once', and on the door 'Rubber Goods Supplied'. I think that previously only about two places in the town sold 'French letters' and 'pessaries'. Certainly nothing quite as blatant as this has ever appeared before.

May 9 Friday

Our two swans at Bourne Mill have made a nest on the reeds quite near the road and have laid four eggs. They both spend almost their whole time on the nest, often sitting on it together. I fear that as the nest is so near the road that the eggs will be destroyed by children as they have been every year. It was nicer today, lovely down at the Mill this evening, with the cuckoos calling down by Cannock Mill.

May 10 Saturday

I hear that bombs fell at both Chelmsford and Clacton in the early hours of yesterday morning. At Chelmsford several men were killed at the Marconi works, which received several direct hits, while at Clacton two big bombs fell in the main street near the Pier.

May 11 Sunday

Went round by Stratford and called at Ida Hughes-Stanton's. She told me that Blair Hughes-Stanton is missing in the East and she has heard nothing from him for months.

May 12 Monday

A somewhat confused and exciting night after I got to bed yesterday. At about 3am, during a raid alarm, the watchmen came running down the stairs calling out, 'Are you there, Mr Rudsdale? There's a fire of some sort in Maidenburgh Street.' I leapt out of bed, rushed on gum-boots, helmet and waterproof, grabbed my glasses and torch and ran up the ancient stairs until my heart pounded like a hammer.

From the turret I could see a thick cloud of smoke drifting away over the town. I could hear the sound of crackling and the swish of water, when a sudden burst of flame through the smoke showed me that it was the 'George' [Inn, on High Street] that was on fire. As the smoke lifted we could see not only a patch of flames bursting from a window but also a little patch of glowing red further along the roof. Not unnaturally I supposed this to be an incendiary bomb which had fallen in the gutter so telling the watchman to stay on guard, I rushed out to tell the firemen about this second 'bomb', which I thought probably could not be seen from the ground.

There were few people about, except a few hotel guests in nightclothes and overcoats, one or two wardens and a few people from the houses in George Street. Not many firemen. I spoke to a man who was apparently the landlord, telling him of the 'bomb' which I could see in the gutter. Much to my surprise he said that no bombs had fallen and the fire was quite accidental!

German 'planes were passing south of the town every few minutes and I was very nervous lest they should see the flames. However, the mist thickened and we escaped unharmed. The fire continued for about an hour and a half and finally died down, although not before flames had burst through the roof and thick clouds of smoke poured down towards the north. Shortly after it was out the 'all clear' sounded.

Horrified to find from the evening papers that a woman was killed at the 'George' fire. She was a chambermaid and was suffocated by smoke.

May 13 Tuesday

Much talk all over the place about Rudolph Hess, the Deputy Führer, flying to Scotland on Saturday night. Some state that he has deserted his leader in the hour of triumph. An amazing business but not more so than many things at this time.

May 15 Thursday

The swans' eggs are still safe, although huge crowds stand round gazing at the nest all evening, and I have caught several boys throwing stones at the birds.

May 21 Wednesday

The swans' eggs are still safe. A man spent 3 hours this evening waiting for a chance to photograph the hen turning them over. I believe he got her at last.

May 22 Thursday

Joanna Round [Capt Round's daughter] came [to the office] this morning, to begin part-time war-work. She is a plump, blonde young lady, good looking. She and Nott are apparently old friends and talk hunting incessantly. She helped a little in paying out wages and seemed a sensible girl.

May 27 Tuesday

Very busy all day on Committee affairs. Beautiful Penelope Belfield [from Dedham] came in, very worried as she had just been interviewed regarding war work at the Labour Exchange. Who would have thought that a time would come when young girls like Penelope would be bullied into the Army or the factories?

May 29 Thursday

Cold, wet day. Felt very ill so phoned the office and went home to bed. Lovely to be in a real bed, the first time since last October. Stayed there until dark and then back to bed in the 'Oven'. Very cold tonight. Felt miserable.

May 31 Saturday

Much better. Took Bob out this afternoon and bought a new camp bed, an iron framed one. I got it from Blomfield's [furniture shop], it cost 37/- and was the last one they had. I shall sleep in luxury tonight, after that dreadful canvas thing I have had for the last 7 months.

Notices appeared on the Banks today or yesterday, advising customers to remove their valuables to safer areas.

June 1 Sunday

This evening went to Seymour's. Jeffrey Saunders has now joined the Navy, almost a year after he registered. He is at Harwich. The papers today full of the disaster at Crete, where the British Army has again suffered a staggering defeat.

June 11 Wednesday

Royal Archaeological Institute Annual General Meeting. Capt Folkard gave me a day off to attend.

Going into London, the eye still sees street after street of sordid little houses, interspersed with open spaces containing only a few bricks. An occasional burnt out factory can be seen but it is surprising how many are quite untouched. Balloon barrage much in evidence, the balloons very low or else grounded. No signs of damage on the line – goods depots appeared normal, many horses and motors moving in and out. There was a cattle-truck full of horses near Ilford.

Terribly devastated area near Stratford, I should think quite 50 houses gone. No doubt a parachute mine. But in spite of damage the familiar London skyline appears quite unchanged, Whitbread's and the London Co-operative Society stables were untouched.

At Liverpool Street, the familiar dirt and noise and smell but daylight comes through the roof in unexpected places, and the great station clock is now on the ground, although still working. The station offices at Liverpool Street were burnt out and there are a few buildings burnt near Broad Street Station.

At the Bank, an RAF band was playing Gilbert & Sullivan music alongside the Mansion House. There was a big audience of city workers, among them some extraordinarily pretty girls. RAF sergeants moved among the crowd, handing out recruiting leaflets marked 'To men of 17 or 18'. I was handed one!

Tremendous devastation in Queen Victoria Street and Cheapside but St Paul's stands up grandly, almost unscathed. Except for boarded windows there is no damage to be seen from the outside. Holborn is damaged in parts but Gamages store and the Prudential, both hideous buildings, are quite untouched, not a pane of glass cracked. Looked in Staple Inn and saw that by a miracle a bomb had fallen in the middle of the courtyard, causing little damage. If this lovely place, which survived the Great Fire, also survives this disastrous war it should be protected for all time to come.

Walked past the British Museum. The outside gates are shut but a policeman is on duty. The damage to the west wing is clearly seen. Went by Tottenham Court Road to Piccadilly. Piccadilly Circus normal but St James's Church burnt out, an enormous hole in the road and the 'Fifty Shilling Taylor' on the north side of the street quite gone.

Burlington House was wonderfully normal, except for a notice at the bottom of the stairs leading to the library, which read 'Do not use the stairs; glass roof is unsafe'. The paper and the attendance were both poor. I had a long talk with Philip Corder, who has been temporarily released from St Alban's Museum to take charge of the Antiquaries' affairs at Burlington House. He told me that on one night in April London was bombed ceaselessly for 7 hours. He was at Burlington House the whole time.

Walked in Green Park. Several bomb-craters visible. The damage in front of Buckingham Palace has been quite cleared up and the whole courtyard re-tarred so there is no sign of it visible.

June 14 Saturday

Tonight there was dancing on the Holly Trees lawn to tunes ground out by an amplifier on a gramophone. It was most noticeable that when a polka was announced 'by special request' the crowd laughed and groaned. Not more than a dozen couples attempted it.

June 16 Monday

I hear there was some alarm among people on Friday and Saturday last week, owing to rumours of an immediate invasion. I should imagine that the Germans' attack on Russia should lay the invasion bogey for a time at any rate.

The news tonight is that the United States had closed all German consulates, so presumably another war can be expected very shortly.

June 29 Sunday

Cycled over to the Parringtons at Lawford. Discussion at tea – when the Germans have beaten the Russians, will Stalin come to London and set up a 'Free Russian' Government? A fascinating suggestion. The BBC is said to have stopped playing the dreary 'National Anthems of the Allies' so as to avoid having to play either the 'Red Flag' or the 'Internationale'.

Called on the Sissons. Mrs Sisson had been away for a few days and had met a man named Burrell, who was one of the censors. He told her that 10 per cent of letters from any town that was bombed were opened within the next few days after the bombing, in order to test the morale of that particular place. After being read, the letters were destroyed. She would not believe this at first but he showed her actual letters which he happened to have with him.

July 4 Friday

The American flag was flying on the Town Hall. I wonder if we may expect to see the Hammer and Sickle on a crimson ground flying there on October 20?

July 5 Saturday

The town all decorated with flags today, in honour of War Weapons Week.

July 7 Monday

Joanna Round started work today as a recorder on the Farm Survey. If this work is done properly it will be of the greatest value, both practically and from a historical point of view.

[The National Farm Survey, conducted between 1941-1943, reported on every farm in England and Wales and formed a complete 'Domesday' survey of the state of agriculture in this period.]

July 12 Saturday

End of the War Weapons Week, during which a total of £897,000 has been 'raised'. Actually this has only been 'raised' on paper, by the temporary transferring of stocks and bonds, etc., but it is interesting to compare this figure to the sums raised for humanitarian purposes.

July 13 Sunday

Cycled to Boxted to call on Mr and Mrs Rose. They were having a great struggle to get a large cupboard upstairs. Had a very pleasant supper and a lot of conversation. Mrs Rose very pleased because it has been announced today that we are Russia's allies! Major

Waller came in and was very put out about the same thing – 'By God, never did I think to find myself allied to Godless Russia!'

[Mrs Rose was a Russian émigré who, as a child, had escaped with her mother during the Russian Revolution in 1917.]

July 20 Sunday

Collected an old cob which I bought from Harry Watts and a tub cart and drove over to Thorington Hall. This turnout is for the use of the old people evacuated to Thorington, where they are looked after by the Society of Friends. There is a dear old chap there who drove for Suttons in Southwark for 50 years and he took charge the moment the horse arrived. I was told that he had been eagerly waiting for this moment for the past week.

It looked strange to see Thorington Hall full of these old people. I don't suppose the Penroses will ever see the place again. The whole turnout cost £20, which is very cheap and I shall charge the Friends £15, as a sort of thanks offering for my good fortune.

July 23 Wednesday

Bought some chocolates today. There seem to be quite a lot in the town. Loose chocolates are 1/12 a quarter pound. Before the war they were 6d.

July 25 Friday

Old Mr Death of Sergeant's Farm, Bures called today, complaining he had not had any compensation from the Committee for the land which had been requisitioned. He was rather pathetic, over 70, and 'had been there 35 years, got used to it now.' I will do what I can for him, as I think he has been harshly treated.

July 28 Monday

At about 4.30 this morning I was awakened by a horrible high-pitched scream of a 'plane out of control. I was petrified with fear as it seemed to be right over the town. It died away and there was a dull crump some way off. Went up on the roof and could see a red glare in the direction of Wivenhoe. Learnt later today that the 'plane was German and that it crashed near Wivenhoe Park. The crew were killed.

New girl called Daphne Young started in the office today as clerk to the Farm Survey. I am going to do the Borough Farms with Mr Craig and we went up this evening to do Motts Farm, Lexden. It was most enjoyable.

July 29 Tuesday

The Premier made another of his alarming invasion speeches today, stating that he has ordered all forces to prepare for an attack by September 1.

August 3 Sunday

Cycled over to Lawford for lunch and this afternoon went up to the Belfields' for tea. Penelope very friendly, laughing and chattering, as pretty as always. Called at the Sissons' for a few moments and discussed the photographing of houses and the collecting of old photographs. Home in the moonlight, very warm and lovely.

August 10 Sunday

Clock was put back one hour tonight, making a very obvious difference. This, and an alarm at 10.15pm, shows that winter is approaching.

August 11 Monday

Working on my photos tonight for three hours. Most enjoyable.

[This marked the start of Rudsdale's photographic survey of Colchester's streets and buildings from old and contemporary photographs. The collection is now held at Colchester Museums Resource Centre.]

August 12 Tuesday

The Germans seem to be winning easily now in Russia and many people believe that if the Russians are out of the war within the next fortnight, there will be an invasion before the end of September.

August 13 Wednesday

Rain all day. Terrible for the harvest.

Heard from Mother today, saying they must come home soon. This of course means that they will get back here just in time for the next big invasion scare, just as they did last year.

August 14 Thursday

A fine day at last, warm and sunny. We started a combine-harvester at Brickwall Farm, Stanway but it does not seem to be very satisfactory. This is the first I have ever seen.

August 15 Friday

Torrential rain all day. What will the harvest be? Combine stopped. Cannot be used unless the grain is perfectly dry.

August 18 Monday

Mother and Father have come home. I am glad to see the old people but I wish most heartily that they had not come at this particular time.

August 21 Thursday

Notices were pasted up today, making the whole of the coastal districts a closed area, into which nobody may go unless they are inhabitants. It is, for instance, illegal to visit friends at Clacton, Mersea or Brightlingsea, or even to pass through any of those places.

August 28 Thursday

Cycled towards Boxted and passed one of Mr Page's wagons returning from the harvest field, painted grey and red, with a lovely pair of Suffolks, two boys riding on them and a man leading. Then cycled by way of Langham and met another pair-horse harvest wagon, coming down the hill to Blackbrook, the setting sun picking out golden lights on the horses' coats and on the yellow sheaves piled high in the cart. With the wheel-skid on they slid slowly down into the gloom at the bottom of the valley.

August 30 Saturday

Weather much improved now and I think the harvest will be safe.

'Free' French garden party held today and a Polish Concert in the Albert Hall last Thursday. How cosmopolitan Colchester is becoming.

September 1 Monday

The tramlines in High Street are at last being taken up, after being out of use for 13 years.

September 3 Wednesday

Annual meeting of the Essex Archaeological Society this morning. This afternoon a memorial tablet in memory of P G Laver and his father was unveiled in the Castle. Sir Gurney Benham made a very pleasant little speech. He spoke of 'two lives almost one', covering a century and a quarter and praised the industry of this worthy father and son, whose generous gifts had enriched the Museum's collections.

September 4 Thursday

From my office window at Holly Trees:

Green grass of the Park lawns, green leaves of the ancient trees on the Ramparts, russet and yellow flowers in the beds beneath the windows. Pale green of the distant meadows at Mile End Hall, olive green of High Woods beyond them. The sky a great blue vault, with a few fleecy clouds and the brazen sun beating down.

On the Park benches there are people sitting, some in the sun, others in the cool shade. In the meadow, boys are playing cricket where 1,800 years ago were the streets and houses of the Roman town. At the top end of the field is a 'model allotment' and nearby a notice board indicating ARP shelters which were filled in 6 months ago. Nobody remembered to take the board away. The white stair-rails of the new shelters show up nearby and the dark smudge under the trees is a machine-gun pit, made last year during the invasion alarm. Against it is the Wardens' Post. I can just see the top of the Castle, peeping through the trees. In the distance a little train puffs along towards Ipswich.

A family, father, mother and three little girls in red and yellow walk slowly up the path towards Holly Trees and a soldier and a girl, arm in arm, walk the other way.

Over everything, the brooding lazy heat of a hot summer afternoon. Not a 'plane in the sky. No wind, the trees hardly moving in the still, hot air, the distant woods fading in a haze. The faint sound of sawing comes up from the basement workshop, where Poulter is making something. Where is the war?

September 25 Thursday

Great shock at home – a notice to attend a medical examination on Saturday. Don't know what to do or think. Is this a preliminary to an alteration of the Reserved List? Is it a mistake? Said nothing to Mother or Father, just that it was feeding coupons for Bob.

Worked on old photographs until 11 o'clock, then to bed, full of worry.

September 26 Friday

Slept badly last night. Told Capt Folkard when he came in and he suggested it was a mistake and that I ought to call and see the responsible people. I did so and found the National Service department. I went in boldly and explained the whole matter to a sour faced fellow. At first I asked for a postponement and he agreed that I could have an alternative date. I then suggested mildly that perhaps there was an error that I was on Ministry of Agriculture work, etc.? He went away and came back. There was a mistake. He said calmly 'You won't be called up,' and tore the 'medical' note to pieces before my eyes. I thanked him without emotion and walked out. I felt pounds lighter. The sky, the air, the earth, were normal again. My luck still held good. Went briskly and cheerfully into the Labour Exchange to see about some men who had been sent along.

October 1 Wednesday

Official came from the Air Ministry today, regarding the taking of land at Rowneys Farm, Wakes Colne and at Langham for new aerodromes. What a wicked shame to take all this good farming land, especially at Rowneys, where we have spent so much money reclaiming it. At Langham, the whole of Langham Lodge will go and all the woods. The Air Ministry man made no secret of the business, showed me all the plans and said that these 'dromes would be used by bombers in the great 'second front' offensive next year. It occurs to me that Colchester may not be very healthy with a large aerodrome three miles from the centre of the town.

Dug up my potatoes this evening, then working on photographs.

October 11 Saturday

Just about a year since I began to sleep in this place. It is becoming very monotonous and, at times, the silence at night has a bad effect on my nerves.

Two alarms tonight but only a few 'planes came over and nothing happened. These are the first alarms for 10 days.

October 16 Thursday

Heard that Indian soldiers are coming to Colchester.

October 17 Friday

As I was going to lunch today, I saw in the High Street, 2 Indians, 3 Canadians, 2 Australians and a French sailor, all within a few minutes.

October 24 Friday

One constantly wonders how much people know and what they are really thinking. Some time ago I went with Mr Craig to Mr Hadley's at Roverstye Farm, for the Survey. Hadley grumbled a good deal about ploughing more land and talked of how the whole future was dark, as he felt sure that the Government would let down the farmers after this war just as they did after the last. Mr Craig said, 'No, Mr Hadley, that's not true, and if I thought it was, I would resign from this work at once. I wouldn't come round asking you fellows to do all this if I thought you would be let down.' Yet a few days later he advised the Corporation to sell Severalls Hall [Farm] at once, as it could be nothing but a liability in the future.

October 29 Wednesday

Biting cold north-east wind. After lunch the sky became very dark and an immense black cloud came up from the north. Within a few minutes a violent storm of sleet and snow came sweeping down, swirling and buffeting against the ancient window in front of me. Two little boys, their jackets over their heads, ran across the Park and a woman with a pram tried to find shelter under the trees by the Ramparts. I have never seen snow so early before. Incredible that we are still carting barley at Abraham's Farm, Great Tey.

October 30 Thursday

Weirdly romantic sight in Head Street – a long file of Indians, leading horses up from the station, grey, brown and black, some of them obviously Mongolian. The men wore steel helmets and carried carbines on their backs. The moon shone, making their faces shine as if they were oiled. Strange cries and words of command floated along the line. It was a most extraordinary sight, like a caravan coming into some far eastern city.

November 2 Sunday

Down to Bourne Mill to feed the animals before I turned in. Going down there to bait in the moonlight always reminds me of a Chinese print which I used to see in the British Museum, showing a man feeding two horses in an open manger in a field, by moonlight, dated about 1380. It always seemed to me to be very beautiful, the horses showing such eagerness for the approaching meal and the man such care and tenderness towards them. So nearly 600 years later and 6,000 miles away, horses still feed eagerly in the dusky moonlight, while thin wet clouds race across the face of the moon.

November 3 Monday

Last Thursday the Ministry of Information 'Gas' Exhibition was opened in the Castle by Skelton, Deputy ARP Controller. He said it was not a question of 'if' the Germans would use poison-gas but merely 'when'. Several officials arrived minus their gas masks.

November 4 Tuesday

There are a good many post-women and girl bus-conductors about the town now but not so many as in the last war.

November 6 Thursday

Went to the cinema tonight and sat right through an air raid alarm. First time I have ever done this.

November 13 Thursday

Heather Hall, the accounts clerk, calmly announced today that she was going to be married. She is only 18 now. Most extraordinary, she looks quite a child.

November 22 Saturday

Heather's wedding day. The whole staff arrived in their best clothes. I wore my best (and only) suit, the one I had made to meet the King [at the Royal Show] three years ago. Joanna Round wore a lovely blue coat and a most saucy little hat, Nott in farmer's check suit.

Joanna drove Daphne and me in a car which she had borrowed. There was an element of risk in taking it to Weeley, as she had no permit to take a car into a defence area. We got to Weeley in good time and ploughed up the long muddy lane to the church. There was a big crowd there and a good many cars. All the office staff sat in a row.

At last, just as the sun began to shine in a traditional manner, Heather came in on her father's arm, looking very pleased and proud. The man is a pleasant faced lad of about 22, an officer in the Merchant Service. The ceremony was not long and then away we all went to the Parish Hall, where they had a tremendous feast. How it is done in these times I cannot guess. Joanna was splendid. It was a very mixed crowd, mostly village folks but Joanna was quite at home with them all and made herself very pleasant indeed. Heather and husband left for London about 4. We left soon after and rushed back to Colchester. I met Mr and Mrs Rose at Holly Trees and went out to tea with them, although I did not feel that I wanted much to eat. They both insinuated that I had had too much to drink as well.

November 27 Thursday

The sirens sounded tonight, so I thought I had better go down to the Castle. A 'plane went towards Ardleigh and in a few moments there was a tremendous flash and a roar. Houses shook and windows rattled and two women, dragging children, came trotting down Trinity Street at a waddling run. Two enormous red flashes shot up and lit the whole sky. A few seconds went by and then two mighty explosions shook the town. I felt the earth tremble as I crossed the High Street. Went into the Castle and went onto the roof but there was nothing to see, no sign of any fires.

November 30 Sunday

Went to Dedham today, by way of Crockleford and saw two enormous craters in a field next to Carrington's Farm, where two of the land mines fell on Thursday. The other two were further over towards Bromley. This was apparently an attack on the Bromley pylons, but missed by a long way. A lot of people in the district are complaining because no attempt was made to bring down the attacking 'planes.

[The pylons at Great Bromley formed part of the Chain Home Radar System, which gave the RAF advance warning of the approach of German bombers.]

December 3 Wednesday

Felt ill this morning, so jumped at the chance to go down to Mersea to find out if some Land Girls had arrived with a thatching machine.

Went right down to East Mersea but no sign of any Land Girls. Coming back, met them with a tractor, a trailer carrying the thatch-making machine, and a living-van hitched on the back. They were two formidable females, nearer 40 than 30, but the tractor driver was a nice little dark girl. I hauled my cycle onto the trailer and rode back with them to the yard where we had a lot of trouble to get in. The girl driving was very young and inexperienced and finally managed to bring down one of the gateposts besides denting the living van. At last we got the van settled under the lea of a barley stack (I discovered when I told Nott this evening that I had put it right on top of a cess-pit). Then there was much grumbling on the part of the ladies because there was no means of getting the machine unloaded, with the result that the tractor had to set off without its trailer. Our organisation is very bad if we cannot arrange for a few men to be on hand when wanted. The ladies seemed to be very dissatisfied with the whole affair. I left them to make their tea in this lonely spot amidst the rising mist.

December 6 Saturday

Great manoeuvres today. The town was 'attacked' by 'invaders' and the whole of the Civil Defence Organisation was on duty to deal with the various 'incidents' which were to occur. The original scheme was that the 'defence' of the town would hold out until nightfall, by which time the ARP people would have left their various businesses and shops and would be ready to deal with 'raids' on a big scale. Unfortunately, the town 'fell' within an hour or two and the 'invaders' swept through. The result was that although the town was occupied by the 'enemy' tonight, the various ARP incidents were carried out as if the 'enemy' was still trying to battle his way in, which made the whole thing rather ludicrous. I decided that in view of the danger from people indulging in too realistic ARP work I should go to the Castle this evening, which I did. The doors were kept locked and I unrolled the hose-pipe so as to be ready to repel any persons who might try to force a way in. About 8 o'clock the view from the turret was quite spectacular. There were bangs and flashes all over the town, for all the world like Guy Fawkes Night, and a considerable fire was burning near the Town Hall. I could not help hoping that there were no German 'planes about to see such a display of light. About 9pm tear-gas was released in High Street but the wind was so strong that it quickly blew away. The public were expected to put on gas masks when the rattles were sounded but I do not think many people did.

At 11 tonight it is still raining and I can still hear fireworks exploding in the distance and the faint sound of gas-rattles, where some determined official, quite undeterred by the wind, which is now half a gale, is letting off tear-gas bombs.

December 7 Sunday

Cycled over to Dedham this afternoon. No sign of the 'war' in Colchester or district – the tide of the battle seems to have flowed towards London. At Dedham, Sisson told me that it had been arranged for him to let off fireworks at various places, so as to provide the incidents for the village ARP services. Unfortunately, the fireworks never arrived, with the results that the whole of the wardens, firemen etc. spent last night keyed-up ready for incidents which never occurred. Sisson was very disappointed, as he was looking forward to putting crackers in the front gardens of people he disliked.

Had tea there and then called at Birchetts Wood. Penelope is definitely joining the WRNS as a volunteer. Mrs Belfield is worried and feels that this must be the end of her home.

December 8 Monday

Committee meeting at Birch. I was most surprised to hear both the Chairman and Frank Warren say very nice things about me. I had no idea that they had any opinion of me at all.

Papers full of the Japanese attack on America and their great successes. No doubt they are determined to clear the white races out of Asia forever and a good thing too.

December 9 Tuesday

Raid alarm today, at noon, the first for 10 days. Nothing came over. The Japanese seem to be making tremendous headway in the Pacific and the situation there must be very serious. How strange that war should come to those tiny remote islands, set far away in that enormous ocean.

Rang Penelope tonight, to enquire how she got on at her interview yesterday. She is accepted and will almost certainly be going to Harwich, so that she ought to be able to get home fairly frequently.

December 10 Wednesday

News today that the 'Prince of Wales' and the 'Repulse' have been sunk in the China Seas by Japanese 'planes. Quite incredible. Apparently these huge ships were sent out without air escort into a region infested with Japanese aircraft carriers. There was a large notice in the 'County Telegraph' window at lunchtime, headed 'Naval Losses'.

December 11 Thursday

Went out to Boxted this evening to see Mr and Mrs Rose, who were just going off to do their turn at fire watching. Each night two people go to the village school and remain awake all night in case incendiary bombs fall in the parish. I went along with them, getting there just at 9pm. They were anxious to hear the news and had brought their radio with them. As it was so near time, they switched it on in the school yard and standing there, under the stars, with searchlights waving far away to the south, I heard the chimes of Big Ben, as clearly as if I had been on the Embankment, followed by the information that the United States is now at war with both Germany and Italy. So another chapter of misery and death begins.

December 14 Sunday

Went to [the Belfields' at] Dedham. Poor Mrs Belfield was worried over Penelope's departure. Who could have imagined that such things would ever come about in England? Penelope had heard nothing definite from the Navy people but she is quite sure that she will go. Her mother said she had packed up all her clothes and belongings.

December 15 Monday

People becoming very depressed owing to the great successes of the Japanese in the Far East.

Went to the Moot Hall with Poulter to see Councillor Blomfield. We had a long talk about the proposed gift to Alderman Sir Gurney Benham when he completes 50 years on the Council next month. I think we persuaded him that a portrait is the only thing.

December 17 Wednesday

A very busy day. Went out with Joanna to examine various pieces of land about the Borough which must be recorded in the Farm Survey. First we went to the Drawing Office [where] Joanna in a riding jacket and green slacks, made a considerable sensation. Then we went down to the Moors at Hythe Hill. There were half a dozen horses and cobs there, wonderfully fat considering there is nothing worth eating, wandering about among masses of barbed wire. Joanna was quite enthralled with it all, the horses grazing, the river, with a barge being poled upstream, Joseph Francis's shipyard and the distant buildings in East Street, Marriage's Mill towering above them. As we came back, the biggest tank I have ever seen came up the Hill, an enormous brute with 'Lapwing' painted on the turret.

This afternoon we had a visit from Mr Thorpe of Bounstead Hill, whose field was taken in possession by the Committee. He was very indignant and very drunk. He swore he had never had the official possession notice and had no idea of the Committee's intention to take possession, being away in Shropshire at the time. On returning to Colchester he finds he has no field and that Mr Stammers, whom he heartily dislikes, is cultivating it for the Committee – 'a man I wouldn't trust to judge a baby show, let alone to farm land.' He begged me to take no notice of the fact that he had 'had a few', and finally left, shaking me warmly by the hand, twice. Supposing he is speaking the truth? We hear a lot about German atrocities in turning people off their own land but what are we doing here? Is not this the same thing? Thorpe bought this 10 acre field after the last war, to keep poultry. Now he has lost it and has very little chance of compensation, as it is regarded as derelict and valueless.

Just before 5pm, we saw a most extraordinary sight on the lawn behind Holly Trees. The sun was sinking low and casting long shadows of the bare trees across the grass and we saw in the gathering dusk two tall Indian soldiers, solemnly prostrating themselves just below our windows. They were facing towards the south-west, which I suppose they imagined was the direction of Mecca. They bowed their heads to the ground six or seven times and then got up and walked away across the Park. It was a strange sight to see Mohammedans at prayer on the Holly Trees lawn but perhaps it is no stranger than the fact that both Moslems and Hindus are enlisted to help England and 'godless Russia' to 'save Christianity'.

December 19 Friday

Great rush of work and hurrying around to get to Writtle, [where] we were lectured to from 11am until 4.30pm but were not told very much of interest. Coope, the new Office Manager, was quite affable, although entirely ignorant of the many difficulties with which we have to contend. I tried to make him see that farming cannot be run from a central office, nor can it be organised by 'efficiency experts'.

December 20 Saturday

Labelling and mounting photos [tonight]. I am going to call this collection 'The Prospect of Colchester'.

December 22 Monday

Christmas cards now have pictures of bombs, aeroplanes, tanks, wardens, etc., all decked out with holly, snow and all the usual decorations. There is even Father Christmas in a 'tin hat'.

December 23 Tuesday

Went out with Joanna this afternoon to do the survey of Brick Kiln Farm. Hadley has a nice little farm, with 6 cows and a few pigs. He told me that he wanted his son, aged 14 next month, to leave school at the end of this term so as to help him on the farm. He applied to the Headmaster to be allowed to leave, as he can legally be compelled to remain at school until the end of the term in which he becomes 14. The Headmaster, on hearing that he was wanted on the farm, refused to let him go, as he had 'not been educated at the public expense to be a farm labourer.' I advised Hadley to complain to the Director of Education but he won't, of course.

Went on to Dedham. Mrs Sisson's cook had been interviewed today by the Ministry of Labour. She is 29, is a trained nurse, cooks for two families and looks after her grandmother, aged 90. She was told that all this was useless, unnecessary work and that she must be prepared to be moved elsewhere. She seems a very astute girl and is confident that she will find a way out of the difficulty.

December 24 Wednesday

Poulter gave us all tea in the office today, his best Lapsang. I bought a cake and we had quite a party. Joanna was in very good form and Poulter enjoyed himself immensely.

Tonight took the evening off, although there was much to be done, and went to see a Marx Brothers film at the Playhouse. The streets were packed with howling mobs of soldiers and ATS girls. Everywhere one saw drunken soldiers sprawling on the pavements, or reeling along, singing.

Army lorries were going slowly up the High Street, collecting those men who were quite incapable. The inert bodies were being heaved over tailboards, respirators and tin-helmets following with a metallic crash. I noticed that the civil police kept well in the background.

December 25 Thursday

At home most of the day. Mother still managed to provide a 'Christmas dinner', turkey, plum pudding, everything. She has never failed yet and I don't believe she ever failed in the last war.

No raids day or night. This is the third Christmas Day during the war and there have never been raids by either side on that day yet.

December 26 Friday

Had to go to the office all day. Only Joanna and Peter Folkard [Capt Folkard's son] came in, to work on the Farm Survey, which is rather behindhand. One phone call came through from Writtle, just to make sure we were there, I suppose.

Mother had a party today but I stayed away as long as I could, very reluctantly putting in an appearance about half past 7. The whole Ralling family were there in force, seven of them altogether. Poor dear Mother, I wonder she does not kill herself with all the work. I suppose this must be about the last of these parties which she has always so enjoyed arranging. She enjoyed this one immensely. Father sat it out quietly, perhaps thinking of all the washing up to do later. I waited until the guests had all gone, helped clear away and then went back to the Castle.

December 31 Wednesday

So ends 1941 and so we look into the vague vista of 1942, a year which will no doubt bring as many disasters and terrors as that now finished. Colchester has been very lucky indeed, in fact since those two days in the autumn of 1940 there have been few really terrifying moments and the wail of the siren no longer turns my stomach. If this luck holds until the end of the war it will be a wonderful thing. There are rumours that aerodromes are to be built at Langham and Colne. If this is done I am afraid the town will be in considerable danger but they are nothing more than rumours so far.

Chapter 4

❧ 1942 ❧

January 1 Thursday

For some reason I do not feel quite so surprised to find myself still alive as I was on this day a year ago. My luck has held well and although this disastrous war becomes daily more disastrous, that extraordinary good fortune which came to me on January 1 last year still maintains.

I am in a good job, one that I enjoy, still in and about my beloved Museum and still owning dear Bob. The prospects are admittedly not good. Today I am 'de-reserved' and am liable for military service at any moment, although I hope the Executive Committee will ask for my deferment.

My parents keep fairly well, although old age begins to tell on both.

Just as we were all leaving the office tonight I plucked up courage and asked Joanna Round to come to a cinema with me tomorrow. She accepted. I rode away up the High Street in great glee.

January 2 Friday

Out on Survey work at Parsons Heath and Old Heath with Joanna this afternoon. Then we had tea and went to the Hippodrome. I enjoyed myself immensely. She said she would come again.

January 8 Thursday

Spencer came in this morning to say that when he was down at Mersea he saw two Army deserters who had been caught at the depot at Mortimer's Farm. They were found among the straw by the storewoman and asked her for a cup of tea, whereupon she screamed and threw them her lunch, rather as one would endeavour to placate dangerous wolves, and fled to fetch help. She shortly came back with a tractor driver and they told him what they were and asked for food and a cup of tea, at the same time begging him not to give them away. He promised he would not and left, ostensibly to get some tea, only to return a few minutes later with the West Mersea police-sergeant.

Spencer arrived just as the sergeant came and saw the heroic arrest. He seemed to think that the tractor driver had been awfully clever but I am glad that Heather and Daphne both violently disagreed and expressed the view that the man was a frightful swine. Joanna simply said how frightfully exciting and did the men run? Spencer said they were finally removed in a car, offering no violence but uttering the most awful threats against the informer.

At lunch I mentioned the affair to Hervey Benham and asked him what he would have done? He said, very languidly, that if there was a reward he supposed one might as well have it or not. Of course, one might actually help an escaped murderer or a thief or some other poor devil out of prison but not a deserter. After all, it was so silly and troublesome of them – escorts having to be sent from all over the place, court martial to be arranged, etc. So damned expensive. They were sure to be caught, anyhow.

It appears that these men broke away from a guard in Colchester Barracks and bolted in what they thought was the direction of London. It is of amusing interest that, in dirty battledress and gym shoes they crossed the Strood [Causeway] unchallenged and without even being aware that sentries were posted there. Our guarded realm!

January 9 Friday

Went down to Mersea this afternoon, to see North Farm at the East end of the Island. A very dilapidated place. The buildings are very poor and the house is so bad that the three old [Woods brothers] who work it live in a modern house along the road. They are dear old men, who can hardly read or write. All use flails, of which they have some beautiful examples. The cold was terrible and made me feel ill.

January 11 Sunday

Just after 1pm the sky clouded over rapidly with thick grey snow-like clouds and grey fat flakes came whirling down thick and fast. I went down to Bourne Mill. Bob and the donkey were in the low part of the meadow, nibbling through the snow. I fed the two, who came trotting up through the swirling flakes, old Bob as brisk and eager as ever, clumping over the frozen ruts. I could not but help standing to admire the scene, which with pond, mill, distant trees and feeding animals looked so like a Breughel as to be almost incredible.

It is extraordinary how the snow seems to change everybody. In appearance they become ageless and from a little distance it is impossible to say to which century they might belong. The girls become prettier, wearing bright hoods or head scarves and fur-lined boots. Everybody seems so cheerful, laughing, snowballing.

January 13 Tuesday

Terribly cold, more snow fell last night. Mines going off at Abberton [Reservoir] about every ten minutes, last night. It is the ice that does it, I think.

Today in the office Joanna made a remark, 'When I think I have three brothers fighting for a fat lump like him' speaking of some man. To hear a thing like that fills me with awful depression.

Felt so ill tonight, internal chill and pains all over. I am really determined to get out of this damned hole [at the Castle]. My health is being quite ruined.

January 19 Monday

Councillor Blomfield brought in some most interesting stereoscopic views of the town, taken about 1857-58. Very glad to have them and shall have them copied for my series.

One is very fine, showing the 'Top of the Town' on market day. You can see the pigs and sheep, cabs coming through them, a man selling a sack-cloth. It is funny to think that everything and everybody in that scene must be dead by now, unless some of the little children are now old men over 90. It fascinates me to think that those people never knew they would be stared at, just as they were that moment, nearly 90 years after. And when the picture had been taken they all moved on and did other things of which we know nothing and never shall. Yet we can see them for just one second, bargaining, selling, driving sheep, oblivious that their tiniest action was being immortalised.

[See Image 21]

January 20 Tuesday

Hervey Benham was talking today about the decay of the [Colchester] Oyster Fishery. He says that only four dredgers are at work now, while there were about 150 some 30 years ago. It is an intensely close corporation and no strangers can get a permit to dredge under any circumstances. He thinks that unless the Charter is changed, the whole fishery will be extinct in 10 years time. Education does much to dissuade young freemen from taking up the work.

January 23 Friday

Today there was a column in the 'Essex County Standard' issued by the Regional Commissioner, Spens, regarding an invasion: 'Quite probable …Not probably now but possible and probable in a few weeks time. If not then, later on in spring. Stay put. Don't panic. Heavy bombing and gas expected.' All very alarming, even if you don't believe it.

January 24 Saturday

Had tea with Mr and Mrs Rose at the café. I think I have got him a job with the Agricultural Committee at the Fordham Orchards. They are both excited about it.

January 31 Saturday

The Executive Officer [Leslie] addressed local farmers in the Corn Exchange this afternoon but did not tell them very much, except that the meat ration would probably be reduced to 6d per week and that in event of an invasion there was to be no destruction of buildings or food stocks, quite contrary to the 'Scorch our Earth' campaign run by the daily papers.

An old farmer, called McKerracher, talked a great deal about the impossibility of growing corn at present prices but Leslie, a Scotsman too, quickly turned laughter on him, which I thought was rather silly. A great deal of what the old man says is true and I believe quite 25 per cent of the farmers in this district are insolvent, or nearly so.

February 9 Monday

Went down to Mersea this afternoon with Capt Folkard and Nott. We stopped at Pete Tye Common and I affixed a notice to one of the telegraph poles, stating that possession had now been taken by the War Agricultural Committee. Rather a pity, although the whole place is now in a terrible state. I wonder if it will ever be laid down to grass again? At present I believe Nymann the Dane is the only 'commoner', although sometimes Spall at Pete Tye Farm puts a few cows there. I could see Nymann's cows moving across in the mist as I nailed up the notice. There are about 40 acres altogether and we have taken 37. It was really the increase of traffic on the Colchester-Mersea road which led to the Common becoming disused as it is unsafe to leave stock unattended there.

Crossed the Strood, very misty. The sentry was standing against Strood House, his rifle, with bayonet fixed, hung over his shoulder by the sling. He looked terribly cold.

Went down to North Farm. The three old Woods brothers were clearing out a ditch, watched from the hedge bank by their little dog and cat who follow them everywhere.

We talked about flails. They promised to let me know when they would be knocking out beans, so that I may get a photograph. Though they have been tenants of this farm for 40 years they seem to take kindly to working for the Committee.

The crops do not look too bad, in spite of frost and snow. The beans hang their heads a bit. Went down to the depot at Hall Barn, West Mersea. Tremendous activity there, steam engines dismantled, a forge working, men making new irons to repair a tractor-trailer, their faces glowing in the red glare of the fire. In the sheds round the stables are tractors, ploughs, binders, all stored away waiting for spring and summer. I climbed into the old [riding school] stable. All silent and empty. A few show numbers still hang on the wall, an empty liniment bottle and a worn body brush on a window sill. How often has Bob come in here, steaming after his run from Colchester.

February 11 Wednesday

Evening papers all preparing the public for the loss of Singapore. The majority of people seem to view the rapid disintegration of the Empire very calmly. Perhaps they are really as sick and tired of the whole thing as I am.

February 13 Friday

Meeting of both the Lexden & Winstree and the Tendring Committees to hear Mansfield give a talk on future agricultural policy [Mansfield was a civil servant working for the then Minister of Agriculture and Fisheries, Robert Hudson].

Frank Girling of Lawford [told Mansfield] that the farmers in his parts had no confidence in the Minister whatever. Mansfield's reply was remarkable. He said that such farmers obviously did not realise what a friend they had in Mr Hudson and they 'should be very glad he is not a weaker man than he is.' Those were his very words. Furthermore, when discussing prices, he said that farmers should be very grateful to Hudson, without whose support they would not have got anything like as good prices as they had, and he (Hudson) 'had always and was now, standing up for the farmers' interests against his colleagues in the Cabinet.' Once again his very words. I have no doubt this does indeed reveal the true state of affairs.

J S Blyth of Walton and Frank Girling both urged that more help should be given by the schools and that War Agricultural Committees should be empowered to take children out wherever they might be urgently needed. I have suggested this for years but in fact the Education Authorities oppose agriculture wherever they can.

It was only when I saw the evening paper tonight that I realised what a staggering victory had been won by the Germans yesterday, when they brought their three biggest warships up the Channel in the face of great opposition, which no doubt would have been greater but for the usual refusal on the part of the Navy and the RAF to co-operate. Forty-two RAF 'planes were shot down. The audacity of the affair [known as 'Operation Cerberus' by the German forces] was amazing. I hear several destroyers went out from Harwich and one on returning landed a number of dead. Almost all the German Navy is now in the North Sea, which looks more like a prelude to an invasion than anything I have seen yet.

February 14 Saturday

My birthday. 32 years old. Well into middle-age now. How remote and ancient such an age appeared to me this day ten years ago. Now I have reached it, with nothing more done than at 22, I feel quite apathetic and would not mind if I was indeed 42. I cannot bring myself to believe that anything matters except to end the war or alternatively to get out of it. I fear to die (physically) and I have a great desire to remain alive until the end of the war for no other reason than to see what the devil is going to happen next.

Mother gave me a pair of socks and a tie and Father gave the usual 5/- as he always does. Bless the dears.

February 22 Sunday

Saw a glorious sight this morning. As I was coming out of Holly Trees I heard the sound of several horses and saw two white officers of the Indian Army Service Corps with an Indian orderly, coming up the street at a rousing canter. The leading officer, a typical looking cavalryman, rode a beautiful chestnut with three white legs and a white face. The other was on a dark bay, which pulled and frothed a good deal, with its head sometimes almost between its legs. The orderly rode a bay troop-horse. He was a fine picturesque figure with his turban floating in the wind. The cavalcade swept up High Street in great style, hooves echoing thunderously on the wood blocks, very loud in the Sabbath calm.

After tea to Seymour's. Jeff Saunders came in, home on leave from the Navy, a little thinner but very well. He is tired of the war and the Navy and has no hope, sees no sign of the end. He has been to the Arctic Circle since I saw him last.

February 24 Tuesday

Went down to Mersea with Nott this afternoon, to see North Farm. The three old Woods brothers were round the lee of a stack, knocking out beans with their flails. The sight and sound of flails fascinates me. The beans looked like pebbles of marble, veined and blotched purple, red and black. It was extraordinary to watch these old men, their tools and method quite unchanged since the days of the Egyptians and to realise that an identical scene could have been seen there as far back as 'The year when the Danes first wintered in Mersea.'

March 4 Wednesday

To London to find harvest carts. Crowds of people travelling, thousands of soldiers as usual. You would think that the whole Army was going on leave. Liverpool Street soon after 9. Dirty and misty, with rain pouring through the holes in the roof. Went out into Bishopsgate, where there is remarkably little damage visible. The traffic just the same, still the great pair-horse drays rumbling along, still the endless processions of buses.

Walked out in the rain down Petticoat Lane. Buildings down and burnt out in places. ARP notices in Yiddish on the walls. At Whitechapel Road took a trolleybus to Brady Street. Considerable damage all along on both sides.

Walked past Mann, Crossman's Brewery and decided to go in and make enquiries there. The main office was palatial – solid mahogany, shining brass. Literally dozens of male clerks, some old, some young. The staff was amazed at my question as to whether they had any carts to dispose of but I was handed onto the Stable Manager, Mr Sweeting. This gentleman is a proper horseman, not more than 30 or 32, in charge of more than 100 of the finest Shire horses in England. He had no lorries to sell as he was in fact buying them himself, as in this firm horses are now to replace motor [on deliveries] up to 7 miles. However, we had a long and most interesting talk and he showed me round the place. There were three new horses in the stables and an old grey, 20 hands high, who was badly hurt in a raid but extricated himself and had made a fine recovery. The destroyed part of the stable looks very pathetic. The damage was caused by a mine which fell directly on it, killing 25 out of 120 horses.

After all this he took me in his car to see a friend in Commercial Road who had carts to sell. Mr Pritchard at Norway Wharf was large, fat and hearty, a real East End Cockney, wearing two overcoats and a bowler hat. His office, a tiny little cupboard, was hung with photos of brakes and coaches going to Derbys 30 and 40 years ago.

He had several carts, vans and trolleys. I finally settled on five, three trolleys and two vans. I suggested £15 each but he asked £20 each for four and £10 for the last, to which I finally agreed. All the sheds and stables were in a dreadful state and the yard full of muck and rubbish. 'Ah,' said Mr Pritchard, 'You ought to have seen this place before it got "blitzed". Lovely set of stables, lovely place.' But you could see it had been falling down for years.

When the deal had been to all intents settled, we all went off for a drink in a pub called the White Swan, almost under some railway arches. It is a typical London drink-shop, garish, gaudy, warm and full of mysterious people. The rather passé barmaid said to me 'My word, you don't half look wet, sonny.' I fear I must look depressingly young. The other two drank double Scotches but I stuck to beer and had three half pints, quite enough for me.

Then we all went back to Whitechapel, old Pritchard coming along to see a new horse. All the way back I saw singles, pairs, unicorns, cobs and ponies, a most cheerful sight. The amount of business which still goes on in this badly bombed city must be very considerable. Everywhere you see demolition sites, damaged buildings, burnt buildings and people hurrying along through drifting rain.

Got the tube to Charing Cross and walked up to Trafalgar Square, where everything seemed normal so far as architecture was concerned. Great posters all round Nelson and the lions, demanding you to save money and so forth. Went into the National Gallery to see the new Rembrandt and the War Artists' Exhibition. Rembrandt all alone, staid, severe. Wish I could appreciate its finer points. War Artists very mixed. Considerable number of the exhibits are portraits of tough, intense women in various uniforms. Many are of air raids but none very remarkable.

[Rembrandt's portrait 'Margaretha de Geer' had been purchased for the National Gallery by the National Art Collections Fund and was being exhibited for the first time. The portrait was shown in isolation and became the first of a series of 'Pictures of the Month' at the National Gallery, in which individual masterpieces were brought back from their wartime storage in Wales to be exhibited in the gallery for a month at a time.]

March 6 Friday

Poulter told me a most interesting story today. It appears that last night he dreamt he was downstairs in the Holly Trees workshop when the old Doctor walked in and sat down in the armchair as he always did in life. In the dream Poulter knew that he was dead but talked to him normally on various matters. Suddenly he thought to ask him a question and said, 'Tell me, Doc, is there really another life?'

The Doctor, in a manner so characteristic of him, got up, put his head on one side, his eyes twinkling, and said, 'I shan't tell you,' so absolutely lifelike. Many a time have I heard him reply to some inquisitive person in just that way.

March 9 Monday

The first of the Land Army Girls arrived at Peldon Hostel today.

March 10 Tuesday

Went over to Boxted tonight, to Mr and Mrs Rose. Almost all the talk was on 'invasion', or at least the invasion of Boxted. I never heard such nonsense. They have been holding meetings, arranging billets for refugees, scaring old people half out of their wits, instructing people to burn their houses, bury food in the garden and perform all manner of strange antics. The parson has been asked to prepare grave spaces for the dead and to be ready to arrange committal services. Major Waller of course is enjoying himself immensely but I believe he does it all with his tongue in his cheek. I cannot understand why Mrs Rose has anything to do with this sort of thing.

After this there was talk of the disasters in the East, where at least 150,000 men have been lost. At least 90,000 are prisoners in Singapore and about 50,000 more in Hong Kong. The Burmese are now, after 50 years of British rule, beginning to get a little of their own back. Rumours hint at grave troubles in India. I rather believe we shall see a vast coloured Army, all united to get the whites out of India and the rest of Asia. I think this would be a good thing and I believe England would be very happy without an Empire. If only the Empire would go, I believe there would not be another war during the present century.

March 15 Sunday

Great church parade today to pray for the success of Colchester's 'Navy Week'. The town is to buy a submarine at the cost of £250,000. As I came along the High Street, the band struck up and out came the Mayor, the Town Sergeant, Sir W Gurney Benham hobbling dead lame, about six aldermen of all shapes and sizes, the usual military officers, an Admiral from Harwich, Oswald Lewis our Jew MP, and councillors shambling along behind. Away they went, very slow march so that poor Gurney could keep up, the band playing 'Marching through Georgia' as slowly as they could.

It was all rather pathetic – not more than a third of the whole Corporation had bothered to turn out and what there was raised giggles from the onlookers. A girl near me called out 'Come and look at the pretties!' And I heard a voice say, 'Oh, they do look funny.'

I could not help wondering how long this will go on after Gurney's death. He invented a good deal of the ceremonial of the Council as well as the robes and hats worn by the Aldermen and Councillors. His High Steward's robe he designed entirely by himself. There is, of course, genuine authority for the Aldermen and Councillors robes but until Gurney made a great point of it about 40 years ago there was very little 'dressing up' in the Council. The hats were quite his idea and as far as the rest of the dress goes are a fearful anachronism. I believe that within a year of the old man's death all this will go.

March 18 Wednesday

Long talk with Poulter tonight about Museum affairs. The latest insanity is that at the Museum Committee yesterday they accidentally passed some of the Harbour Bills in mistake for Museum Bills and only Councillor Blomfield noticed anything wrong! Hull's mind was wandering and poor old Gurney was half asleep.

March 29 Sunday

This afternoon two Army co-operation 'planes flew over towing gliders. This is the first time I have ever seen such things. They flew round for a time and then released the gliders away to the north, probably over Wattisham Aerodrome I imagine.

Called in at home. Mother has had a letter from Aunt Hetty to say that Maitland has joined the RAF as a photographer and expects to leave within a few weeks. I remember Aunt said several times last year that he had tried to join the RAF, 'as all his friends had gone'.

March 30 Monday

Committee at Birch. The Committee are determined that Joanna Round shall work with the Land Army.

March 31 Tuesday

I have now been 'de-reserved' for three clear months and it is four months since application was made for my deferment by the Executive Committee. Will my luck hold for another three months?

April 1 Wednesday

Joanna came in early this morning to say that Frank Warren had insisted that she began work at Peldon WLA Hostel at once, which she has done. She came in again this afternoon and we cycled over to Fingringhoe. There was a terribly strong south-west wind, blowing right against us and it was very cold. We went right down to the Wick and stood watching the birds, of which there were hundreds on the edge of the mud, geese, mallards, gulls, etc., others riding on the water or wheeling about over the estuary, crying and calling. The view was magnificent and we spent some time looking towards Colne Bar through my field glasses, where there were quite 20 barges at anchor between Mersea and Brightlingsea, together with several Naval Patrol boats.

Next we went over to the [gravel] pits, where to my surprise I saw that hundreds of middens had been cut through, the whole place being littered with sherds, bones and pieces of tile. At first Joanna would not believe what they were but she soon became convinced and I had the exquisite pleasure, which I have not had for years, of showing a novice her first Roman pottery. Most of the pottery was 1st century, Claudian period.

I went on with Joanna, in gathering dusk, to Layer Cross and left her at the bend before you turn down to Layer Breton. She thanked me for my kindness towards her during the last year and I said what a pleasure it had been to have her working in the office, because had it not been for that, I should never have known her. She said, 'Yes, isn't it funny how if certain things had not happened we might never have been friends at all.' She promised to come to tea sometimes. I said it might be rather unwise, as people would be sure to talk but she said she did not care in the least. I thought, 'No, but your people might!'

Then I said, 'Well, I must go back to Colchester now.' She said, 'Yes, I suppose so.' I took her hand and said, 'There's just one thing. Can I kiss you goodbye?' She smiled, put her cheek forward, I kissed her, she laughed got on her cycle and rode away, just as the moon rose round and red through the trees behind us. I got on my cycle and rode back to Colchester feeling rather depressed.

April 2 Thursday

Telephone message from Writtle this morning to say that the Executive Committee had approved Joanna's appointment as supervisor for the Land Army at Peldon. I was glad to be able to tell the Chairman the news at once, as he happened to be in the office. Before he left he passed a remark on last night's outing – '… fossil hunting daughter didn't get in until half-past eight' (which caused the District Officer to raise his eyebrows a little).

April 6 Monday

Curious and rather repulsive sight in St Botolph's Street – about a dozen girl conscripts, carrying pathetic little bundles and boxes, being marched up from the station by an escort of soldiers. All the soldiers walking up town laughed and jeeringly shouted military commands and passers-by gave silly grins. The escort (as a compliment to the sex of their charges?) carried neither rifles nor side-arms but for some odd reason wore packs and ammunition belts.

April 8 Wednesday

The Chairman had a story about a girl evacuee at Layer Marney. A very prim old farrier, with full beard and clothes of old fashioned cut, saw her in the village shop, staring at him very hard and said genially, 'Well my dear, what do you think of me?' 'Blimey,' replied the child (aged about 8), 'you're a funny old bugger!'

April 11 Saturday

Had a letter this morning from Joan Blomfield about her cob Robin, saying that she must get rid of him at once, as he is such a nuisance. Sent a telegram to say send him over at once, as I always promised I would. I never felt less like taking a horse than I do now but I shall have to give him a trial.

Joanna had a most amusing story about the trouble she has with the Land Girls regarding the lack of lavatories in the country. She says no girl ever goes to the lavatory by herself. Always two go, one to 'keep guard'. One day this week Joanna had to go to Capt Maughfling at Pete Hall to see what 'amenities' there were there. She asked for the 'lady of the house' but as there is not one, found herself compelled to put the delicate question to the gallant captain. Unfortunately, she was so tongue-tied over the whole business that the captain missed the point and thought she was trying to find somewhere for the girls to eat their lunch. Joanna had to give up altogether.

No more white bread now, all flour being a light brown colour. Everybody esteems this to be a great hardship – only pure white flour being suitable for Englishmen. For many years past the millers have produced white flour by extracting the wheat-germ. Bread made from this flour causes digestive ailments, which can be cured by taking wheat-germ in the form of 'Beemax'. This is only one of the thousands of ways in which great combines and vested interests fool the public.

April 12 Sunday

Tonight I made a thorough inspection of the Castle and I find that there is not one drop of water on the roof and only two buckets of sand. The hose pipe, which was fitted months ago after I had agitated for a year, does not work. I reported all this to Poulter this evening but he still takes the view that Hull alone is responsible and that he will not interfere with Castle affairs.

April 21 Tuesday

Telephone from the station this afternoon to say Robin had arrived. Great excitement. Went down to the station with Joanna at 6.30pm and there he was – a lovely russet red, with a white blaze and one white foreleg, rather thin and ragged, no shoes on, in a tremendous way to get out of the box where he had been shut up in the dark since early morning. We saddled and bridled him in the station yard and Joanna rode him away. His action is lovely, head up, tail out, feet put down firmly, the typical Welsh cob. I immediately decided I must give Joan £20 for him, anything less would be robbery. She only suggested £15, which was what she paid for him.

April 25 Saturday

Mr Craig came in this morning and talked about old McKerracher drowning himself at Ewell Farm, Kelvedon last Monday. It seems that he had always threatened to kill himself if the WAC took possession of his farm and when John Fenn went over last Monday to make a record of condition, the old man greeted him and then disappeared. After a while they found a chalk written message in the garage, saying, 'You will find me in the river' and there he was, quite dead. This is the old man who spoke at the farmers' meeting on January 31 last. It seems very sad but perhaps the poor old chap was right.

April 26 Sunday

Called at Seymour's this evening and heard for the first time that there had been an air raid at Bath last night, as a reprisal for the destruction of the ancient medieval cities of Rostock and Lübeck. [These cities had been bombed by the RAF in April and March 1942. The raid on Bath formed part of a series of 'Baedeker raids' by the Luftwaffe, which targeted historic British cities.] There do not seem to be any details of damage. No doubt this will be made an excuse for a further 'reprisal' on Rome. Many people have for a long time advocated raids on Rome 'to show the Italians what ruins really are'.

April 27 Monday

Raid on Bath the main item in all the papers today. Casualties 'fairly heavy'. 'Indiscriminate bombing,' 'widespread damage among working-class houses.' No mention of any historic buildings being hit. Several West Country towns appear to have been attacked during this weekend, including Bristol and Exeter. I heard someone at lunch today saying with gloomy joy, 'Ah well, I suppose we shall get our packet before long.'

I went with Capt Folkard and Mr Craig to see Rodd's land at Lexden Garden Village. It is in a terrible state. One of the Rodds was there harrowing with a tractor. Some talk after of serving orders and then taking possession of the land. It seemed rather awful to me with Rodd working away in front of us, trying to do his pathetic best with this field, while we stood outside, calmly discussing his fate. A girl came riding up on a pony and watched him. I wondered if it was his wife.

Evening papers report a second raid on Bath last night, with heavy casualties, much damage to historic buildings. The Germans, in their official reports, say it was a 'reprisal' on 'aristocratic Bath' and that 'huge fires' were caused in the northern part of the city.

How much has really been destroyed? How is it that on a clear, moonlit night not a single raider seems to have been brought down? Has the whole Air Force gone to the east? How long, how long, before somebody is brave enough to make an effort to stop this war?

April 28 Tuesday

Vague news this morning of a raid on Norwich last night. 'Many casualties feared,' 'widespread damage.' An article in the 'Mail' today describes Bath in the past tense. Never before during this war have I felt so depressed. It is obvious that comparatively few 'planes have been used in these raids. Perhaps the defence system has quite collapsed.

Colchester now begins to wonder quite seriously whether or not it is an 'historic town'. It would certainly be ironical, if after all these years of senseless destruction leaving so few buildings still standing, if the Germans attacked the place as a town of British culture.

I am in a most depressed state in the 'Oven' tonight. It is gone 11pm and the silence is so intense one can almost 'hear' it. I am straining my ears to catch any friendly sounds, a car, a lorry, a drunken soldier, or even a ghostly noise in this 'crumbling ruin' would be better than a silence which presses all round you. I cannot forget our lack of sand and water.

There is nothing to do but try to go to sleep. The telephone has rung with startling suddenness, almost scaring me out of my wits but it was nothing but the wind crossing the wires. How much longer shall I stand these nights? There is a noise now, at last – the wind moaning under the Castle door.

April 29 Wednesday

Felt quite glad to be alive this morning. Just at midnight last night there were four tremendous explosions, so I grabbed my helmet, boots, trousers, coat, torch and binoculars and rushed up the stairs to the turret, heart pounding, fit to burst. The town lay peacefully in the moonlight, the only sounds coming from trains and distant cars. There was nothing in the sky. All was so quiet I concluded that the noises must have been mines exploding at Abberton Reservoir and so descended again, considerably shaken.

April 30 Thursday

Mr Craig told me there was a general alarm last night and the Canadians were all called out to stand by in case of a raid. We saw some at West Bergholt with a Bren gun mounted on a lorry, rather a pathetic protection. A lot more are on Lexden Lodge Lane. If these are our only defence, God help us. Mr Craig says the Colchester authorities all expected a raid. Major Vickers has put all ARP staffs on double shifts.

A brilliant full moon [tonight]. As I came across the Park at 11pm the Castle stood out as if it was midday. I hope to God nothing comes over tonight. Somehow I don't really feel so scared as I did on Wednesday but I wish it was morning. It is no joke being here alone, hour after hour (although not quite alone, as there is a large rat under the floor). My nerves are not very good now. How I wish it was morning or that the moon would be covered by thick clouds. There was an attack on Norwich last night but not much damage. A few people killed.

May 1 Friday

The evening papers tonight say that there were attacks last night all along the East Coast as far up as Sunderland and that out of about 50 German 'planes attacking, 11 were brought down.

May 2 Saturday

Hull apparently has no intention of doing any more fire watching at all. Under the circumstances, I really do not think I can go on much longer. When I think of the work

I could get done away from this ruin, it makes me realise what a fool I am to stay here night after night, often in a sweat of fear, when not a single soul comes to see whether I am there or not. I can hear a 'plane going over now, fairly low, probably an RAF going across the sea, or else a night-fighter on patrol.

How fantastic it is to sit scribbling in this tiny cell, wondering whether you will ever see daylight again or whether this domed roof will be the last sight your eyes will see, just as it was poor James Parnell's last, 286 years ago. It is difficult to appreciate what noble sentiments must have filled him, even when sitting in the very place where he breathed his last.

I can now hear drunken soldiers singing and shouting in the darkness, just as he must have done as he lay here on a heap of straw all those years ago. Perhaps he really enjoyed dying, so sure was he that he would gain the life everlasting. He was only 20, just the right age for a fighter pilot. I wonder what they think about as they take off?

May 3 Sunday

This afternoon about 50 fighters and bombers flew over in three formations. I suppose on their way to attack targets in France. The sun shone, people in their best clothes walked down Wimpole Road and children played on the Recreation Ground, just behind the parked ambulances with corpse-baskets on the roofs, while 5,000 feet above them sailed mighty weapons of destruction.

May 5 Tuesday

Had a run down to Mersea this afternoon with Capt Folkard. Brilliant sunny day, everything dry and parched. Some crops look well but others not. We went on to Abbott's Hall, Wigborough. This is a wonderful farm, with enormous buildings, much damaged by bombs 18 months ago. There were two of the Committee's tractors there, great crawlers, tearing up the old grassland in a wonderful way.

I always feel depressed at teatime now, as that is when the evening papers come out with their alarming and morbid placards. The last raid on Exeter is now said to be 'serious', with heavy casualties, more than in previous raids. Rumours about Norwich have been so bad that the Regional Commissioner has issued a sort of manifesto, asking people not to believe the rumours but as he still refuses to give any details, this is hardly likely to do very much good, in fact he makes the matter much worse by such announcements.

Tonight I took a decisive step and wrote to Hull asking to be relieved of Castle duties [due to ill health and the additional workload at the EWAC].

May 8 Friday

Lowering clouds! Rain! It began at 8 this morning and soon fell steadily. This will bring the grass on tremendously.

Rang up Mrs Parrington tonight and discussed the possibility of going over to Lawford. Hull has made no reply to my letter and I no longer feel bound to carry out duties at the Castle [every night].

May 9 Saturday

Rang Mrs Parrington again tonight and settled to move over to Lawford on Sunday. Now I have made the decision I feel very much better.

May 10 Sunday

I cycled to Lawford. Langham Lane looks lovely. It will all be destroyed if the proposed aerodrome is built there. Had supper and then bed, a lovely soft white bed. Before I fell asleep I lay listening to rain falling in torrents.

May 11 Monday

Up at 6.30am, into a world smelling of damp earth. Everything already looks much greener.

Committee meeting at Birch today and I drove over with Robin. He went quite well, although rather troublesome when we met the Indians with their horses and also with lorries. However, he got me there in 35 minutes. The Committee were all lined up outside when I arrived and gave a mighty cheer but I was glad to see they all admired him.

May 16 Saturday

Raid alarm at Colchester this afternoon but nothing happened. Got some shopping done and was then on duty at the Castle tonight. The cell seems very unpleasant to me now.

May 17 Sunday

Went down to Dedham and called at Sisson's. He told me that hardly an ancient building had been touched in Norwich but some windows are broken at the Cathedral and St Peter Mancroft's and St Benedict's Church was burnt. None of the Museums nor the Castle was touched. There is considerable damage on the west side of the city, houses and factories burnt out and one of the railway stations almost useless. There are several thousand people homeless. The odd thing is that these raids were widely publicised as being directed against ancient monuments, yet three successive efforts were all against industrial quarters.

Stabled my pony in the cowshed at Sherbourne Mill and had a wonderful supper, then ground some flour and some cow-cake, chopped some mangold, brought up the cows and so to bed.

This is the end of the first week of this experiment and as far as I can see it works very well. I have never felt so well in years and, for the first time in my life, I find getting up in the morning a real pleasure. The Parringtons could not be kinder.

May 27 Wednesday

The District Officer had to spend the whole morning at Writtle, in response to an urgent phone call, considering a ridiculous 'exercise' for the immobilisation of tractors in case of invasion. I never heard such rubbish in my life, because if there was an invasion the whole scheme is unworkable, as it depends on the free use of telephones. It is most depressing that all these schemes of 'what-to-do-when-the-Germans-come' assume that an enemy invasion will be completely successful.

May 31 Sunday

This evening I went to see the Sissons. He was very depressed over the raid by 1,000 RAF machines on Cologne as he fears this great medieval city must be entirely destroyed.

He also fears that reprisals will result in the total destruction of any English towns which contain antiquities, in fact as I parted from him at his front door, he looked up at the full moon riding above the church tower and said, 'I wonder which it will be tonight? Cambridge or Canterbury?'

June 1 Monday

Saw in the evening papers, with a sense of shock, that Canterbury was attacked last night, just 2 hours after Sisson had spoken of it. No details, except that the Town Clerk was killed and 'considerable damage' done. Nothing about the Cathedral. People seem horrified at the Cologne raid. The papers try to whip up enthusiasm about 'revenge' but it seems to fall a bit flat.

[The Cologne raid formed part of the RAF's 'area bombing' strategy from 1942.]

June 5 Friday

Got to Lawford at 8.30pm and fed all the animals. Mrs Parrington came back at 10.30pm, after a 3 hour meeting of the parish invasion committee. What a fantastic waste of time. The latest problem (like so many of their problems) still concerns the dead. It has already been decided what to do with the dead and who shall do it but it has now been pointed out that, if any persons are killed before an invasion has 'officially' begun, it will be necessary to hold an inquest upon them and in that case, how can the Coroner be brought to the spot? Further investigations into this important point will now be made.

June 8 Monday

To Birch for a Committee meeting. Nothing special but in conversation at tea I heard it said that the raids on Cologne etc. were of little value and had little effect on the war effort, just as the raids on England two years ago had little or no effect. I expect this is true. I also heard that most of the big houses now requisitioned by the Army would soon be vacated, as almost the whole of the regular Army will be sent abroad in the near future, leaving the country in the hands of the Home Guard (God help us!). I have heard several rumours of this during the last week.

June 9 Tuesday

Serious news about Joanna today – the Local Manpower Board has refused to allow her to continue her work and she has received notice for a medical examination for the ATS.

This is a most scandalous thing, as she is doing excellent work and I do not see how she can be replaced. The poor girl is very upset, as well she may be.

June 10 Wednesday

Great business all day today about Joanna. Poor Joanna has been most miserable but I gave her tea tonight and took her for a drive with Robin and I think she felt a little better. I called at home and we spoke to Mother, who was so pleased to chat with Miss Round! Dear Joanna said afterwards she thought my parents were charming and that I ought to see them more often and not neglect them.

June 14 Sunday

Lay in bed late, reading Bell's 'Great Fire of London'. How much that fire exceeded anything that the Germans have been able to do so far.

Before lunch I put on my new corduroy trousers which I bought yesterday for 50/- and 5 coupons. They look very well and ought to last 10 years. These trousers and a jacket which I bought 6 weeks ago are the only clothes I have bought since rationing began more than a year ago. Of course, I was very lucky to have bought four shirts on the day before the scheme started.

This evening I went down to Bourne Mill. Suddenly a tremendous storm burst without the slightest warning. First came torrential rain for a few seconds. Then a violent storm of hail or rather lumps of ice half an inch across. The noise on the tin roof of the stable was frightful and what with that and peals of thunder, Bob and the donkey fled out into the storm, where they stood in abject misery, tails to wind, heads nearly touching the ground.

The temperature must have fallen 10 degrees in a matter of seconds and the ground and house roof became white as if covered with snow. It was most incongruous to see green trees and thick grass in such a scene. I have never seen anything like it in my life. I fear much damage will have been done to crops, especially in the market gardens.

June 15 Monday

Joanna came in very upset and wanted me to do something about the Manpower Board. Capt Folkard agreed that I had best try to arrange an interview at once. I was put in touch with a Miss Downie, who had dealt with Joanna's case. She was about 50, grey, very severely dressed in black and white and obviously with no nonsense. I explained the whole business from the very start. She asked me many questions and took down all my answers in a notebook, a detestable habit guaranteed to upset any interview, however friendly.

Gradually it dawned upon me that this woman, who has immense power over the future of young girls in this town, was quite ignorant of the whole matter. She knew nothing whatever of the work Joanna was doing. She knew nothing about farming. As a matter of fact, she had never heard of the local War Agricultural Committees at all. I tried to explain but her brain could not take it in and I soon began to feel quite overwhelmed with the impossibility of persuading her of the facts of the situation.

We got to such an impasse that at last Miss Downie suggested I had better see Mr Dymond, 'although members of the Board do not as a rule see callers.' Mr Dymond is a dark little man, hard as nails, giving away neither information or help. We had the whole thing all over again, with the same result – he had not the slightest idea what I was talking about. He was quite pleasant but he obviously regarded me as a strange visitant from another land. It appears that Writtle have made two separate appeals for Joanna, both of which have been rejected. I finally left after one and a half hours talking and felt very glad to get away from the place. Here is a vast body and a complex organisation, yet when a case is put before them they have nothing to say and have no actual knowledge of the matter under discussion. It reminds one of a seemingly wonderful machine, which, when you try to find out how it works, you discover that it has no works.

I saw Joanna when I got back, very white and anxious, poor dear and did my best to reassure her, although to myself I cannot admit that her chances are good. There was an atmosphere of enmity towards her about the whole place.

There was terrible damage done by the storm yesterday, especially at Dedham and East Bergholt. Tomatoes, fruit, rhubarb, peas and some oats were quite ruined.

June 16 Tuesday

Went out with Mr Stanley Webb [from the Essex Agricultural Executive Committee] and the Chairman this afternoon to inspect farms at Mersea. We went to Bower Hall first. Poor old Vigne came out, looking a physical wreck. The first field we went into was just a sea of thistles. Webb said, 'What have you got here, Mr Vigne?' 'Oats' was the reply and there was in fact an oat or two sticking up. 'Well,' said Webb, 'I'll tell you what you've got here Mr Vigne. You've got a bloody mess!'

They decided to recommend possession at Michaelmas and Vigne made no objection as he is due to leave there in any case. His poor worn out old horses were still working, just as I saw them a year ago. The buildings seem to have collapsed a little more.

June 19 Friday

Very busy day. Went down to Mersea with Joanna and then on to Fingringhoe where I paid a gang. Out of 10 men, 4 could not sign their names.

In the papers tonight nothing but military disasters. One article describes 'mass produced' houses which are to be made after the war. There is a good deal of 'after-the-war' stuff in the press now, I suppose to encourage the people.

Drove out to Lawford. Great excitement. The sweep had been. It seems he must come on Fridays now, because, owing to the shortage of soap, that is the only night he can have a wash.

June 21 Sunday

Cycled to Dedham, taking spring onions to the Sissons [who were] both full of rumours that 2,000,000 American troops would be brought into the district and the whole civil population removed to make room for them. This of course is for the 'Second Front'. One sees 'Open a Second Front NOW' chalked all over walls and railway bridges in Colchester.

Drove back to Colchester in the cool of the evening. At Holly Trees Poulter was very depressed about the capture of Tobruk and the surrender of 25,000 men.

June 28 Sunday

When I got in [to Colchester tonight] I found that my journey had been quite unnecessary, as a new arrangement has now been made whereby a fire watching gang has been transferred to the Castle, so that two men were doing duty there tonight, besides myself. They were supposed to be there by 10 but eventually arrived at 10.45pm, grumbling and complaining that they had not received proper instructions. I presume that under these circumstances my services are no longer required.

June 29 Monday

Unpleasant news in the papers today that a tremendous 'comb out' is to take place of all men of military age. Mr Bevin states that all individual deferments must go by the board. Well, it is now six months since I was de-reserved and I do not know yet how I stand as regards deferment.

Notice that some railings have been removed in Winchester and Canterbury Roads, as well as those of the Wesleyan Chapel in Wimpole Road [for salvage]. Why a whole street cannot be cleared at once, I do not know but I suppose the railings given voluntarily will be removed first, so as to make the whole business more complicated than it would otherwise have been. This 'spirit of sacrifice' about gates and railings is very interesting. It is considered to be a much greater sacrifice if the railings are old and beautiful so people tear down lovely gates or throw out rare books to be pulped in order to appease the Gods.

'Sacrifice' has always been something of a mystery to me. If a man is conscripted like a criminal, thrown into the Army, hustled into a foreign country and there killed, he is said to have 'given his life for his motherland'. If, however, he is run over by a lorry on the way to the barracks, that is simply a regrettable accident.

July 5 Sunday

Drove out today by Dedham and called at the Sissons'. Mrs Sisson told me that last Christmas a lady in the village decided to send a Christmas card to every Dedham man serving in the Army. The card she chose was a view of the Dedham War Memorial.

July 6 Monday

Committee at Birch. More 'secret' sub-committees about Joanna. The Chairman has written to R A Butler, MP for Saffron Walden, asking him to bring the matter before the Ministry of Labour and Agriculture.

July 23 Thursday

Man from the Air Ministry in today regarding new aerodromes. It seems that the three in this district, Langham, Wormingford and Birch, will take about 1,500 acres of arable land, which is just the amount of extra grassland ploughed this summer, so we are back where we started. How can the land support the people?

Two alarms this morning in quick succession. I was cruelly amused to see the Air Ministry fellow blanch when the siren sounded and to notice that his voice shook a little.

Drove out to Lawford. Mrs Parrington had been to Manningtree to attend a lecture on fire fighting, which she said was rather silly. The lecturer made everything as simple as possible, beginning by saying that when bombs are released from an aeroplane, they fall to the ground.

July 27 Monday

Busy day at the office. Barker came in from White House Farm, Langham, to say that the Air Ministry's contractor had entered upon the Committee's land there without warning and had told him that some 15 acres were requisitioned forthwith. I have sent a full report to the Executive Officer but I don't suppose anything will be done.

July 29 Wednesday

Went to the presentation of Sir Gurney Benham's portrait at the Moot Hall this afternoon. The Mayor, Alderman Alec Blaxill and S A Courtauld made three of the worst speeches I have ever heard in my life, incredibly dull and tactless. All three seemed to forget that not only was the old man not dead but that he was sitting on the platform beside them. The Mayor went so far as to congratulate Lady Benham for her efforts in keeping the old chap alive!

Then Sir Gurney spoke himself and his was the best speech of the lot. He was clear, concise and witty, saying among other things that the portrait would be valuable in years to come not because of the subject but because of the artist [Maurice Codner] and that while apologising for all the trouble he had given his friends today, he could safely promise it should not occur again.

So ends his half century of civic life, begun in the calm solidarity of 1892 and now drawing to a close as our civilisation crumbles. When he first sat on the Council the old Town Hall was standing and there were persons still active who were familiar with the Corporation before the Reform Act.

As I write these words the moon is rising, ruddy gold, behind the farm and the trees cast long shadows across the little paddock. Far above, it seems almost amongst the faint stars themselves, bombers are passing over on their way to Germany. It is impossible to prevent oneself from wondering how many people at present peacefully asleep in Germany will never see the morning and how many of the crews of these bombers are seeing England for the last time. Last night 32 machines were lost at Hamburg.

There is a very pleasant Canadian staying at the farm with his sister-in-law. We sat outside in the dusk talking about farming, about which he knew a good deal. He was quite impressed with the harvest. I was thinking as I cycled out tonight how suddenly the harvest bursts upon one. All along through Crockleford and Ardleigh they were cutting oats tonight. Many fields are traved up already and I suppose will be carted within a fortnight.

August 4 Tuesday

Heard today that the Manpower Board has finally refused to allow Joanna to remain in her present work. It seems, therefore, that all our efforts have failed.

August 5 Wednesday

Major Round came in today and showed me a letter from Bevin's private secretary to R A Butler, stating that there seemed to be no grounds for giving Joanna any deferment. [Ernest Bevin was the Minister of Labour and National Service].

I am becoming more and more convinced that this is merely a tiny episode in 'Britain's Silent Revolution'. The landed gentry is not to be massacred, it is to be merely squeezed out of existence and breaking up its family life is an important step towards this.

August 11 Tuesday

As I cycled in [this morning] I was vaguely aware that I had heard gunfire during the night but it was not until I overheard conversations on Hythe Hill that I realised something had happened in Colchester. I was shocked to see a notice on the Casualty Board which read 'No Information Yet' and at the office Nott and Harding both said that bombs had fallen on Severalls Asylum.

At teatime a list was on the Casualty Board giving 26 names, all women, mostly between 50 and 70 years of age, all dead. I understand these are all patients and that not one of the staff was killed or injured. Apparently there was a direct hit on the infirmary.

This afternoon I went down to Mersea with Capt Folkard and did a full round of the island. Our glorious wheat is now traved, the stooks standing so close it appears impossible to get a cart into the field.

Back [to Colchester] at 6pm. Saw the West Mersea Demolition Squad coming back up North Hill in their lorry, very grimly and looking tired. Two more names have now been added to the official list, also women.

These affairs make me very gloomy. Strange contrast to Colchester to get back to Lawford and have supper in the candlelit room, with everybody talking harvest and farming.

August 12 Wednesday

Joanna came in early to say she was finished. It must be admitted that this business will not stop production on the Committee's land but it will cause the greatest inconvenience. The Land Army will undoubtedly do less work and there will be endless trouble with time sheets and allocations. The important point is that this cannot be an isolated case – these things must be done all over the country. The whole organisation of the nation's labour is in the hands of embittered socialists and conscious-less civil servants. I feel nothing but anger at the sight of Government officials working hard and systematically to undermine the agricultural organisation, upon which rests literally, the whole future of the British people.

At lunchtime today figures were put on the Casualty Board showing that 36 were killed [at Severalls], 4 can't be found and 19 were hurt. Every one women, all patients.

August 14 Friday

The news tonight is that Mainz Cathedral has been burnt by the RAF, so one must suppose that York, Canterbury or Salisbury must be burnt in revenge. And so we shall go on until not a single building remains in England or Germany.

August 16 Sunday

At 9 o'clock this morning I could hear through the walls of my room the smooth tones of the BBC announcer from the Hooper's portable radio. They carry this damn thing with them wherever they go and insist on turning it on for every news bulletin. People like this suffer great agonies if they are separated from their radios for a single day, yet the Sissons, the Parringtons, my parents and myself, to name only a few, live quite happily without this blessing of our times. Hundreds of thousands of people never miss a news bulletin all through the day. I hate to hear news on the radio. It is always either depressing or alarming.

This afternoon eight people came to tea at Lawford. There were three 'Wrens' from Harwich. Apparently these girls are in future to man picket boats and mail boats. Who would have thought that a time would come when girls of 19 and 20 would navigate naval vessels in wartime?

August 19 Wednesday

Coming up North Hill this morning I heard the skirl of pipes and saw the Cameronians marching away to the station. They are to be trained as parachute-troops.

It was announced on the 8am news that a landing had been made at Dieppe about 1am and that the invading force was still there. Some wonder if this is the beginning of the 'Second Front'.

Just after 5 tonight I saw a contractor's lorry go up the town full of American soldiers, all in working dress. I believe they are employed on several aerodrome sites in the district.

Capt Folkard told me that at the Lexden & Winstree Rural District Council meeting today, the medical officer submitted a letter from the Ministry of Health expressing grave concern about the falling birth rate and urging all members of RDC's to do their best to remedy this state of affairs. He said the faces of some of the elderly lady members were very funny.

August 24 Monday

Capt Folkard came in to say he had just had a telephone message from Joanna to say she was engaged. I have never heard such good news! The young man is a fellow named Tritton, a Sub-Lieutenant in the Fleet Air Arm. She has known him a good many years, I believe.

August 31 Monday

Drove over to Birch for the Committee Meeting. Cooper-Bland [EWAC District Committee Member] was late at the meeting owing to his having had to attend an inquest upon two of his Home Guards who were killed at bomb practice on Sunday. He said everybody in the company felt it very badly – nobody minded when men were killed in battle but this sort of thing was different.

Mr Craig mentioned that 8,000 recruits were coming to Colchester for initial training, so I suppose no enemy invasion is now thought likely. Mr Craig has just been over to Wales by car, buying cattle and, when at a petrol station somewhere near the Welsh border, he happened to meet R L Hudson, the Minister of Agriculture and had a few minutes talk with him.

September 1 Tuesday

The Hoopers came back to the Mill today. They have come for the threshing. He said he had been told that in all 12,000 troops went to Dieppe and suffered serious losses. Over 2,000 were taken prisoner.

September 2 Wednesday

Confidential letter from the Executive Officer today, stating that a report was required on why Mr Craig had taken a car to Wales. Apparently, the Minister, after an interesting talk with a member of a War Agricultural Committee, had rushed back to London to report him for misusing petrol! Who would have ever believed a British Cabinet Minister would behave in that way? The Executive Officer now wants a private report as to what Craig really did. Craig said that he had been in touch with the Petroleum Board and no objections were raised by them. He has actually made no secret of the business.

September 3 Thursday

Third anniversary of the beginning of the war. For three full years my family, cob and myself have survived unharmed. There were services at 11 o'clock this morning and most factories and businesses stopped work. We were too busy to notice.

September 10 Thursday

The telegraph wires along Dedham Long Road were all lined with birds this morning, waiting to fly south. Perhaps in a few days they will be flying over the Libyan deserts and will perhaps be seen by men whose homes are in Essex.

September 19 Saturday

Both Mother and Father seemed rather unwell today. Poor Father now gets out of bed for every bomb or burst of gunfire. I can't think why he doesn't get pneumonia. It is very bad for Mother to be so disturbed. He said there were 'bombs' at midnight last night but I heard nothing at Lawford.

September 25 Friday

Received information today that Smith, the farrier at the Prince of Wales Yard, St Botolph's corner, had refused to shoe any more heavy horses and proposed to confine himself to ponies and light iron work. I went to see him and he said he sees no future whatever for the trade and that within 6 months of the end of the war there would not be a horse in Colchester. I did all I could to show him that he was wrong but could not convince him.

Since the war began, the smithies at Heckford Bridge, Chappel, Great Horkesley, Lawford and West Bergholt have all shut or are shutting. The seriousness of the position lies in the fact that the Ministry of Labour has no control whatever over blacksmiths, so that there is no means of compelling these people to keep at their work. I have frequently noticed that once a man stops shoeing horses, nothing on earth will ever persuade him to do so again.

September 28 Monday

Went down to the stable and fetched Robin up to the Bull Yard, so as to be ready to go to Birch. About 11am, I heard a 'plane flying very low and at once a tremendous crash of bombs. Capt Folkard and I jumped up and backed away from the windows. I put on a coat and ran out into the street. A policeman asked people nearby if they knew where the bombs had fallen. He said there were pieces on the steps of the police station and thought they must have been 'anti-personnel' bombs, exploding in mid-air. I thought this must be the explanation and walked back to Holly Trees, feeling very glad and relieved that no damage seemed to have been done.

It was not until after 12 that Harding came in with the news or what had really happened – a terrible disaster. Four or five huge bombs had fallen across South Street, Chapel Street, Wellington Street and Essex Street. Harding said there were 'dozens of houses down – bodies all over the place – still digging 'em out.' Capt Folkard said he didn't suppose the cob would be in any state to drive to Birch, so he thought he had better drive me round to 'The Bull' in his car. The Bull Yard was covered with glass but Robin was safe and sound, quite unperturbed.

The ostler was a bit upset and shaken and was busy sweeping up glass. I went down to the Essex Arms, broken windows all the way. There was a rope across Essex Street. About halfway along I could see wreckage, police, ARP men, ambulances and all the sickening paraphernalia of an incident. A continual stream of people came out of Essex Street carrying bundles and boxes, going away to find somewhere to sleep and all the while it rained steadily.

Two girls came along, white as ghosts, one wheeling a cycle, and an old woman said, 'Come on in dear, you're alright, you come in.' From overheard remarks I gathered that they had come home from work to find their house had entirely vanished.

No rope at Chapel Street, so I pushed into a crowd and began to see what had happened. There are in all quite twenty houses gone and I should think another fifty are uninhabitable.

September 29 Tuesday

Went to Essex Street first thing this morning. Altogether there are either 7 or 8 people dead and 6 hurt badly, besides a good number cut and bruised. The damage is tremendous. One bomb brought down 4 houses on South Street, the next demolished 3 or 4 houses in Chapel Street, the third passed almost horizontally through a house on Wellington Street, struck the roadway, leaving a perfect impression on the tar of its shape and tail-fins, bounced over a fence and burst in the gardens between Essex Street and Wellington Street, demolishing 9 houses. Half a dozen houses have the fronts blown out and cascades of furniture and bedding are tumbling into the front gardens.

Many houses have either broken windows, slates off or chimney stacks down and windows are broken all along Butt Road as far as Mill Place (where the bomb dropped in

1915). Bomb fragments were found in many streets and this morning one small piece on the Castle roof. There is tremendous activity – bricklayers, ARP demolition men, firemen, all over the place. A Salvation Army mobile canteen was at the top of Chapel Street. It is very risky to cycle in any of these streets as the road surface is covered with tiny fragments of glass.

Not much furniture seems to have been moved and tables, chairs, beds, mattresses, pianos etc. stand on the pavements forlorn in the rain, which has been almost continuous today. It seems such a pity that in this vast ARP organisation so little provision has been made for people's belongings. There were several motor pantechnicons there today and a number of pony carts and hand barrows.

[See Image 22]

September 30 Wednesday

Dull, grey morning, wet. About the middle of the morning I heard the noise of a 'plane diving out of the clouds and just had time to say 'Hullo, I don't like the sound of that' when heavy gunfire shook the building. Everybody got up and began to go downstairs when we heard the whistle of bombs and four tremendous explosions. The building shook and windows rattled. I looked out and saw the sky quite full of bursting shells, right overhead but hurriedly withdrew as I heard the noise of a 'plane returning. The 'plane went into a shrieking dive and we all heard the bursts of its machine-guns. There was more AA fire and the noise died away. I had a glimpse of people running this way and that in the street and across the Park towards the shelters. Harding came in to say that the bombs seemed to have fallen in the Hythe direction so got leave from Capt Folkard to go and see what had happened, in case there was damage at the stables.

The alarm had sounded just after the bombs fell and the 'all clear' came as I cycled along Magdalen Street. St Botolph's coal yard gates were shut and police and wardens about. Bombs had fallen right in the coal yard, on the sidings, but although there were 8 or 10 horses there, not one was hurt and the only casualty was Bert Humphreys the coalman, whose arm was broken by being buried under loose coal.

A man on a cycle, by appearance an engineer, whom I did not know, came up to me at Magdalen Church and said, 'If you ask me we're all crazy. We bomb them and they bomb us. We're all of us a lot of barmy buggers. The Stone Age men had more sense, I reckon.' I agreed mildly. This is the first time I have known a total stranger to say this kind of thing.

Rushed down to the stable, where all was well, and then home, where Mother was rather upset. Jollied her a bit and assured her the damage was nothing. She had had a letter from Aunt Het to say that Maitland was 'very happy' with the RAF and would soon be getting married to a girl from Reading.

At lunchtime I went through Childwell Alley, onto the iron bridge, from where I could see the bomb craters at the far end of the coal yards. A number of trucks, standing on the last line, had been blown down the embankment onto the main track. A breakdown train and a large gang of men were busy moving the wreckage.

This afternoon I felt ill and shaken and went home again for a cup of tea. Mother was much more cheerful, having had a good gossip with all the neighbours. All the old ladies are agreed that the Germans are very wicked people and nothing is too bad for them.

Rang Mrs Parrington who seemed quite anxious about me. Cycled to Sherbourne Mill at 11pm. A few 'planes about and some searchlights waving. Strange how one's anxieties change in a few days. Up to last week one prayed for a dirty night and never thought of daytime weather. Now we shall fear cloudy, wet days.

October 1 Thursday

All day I have felt anxious and uncomfortable every time a British 'plane flew over very low as we have so little faith in the reliability of the warnings. There is a good deal of talk in the town about the absurdity of sounding alarms after the damage has been done. It is typical of this war and this country that although they are spending £14,000,000 a day they cannot devise a means of warning the public of enemy 'planes until the attack is half over.

October 2 Friday

A good deal in the papers this week about the Colchester 'incidents' and above all complaints about the sounding of the alarm. Many people point out that the Observer Corps 'Crash' warning is relayed to all factories, many large shops and some schools, so that everybody who happens to be in such places has a chance to get cover, while the general public knows nothing of the impending danger until the bombs explode. Exactly the same state of affairs maintained two years ago when the bombs fell in Old Heath Road and on the laundry and during those two years not the slightest effort has been made to effect any improvement.

October 3 Saturday

Very foggy. Went in by car this morning as there was a load of watercress to be taken in. Much joking about it not being the sort of day to go to Colchester.

There were a good many country people walking through Essex Street to see the ruins. There is still a lot of furniture laying about. It does seem a pity to leave it there. On one heap of rubble somebody had put a coloured print of the King and Queen and on another a small Union Jack.

There is great indignation about the slowness in sounding an alarm. It is only natural that there should be delay, as the Observers' reports go first to Colchester, from where they are sent to schools, factories, shops, etc. then to Cambridge, then (I believe) to Fighter Command at Uxbridge and finally back to Colchester, where the police are ordered to sound the sirens. Only in England could such an insane system be worked. On previous occasions in Colchester when bombs have fallen and no alarm sounded, the public have been given to understand that the alarm was withheld so as not to stop 'vital work' – yet all the while the people engaged on the 'vital work' have been safe in their shelters!

October 6 Tuesday

Heard today that the Mayor has taken action with regard to air raid alarms so that in future the sirens will be sounded direct from the Observer Corps warning, thus saving about five minutes. Notices were pasted up today all over the town, informing the public that steps had been taken and urging them to take cover as soon as the alarm is given.

This is likely to be a great improvement and the credit must be given to the Mayor for bringing this about in the face of considerable opposition from the Regional Commissioner at Cambridge.

October 9 Friday

Joanna came in this morning to say goodbye. She looked absolutely radiant and happier than I have ever seen her.

October 10 Saturday (Joanna's Wedding)

The great day. I got away before 12pm, harnessed Robin and went to Boast's for the trap. It looked superb. The whole outfit shone and glittered as we drove up to Holly Trees, just as the sun came through the clouds. I picked up Heather and Daphne and away we went up the town at a spanking trot. Neither of the girls had ever been behind a horse before and enjoyed it immensely.

We went through Birch Park passing many of the local people, all in their best clothes, walking to church. I was amazed at the number of cars – there seemed to be hundreds. I put Robin across the road in Theobald's buildings and went into church through lines of Land Girls. Joanna's eldest brother was one of the ushers, all of whom were in Army or Air Force uniform.

Mrs Round came in and sat up in front. The bridegroom's mother and relations came and then Tritton himself in Naval uniform. The organ played and everybody fidgeted about, turning to look at the door, through which you could see the Land Girls forming the 'guard of honour'. Major Jim Round came up and sat next to Mrs Round. I wondered if she was thinking of her other boy, far away across the world, or of Oliver, dead two years [whilst on active service in the Navy].

At last, the expected stir and bustle and in comes the bride, leaning on her father's arm, tall, fair, lovely in a beautiful white lace dress. Tritton moved towards her and the service began. Both spoke very quietly and I could not hear the responses. Then Mrs Round and the others going up into the vestry. A long pause and Major Round comes hurrying down the chancel to signal to the organist, who does not notice him and has to be prodded by a woman sitting nearby. The wedding march bursts out and down the aisle they come, Joanna smiling and bowing to her friends, Tritton looking a little shy and nervous.

A tremendous crush to get out. I wormed my way out as soon as I could to fetch the horse. Heard people saying 'Oh I had a lovely view. Didn't she look beautiful?' Got Heather and Daphne on board and away we went, overtaking girls on ponies and cyclists, one of whom was Poulter. Robin went smashing across the Park and up the drive. I was determined to go right up to the door, although the drive was an almost solid mass of cars. It seemed I should never get away again but old George the coachman came rushing out and shouted, 'Make 'em give way Sir! Goodness alive, haven't they ever seen a horse before?' I did not need much telling and soon forced Robin's nose up the stable drive. When I got back to the Hall, the whole place was packed solid. Joanna and her husband stood by the big clock. She seemed ever so pleased to see me and asked how Robin had behaved.

The reception was in the dining room. There was plenty to eat and drink but the crowd was so dense there was hardly room to move one's elbows. Heather and Daphne were there and Spencer and Capt Folkard, while all round 'county' women yelled at one another amid the roar of conversation. Joanna and husband forced their way in. One or other made a quite inaudible speech and the cake was cut. Most of us drifted out and saw as much of the presents as we could. Joanna came round and spoke to us all, her husband carrying her train in his hand. I thought it was very sweet and kind of her to come over, especially when half the county were waiting to have a word with her. She looked wonderful.

About 4pm, I thought we ought to move, so I went round to the stables to harness up. Both the girls were greatly impressed by the size and magnificence of the place. I wondered if they realised that they had seen the end of it all – never again would Birch Hall be filled with such a crowd, until the day when perhaps it will all be sold.

[Birch Hall was demolished in 1954.]

October 12 Monday

Committee Meeting this afternoon. Dreadful row. The Executive Officer phoned through in the morning and said he wished to see the Committee alone, without either the District Officer or myself, in order to hear all the details about the purchase of English and Welsh cattle.

Our Committee are bound to run into trouble from time to time because they cannot or will not realise that they are not farming the 3,000 acres in possession in this District – the Executive Officer does that, under his Committee and the District Committee are only empowered to advise. Our men can't see that – they still think they have a right to order tools or machinery as required.

While the argument went on, Folkard and I walked up and down in the cold Park, watching the sun sink among red and angry clouds and the rooks come flying home. The old house looked noble and forlorn, as the last squire argued with a Government official whom he despises and who in other times he would have ordered off the premises.

At last Leslie went, having got the Committee to make an unconditional withdrawal and an admission that they had done wrong.

October 13 Tuesday

Heard tonight that Penelope Belfield had been severely punished for wearing the wrong stockings at a [Naval] parade. She is compelled to scrub floors every night for two weeks.

October 16 Friday

Felt ill but went in. Had a terrible headache all day. In the 'Standard' tonight that Eric Hucklesby is missing from a flight over Germany. I knew him 25 years ago at Colchester Royal Grammar School. I remember one day, in the last war, he brought a loaded revolver to school with him and sat playing with it under his desk.

October 19 Monday

Up at 7am. Dull, with lowering clouds. Felt nervous but had to go in. Just going into the café for breakfast when the sirens blew. Noticed a good many people in the shelters – Benham's men standing round the works entrance, Woolworth's girls crowding into shelters in Culver Street. Reminded one of 1939.

'All clear' at 9.30am but another alarm at 10 o'clock. Suddenly, soon after 11, we heard guns and I said, 'Time we moved.' We got onto the stairs. Machine-guns rattled. I could hear a 'plane very low, then five tremendous bomb crashes, I ran into the hall. A woman rushed in from the street, white and panting, saying, 'Oh my goodness! What brutes! What swine! Oh dear.' There were great columns of smoke to the north. Boys who had been playing football on the Holly Trees Lawn had dived into shelters and now came popping out, for all the world like young rabbits. I heard the 'plane returning and another burst of machine-gun fire. The boys rushed back into the shelters again, laughing and shouting.

The 'plane died away and there was no more shooting. Smoke drifted across the valley, mingling with engine smoke from the railway. Went up to Poulter's flat and with binoculars could see a house on the By-Pass with tiles off and several ARP men running about. Cars and lorries were going by slowly so it was clear that something had happened down there.

Everybody was a bit shaken. Harding has a sister living on the By-Pass, so he borrowed my cycle to go and see if she was alright. He came back to say 2 dozen houses were badly damaged and Spencer arrived a few minutes later to say 40 were 'quite wrecked'. Nobody dead and only a few hurt.

A third alarm at midday and Capt Folkard laughed and said, 'The bugger's been back for another load.' I could stand no more and made an excuse to go for an early lunch. I heard one 'plane come over in the clouds and dive but nothing happened.

Called at home tonight. Mother did not seem to mind the affair very much. I pooh-poohed the whole thing. Only wish I felt like I talked.

October 20 Tuesday

Mother's birthday today. This morning I rushed up town and bought her a leather writing case. She was delighted. A postcard for me from Maitland showing Whitby Abbey and 'enjoying the RAF'. Long letter today from Joanna, bursting with happiness and asking for news and gossip.

October 25 Sunday

Heard that an RAF 'plane [crashed] in flames on the marshes [last night], near Cattawade Bridge. It got into trouble when going out and turned back, dropping its bombs in the sea near Harwich. The Observer Corps thought it was a German and the alarm was sounded. One man got away by parachute but the rest of the crew, 5 or 6, were killed.

October 31 Saturday

Went home to tea and was upstairs in my old room when 7 or 8 heavy bombers came over, very low, heading south-east. I stood at the window to watch them. I heard a woman in a garden behind ours call out, 'Are they ours? Are they going in or out?' and a man answered, 'Going out. They go a long way when they start early like this.' The woman said, 'Well, good luck to 'em.'

To the Castle at 7 and began my supper early. At 8.05pm the sirens blew. I put on the Vault lights, grabbed helmet, glasses, etc. and went up to the roof, meeting the other two fire-guards coming down as quickly as they could. There were 'planes in the distance and several night-fighters came over rather low. An old man and his wife came in. I remembered them, they used to come in regularly two years ago. The poor old woman was frightened.

At last the 'all clear' sounded just before 9 and I went back to my supper.

November 5 Thursday

Papers today full of a 'great victory in Egypt' [the Battle of El Alamein] but how much of it is true I do not know. We have been told this story so often before. Hundreds of thousands of people must be in agony of mind tonight, wondering if their sons, friends or relatives have been sacrificed to gain this priceless 'victory'.

Guy Fawkes Day but not a single guy appeared. By the time the war is over children will have no knowledge of the old customs and festivity.

November 6 Friday

Caught the 12.50 to Chelmsford. Noticed that Chelmsford now has barrage balloons. There are 29 altogether, as I saw when they were sent up this afternoon. This seems to show that Chelmsford is considered to be a target of some importance [owing to its industrial works].

Looked in at the market. Full horse sale but rather rough stuff. Sad to see so many old hunters and little worn out ponies, all destined to be 'black market' meat.

Train back very full. I went right back to Manningtree and did not stop at Colchester. Stood in the corridor to see the old town come into sight. I can never resist that long downward rush from Chitts Hill to the station, when the town suddenly bursts into view. It looked all blue and grey, the dying sun just touching the towers and spires with pink. It seemed strange not to get out there.

November 8 Sunday

Edward Holloway of the Economic Reform [Club] here for the weekend. Holloway prophesies bloody revolution after the war when the young men returning find that conditions for them are very much worse than they were before the war. I do not think this is very likely. Not one in a hundred of the population has any knowledge of economic affairs (I know nothing whatever about the subject). If the younger men do not consider it worthwhile to revolt against their conscription into the war, which is affecting every one of them, it is hardly likely that they will be prepared to take drastic action on a subject which they cannot understand and which they do not know has any effect on their lives. I do not know what work [Holloway] does but he knew a good deal about the disastrous raid on Dieppe. Apparently the Germans were quite ready for it.

Amongst other things, Holloway considers a permanently prosperous agriculture to be essential in the post-war England but how can this be achieved when the very framework

1 Aerial view looking towards Colchester Castle, taken in the 1940s, from E.J. Rudsdale's wartime photographic collection 'The Prospect of Colchester'. (Colchester and Ipswich Museum Service)

Above left: 2 E.J. Rudsdale's Travel Identity Card photograph, 1948. (Essex Record Office)

Above right: 3 Colchester Castle Museum, 1944. An air-raid shelter sign can be seen in the rose bed in front of the castle. (Essex Record Office)

4 E.J. Rudsdale with his parents, Agnes and John Rudsdale, at Walton Beach, 1929. (Essex Record Office)

5   E.J. Rudsdale collecting archaeological material at Sheepen Farm, Colchester, 1934. (Essex Record Office)

6   Hollytrees Museum in Castle Park, Colchester, with wartime sandbag protection for the basement, c. 1940. Hollytrees is a Georgian townhouse built in 1718. (Colchester and Ipswich Museum Service)

7 E.J. Rudsdale pointing out the intersection of two Roman streets discovered during excavations for Colchester's new public library building, 1938. (Essex Record Office)

8 Bourne Mill, Colchester, c. 1940. Rudsdale's horse, Bob, and a donkey can be seen in the paddock on the left. Bourne Mill was built in 1591 as a fishing lodge and was later converted to a watermill. It is owned by the National Trust. (Colchester and Ipswich Museum Service)

Left: 9 Steps leading down into Colchester Castle's Roman Vaults, which were used as an air-raid shelter during the war. Colchester Castle was built between 1076 and 1125 on the ruined base of the Roman Temple of Claudius, constructed 1,000 years earlier. The Roman Vaults of the temple form the foundations of the castle. (Colchester and Ipswich Museum Service)

Below: 10 The skeleton of the fifteenth-century timber-framed hall in Culver Street, Colchester, prior to demolition in 1939. (Essex Record Office)

Left: 11 The West Bay of the Culver Street hall after it had been re-erected in Colchester Castle Museum in 1940. The Vaughan brothers who undertook the work are standing on the left of the photograph and their two workmen are on the right. (Essex Record Office)

Below: 12 The exterior of the 'Old English Farm' at the Royal Show, Windsor Great Park, 1939. Rudsdale designed this historic farming exhibition and is pictured on the right riding Bob. (Colchester and Ipswich Museum Service)

13 The interior view of the kitchen of the 'Old English Farm' at the Royal Show, furnished in the style of the 1830s with objects from the collections of Colchester Museums, 1939. (Colchester and Ipswich Museum Service)

14 The site of a crashed German mine-laying plane in Victoria Road, Clacton, 1940. (Essex Police Museum)

Issued by the Ministry of Information on behalf of
the War Office and the Ministry of Home Security

STAY WHERE YOU ARE

IF this island is invaded by sea or air everyone who is not under orders must stay where he or she is. This is not simply advice : it is an order from the Government, and you must obey it just as soldiers obey their orders. Your order is " Stay Put ", **but remember that this does not apply until invasion comes.**

Why must I stay put ?

Because in France, Holland and Belgium, the Germans were helped by the people who took flight before them. Great crowds of refugees blocked all roads. The soldiers who could have defended them could not get at the enemy. The enemy used the refugees as a human shield. These refugees were got out on to the roads by rumour and false orders. Do not be caught out in this way. Do not take any notice of any story telling what the enemy has done or where he is. Do not take orders except from the Military, the Police, the Home Guard (L.D.V.) and the A.R.P. authorities or wardens.

What will happen to me if I don't stay put ?

If you do not stay put you will stand a very good chance of being killed. The enemy may machine-gun you from the air in order to increase panic, or you may run into enemy forces which have landed behind you. An official German message was captured in Belgium which ran :

> " Watch for civilian refugees on the roads. Harass them as much as possible."

Our soldiers will be hurrying to drive back the invader and will not be able to stop and help you. On the contrary, they will

15 'Stay Where You Are' leaflet issued to households in Britain in 1940 by the Ministry of Information with instructions on what to do in the event of an invasion. This copy was pasted into Rudsdale's journal in July 1940. (Essex Record Office)

Above: 16 The remains of Little Horkesley Church following a direct hit by a parachute mine, 1940. (H. Benham, *Essex at War*)

Left: 17 The Swynborne Tomb as it was found by Colchester Museum staff on the devastated site of Little Horkesley Church, 1940. (Essex Record Office)

18 The wooden effigies of two knights and a lady, which were restored by Colchester Museum staff and returned to the rebuilt church at Little Horkesley in 1958. (C. Pearson)

19 The remains of the house destroyed by a bomb in Scarletts Road, Colchester, 1940. (H. Benham, *Essex at War*)

Above left: 20 James Parnell's cell, also known as the 'Oven', in the entrance to Colchester Castle where Rudsdale was on wartime night duty from 1940 to 1942. (Colchester and Ipswich Museum Service)

Above right: 21 'The Top of the Town': Colchester on Market Day, *c.* 1858. Taken from a stereoscopic photograph that formed part of Rudsdale's 'The Prospect of Colchester' photographic collection, begun in 1941. (Colchester and Ipswich Museum Service)

22 Houses destroyed in the bombing raid on Colchester's Chapel Street and surrounding residential roads on 28 September 1942. (H. Benham, *Essex at War*)

23 A typical harvest scene in north-east Essex during the 1940s. (Colchester and Ipswich Museum Service)

24 The remains of a tiled Roman drain discovered during the excavation to remove an unexploded bomb that fell within feet of Colchester Castle in December 1943. (Colchester and Ipswich Museum Service)

Above: 25 St Botolph's Corner looking towards Mersea Road, Colchester, following incendiary bomb damage, 1944. (Essex Record Office)

Left: 26 The curve of Colchester's Roman North Gate wall, as discovered by Rudsdale, August 1944. (Essex Record Office)

27 The Royal Observer Corps Post at Great Horkesley showing the view to Stoke by Nayland Church. It was from his observations from this post that Rudsdale discovered a possible location for John Constable's painting 'The Cornfield', 1826. (M. Lees/Essex County Council)

Above left: 28 The fields below the Observer Post, which Rudsdale identified as a possible site for John Constable's painting 'The Cornfield'. The view today shows some striking similarities with the painting. The distinctive oak tree at the centre of the painting remains, although the trees in the foreground of the painting no longer survive. There is a bank and stream on the left of the photograph where the boy in the painting quenches his thirst. The River Stour weaves its way along the bottom of the valley in both the view today and in Constable's painting and the rising valley and field patterns match those shown in the painting. The church in the painting was repositioned by Constable but his preparatory works for 'The Cornfield' depict Stoke by Nayland Church on the horizon, where it can still be glimpsed today. (M. Lees/Essex County Council)

Above right: 29 John Constable 'The Cornfield', 1826. (© The National Gallery, London)

30 Wisbech Museum and Literary Institution, 1940. (Essex Record Office)

31 H.W. Poulter, the Curator of Hollytrees Museum, and US Army soldiers on Colchester Castle walls, 1944. (Essex Record Office)

Above: 32 Visitors to 'The England that America Loves' exhibition by the US Army Air Force at Colchester Castle Museum, February 1945. The exhibition showed photographs and artworks of places in England as seen by the American forces. (Colchester and Ipswich Museum Service)

Left: 33 E.J. Rudsdale at Wisbech Museum during the late 1940s. (Wisbech & Fenland Museum)

of rural life is collapsing before us? The pace at which rural craftsmen are leaving their work, blacksmiths, harness makers and the like, has been hastened since the beginning of the war, not lessened.

November 14 Saturday

Ground fog and a pale blue sky and by 8.30am the sun came through in a golden haze. There was a lovely sight at Ardleigh – six pairs of horses, ploughing and harrowing and three on a drill. They moved in slow, stately silence, with only the voices of the ploughmen coming across the field, each team in a cloud of steam from the horses, the ploughmen leaning on the handles and a flock of sea-gulls fluttering behind. How much more satisfying than tractor-ploughing. How much better too, when one thinks of the muck that these horses will send back to the land in the course of a year.

November 15 Sunday

Carted hay to Bourne Mill and then went up to Barn Hall for a truss of straw. As I came back I heard St Peter's bells begin to chime, slowly at first, then bursting into a peal – the 'great victory' celebration. This is the first time for two and a half years that we have heard bells. As I went home, the other bells began to call to service, the solitary cracked bell of St Mary Magdalene clanging slowly, just as it did when I was a child. A few people in the streets going to church and some children delivering newspapers, exactly like a hundred other November Sundays, a reminder of those lovely days that will never return.

Mrs Belfield called. Penelope is to have a commission. Her crime of wearing the wrong stockings some weeks ago is to be wiped out and forgiven.

November 20 Friday

Since the war in Africa has become so active we have been very free from attacks. There has hardly been a German 'plane over for a fortnight.

November 21 Saturday

Winter seems to have come quite suddenly – cold today and not a leaf left on the trees all their branches stark and naked.

December 1 Tuesday

'Cold December hath come in,' as the Bellman used to call when I was a boy. The Council did away with him long ago. The morning was indeed cold but bright and sunny, with high, windswept clouds. As I went up Jupes Hill, I saw a dozen men loading sugar beet, although it was hardly light.

'O yea O yea O yea
Cold December has set in
Poor people's backs all clothed thin

The trees are bare
The birds are mute
A pint of goode purl
Will very well sute.'

[Purl was a strong, pale aromatic ale brewed in winter, which was said to give labourers nourishment on cold mornings.]

December 2 Wednesday

The great 'Beveridge Report' published at last. No time to read it but noticed the salient points seem to be a greatly increased 'dole' and a 'burial grant' of £20. Rather curious joys in the 'Brave New World'.

December 5 Saturday

I noticed a little shop near the Bus Park has been opened by the British Communist Party and a little group of 'comrades' were standing by the corner of St John's Avenue with a portable 'Pulpit', the sort of thing used in Hyde Park. Apparently a speech was due to be made. Two of the 'comrades' were dark, oily looking young men and another was a young girl, very dark and pretty, wearing slacks, a long grey coat and a scarlet scarf. It rather looked as if she was the speaker but I was unable to wait to see what happened.

December 6 Sunday

About 20 'planes went out towards the sea soon after 6pm. Mother asked, 'Had I heard the 'planes going over?' I said, 'Yes' and she replied, 'Beastly old things, going out to kill more poor people.' I wonder who has suffered tonight?

December 9 Wednesday

This afternoon I went to Wigborough with Capt Folkard. Everything very wet. The most tenacious mud I ever saw. I was told that when the Hutleys had this farm many years ago, it was ploughed up at once, 104 horses being used – 52 pairs. What a sight that must have been.

   A lovely misty day, like autumn. The great barn at Abbott's Hall is now being repaired, the broken end being built up. Old Mortimer [the farmer] was tramping round with his vicious dog, jeering at the Committee's workmen and being as unpleasant as he can. He has done everything he can to obstruct the work.

December 10 Thursday

Glad to have the chance to get out with Nott and went down to Little Wigborough. Picked up Charlie Baldwin [Chief Foreman for the EWAC] and went off down to Copt Hall. As we went down the lane from the Wigborough road, I saw two boarded cottages and suddenly realised that this was the very place where the Zeppelin came down in 1916. I came there with my Mother to see it.

We went right down to the buildings, grouped round the little church, and met Cutting, the new foreman. He seems a very able sort of man. Then we walked across the fields to the Lower Barn. The desolation was superb – a vast sky, filled with racing clouds, gulls wheeling, peewits crying, skeleton trees standing up on the far horizon, ship masts off Mersea and Bradwell shore in the far distance. Not a human being in sight but ourselves.

Below Lower Barn are four fields on a sort of island, which can only be reached by crossing a very wet marsh. They were all ploughed in olden times as can be seen from the ancient stretch marks and now they are to be ploughed again.

Nott mentioned the last war and if the War Agricultural Committees had done any work at Wigborough then? Charlie said, 'There wasn't much for 'em to do, 'cos most everybody was a-farming then.' What a contrast with the present time.

I asked him whether, in his honest opinion, the farm men were content in the old days. He said, 'The good ones were but it was the bad men who were always agitating. Now they all get the same money, good and bad alike, so there is no incentive for the good men to work.' This I believe to be very true. He went on to say that when wages were made higher and higher and the men's unions insisted on shorter hours, and began to lay down conditions of labour, the farmers withdrew all the old prerequisites and privileges.

December 13 Sunday

Langham aerodrome continues, a vast man-made wilderness where less than six months ago were fertile farms. I suppose by this time next year the lovely little cottages in Langham Lane will be empty and derelict or else blown to pieces.

[Langham Aerodrome was officially named Boxted Aerodrome to avoid confusion with an aerodrome of the same name in Norfolk, but Rudsdale mainly refers to it by its local name of Langham.]

December 17 Thursday

Joanna came in this morning. I saw her from the front window, running across the forecourt and up the steps, as she always did. She is as lovely as ever. She could only stay about an hour and had to see everybody, so I had little chance to talk. There is no doubt that she is enjoying herself immensely. Yesterday she went to Buckingham Palace with her husband, to see him receive the Distinguished Flying Cross from the King. Apparently the King chatted to him for a few minutes and Joanna was so pleased.

December 19 Saturday

This afternoon cycled out by Boxted. Called at Stuart Rose's and paid him his wages. I am very glad I was able to get him this job. Saw their new baby. Its name is Harriet, rather nice I thought.

December 24 Thursday

Very busy all day and much behind in my work. This is the first year that I have not bought a Christmas card. The town was very full today, like Saturday, and the shops open in the afternoon. People have got plenty of money but there is so little to be bought without permits or coupons.

Managed to get 4/6 tobacco for Father, from a little shop in East Street and a Christmas cake for Mother, which Rose made for me. Could think of nothing for Joy and Parry [the Parringtons], so suddenly decided to give them my copy of Morant's 'The History and Antiquities of Colchester' for their library.

Army lorries out in the town today, delivering letters and parcels. Not a horse used this year. Bunton did not use his old van, as there are not enough wines and spirits available to make it worthwhile.

December 25 Friday

Lovely not to have to get up early for the next three mornings. Joy gave me a lovely pair of woollen socks, which I thought most kind of her. I cycled into Colchester to have lunch at home – turkey and plum pudding. Mother always has a turkey. Very few Christmas cards.

After lunch went down to Bourne Mill. Very few people about. Then to the office and was appalled at the amount of work not done.

Soldiers shouting and singing in the streets and a few rather drunk Americans about. Home to tea, then down to see Hampshire. Dozens of front windows gleaming in the dusk and everywhere the noise of pianos, radios, fiddlers and gramophones. In one house, a whole family were singing carols and in another, a girl and a young man, both in khaki, and a young sailor, all eating and drinking. In yet another (in complete defiance of any fuel saving) the parlour was strung across with coloured fairy lamps. In every house, paper chains and holly. At Hampshire's there were paper chains all over the room and a big crowd there. He came out, the little boy, now aged 5, with him, shouting and singing at the top of his voice. Hampshire said, 'Shut up, you little bugger,' and to me, 'Don't take no notice of him, he's had half a glass of stout.'

December 31 Thursday

Ulting, the National Service Officer from the Ministry of Labour, came in this afternoon, to say that several of the conscientious objectors who used to be at Langham Oaks are to be prosecuted for refusing to work for the War Agricultural Committee. These men said they would only work on their own farm or on a private farm but no farmer would have them on the place. Half of the Langham Oaks Community has moved up into Suffolk and the rest are going to Frating Abbey in March. The Ministry of Labour are determined to break up these pacifist communities as far as possible. In some countries this would be done by raids, shootings and murders. Here it is done by the slow processes of the law, just as effectively, without any excitement.

As we waited for the bus tonight, 4 or 5 bombers came over very low, heading out to sea. I think there are few things quite so horrible as seeing these murderous monsters sailing slowly along, hardly able to keep up with the great weight of bombs they carry. It depresses me terribly to know that there are people in France, Germany, Holland and Belgium, now alive and well, planning their evening's amusement, arranging their work for tomorrow, who in less than an hour will be dead and I can do nothing about it.

Discussion at supper tonight about inventions. How many are beneficial and harmless? We could only think of anaesthetics, bicycles and telephones. Extraordinary how scientists misspend their time and knowledge.

And so we face 1943, without hope of peace, in fact many of us too bored and apathetic to care what is the outcome of this terrible, disastrous war.

Chapter 5

❧ 1943 ☙

January 1 Friday

Everybody wishing 'Happy New Year' to everybody else, although it is difficult to see where happiness might be expected to be found during the next twelve months. The daily papers, screaming Russian victories on one hand and shouting against undue optimism on the other, tell us very little of what is actually going on.

In Colchester there is a certain measure of prosperity. There is virtually no unemployment and all engineering workers are earning very high wages – £7 a week is common. The population of the town must have greatly increased in the last two years and is probably at the present time about 60,000, besides at least 10,000 troops. There are a large number of Training Units in the barracks, besides some Canadians and a certain number of United States Army. The presence of so many Training Units leads one to suppose that there is little fear of an invasion this coming spring. We still fear air attacks but I don't think anybody expects a large scale raid this winter. Odd raiders are fairly frequent, coming and going quite unhindered. It seems quite extraordinary that the Germans can fly over a garrison town, containing some 10,000 troops, with complete impunity.

The state of the Museum is bad. Poulter becomes more and more morose and retiring, which is a pity to see, as it is quite against his real nature. I cannot even get him to take an interest in photography or in work on the collections in Holly Trees.

My work with the EWAC still goes well. I have now completed a full year as an 'unreserved' person, during which time I have never heard one word as to my true position. I can only assume that I must have been given unlimited deferment, although I cannot imagine why, as the reserved age for my class was put up to 35 on January 1 last year. Such an extended run of luck as this seems too good to be true and I only trust that it will hold for another year, although one hears rumours that all men under 40 must be in the Army by this spring, ready for the 'great offensive'. However, we received notice this morning that my salary has been raised to £4.10.0 per week, making £234 a year. This is the most I have ever earned and is 30/- a week more than I was paid at the Museum.

My old parents still continue fairly well but they are very old. Mother is frail, yet extraordinarily tough. Only today she went up town in the pouring rain. I refuse to look into the future but I sometimes wonder what will happen if they both became quite helpless.

Outside my official work, I do nothing except one night per week at the Castle.

January 8 Friday

Bought 6lbs of candles tonight, for 5/-. They say candles will be very scarce soon and I use a lot at Lawford.

In the Council news, there is already much talk about 'post-war housing'. Without doubt they are planning thousands more hideous council houses. Why it should be necessary to build more houses for a decreasing population is not quite clear. One would have thought that new houses to replace those destroyed in raids should be built on the original sites not elsewhere.

In the early hours of this morning an American soldier came knocking on all the doors, trying to get help, as his car had run into a ditch. He made a tremendous noise and the dogs almost barked themselves into hysterics. Parry carefully bolted the larder door before speaking to him, in case he was an enemy parachutist, the joke being that all the doors were unlocked, so he could have walked in anywhere.

January 13 Wednesday

A very busy, tiring day, yet got very little done. A man called Russell came in this morning and was most extraordinarily rude and abusive and was threatening to assault Capt Folkard. He was annoyed because the Committee had taken possession of his land and had let it to his pet enemy.

A farmer reported by phone this morning that two Land Girls we had sent him walked off the farm because they said it was too cold. Two other girls had failed to report at all today, so that instead of having 20 girls he had only 16.

[Spoke to] Molly Blomfield tonight [daughter of Councillor Sam Blomfield]. Molly shocked me by saying she had heard that Poulter might have cancer in the throat. His voice has become very weak and husky during the last few months but I had not thought this. Poor old man, how terrible for him if it is true.

January 14 Thursday

A day of troubles. At 10.30am a meeting of the Essex War Agricultural Committee and all the parish representatives in the Grand Jury Room, when Sadler spoke at great length on the 1943 Cropping Programme. According to estimates, Essex should this year grow 140,000 acres of wheat and 80,000 acres of barley. If this is done, who is to stack and thatch? However, I suppose that is one of the difficulties which Sadler said the Executive recognised to exist but which they had no doubt would be overcome. These meaningless platitudes are most irritating in times like these.

I went back to the office [and] as I went upstairs, Poulter came down. He looked at me rather oddly and said, 'I have to go to the hospital at 6 o'clock to be operated on for cancer in the throat,' and his face went queerly flushed. For one awful moment I thought he was going to cry. He said, 'They don't think there's much chance.' I was quite horrified and could only say, 'For God's sake don't talk such nonsense man, there's many people get over that easily' with all the vehemence I could.

He pretended to be put out but I could see that was what he wanted to hear. Apparently Dr Rowland had been alarmed at the sound of his voice and had asked him to see Dr Cowan the throat specialist, who at once said he must have a preliminary operation to see what was the trouble. There is no doubt he has a growth on the vocal cords.

Later in the afternoon I found him sitting in the office chair, his feet on the desk, his old hat on the back of his head, his face very white and tired. It seemed incredible that he might be sitting there for the last time. He had just made a new will and said with a faint grin, 'You'd better grab my binoculars if anything happens.' I always said I wanted them.

January 16 Saturday

Phoned Dr Rowland, who said Poulter had had a very successful operation but the result would not be known for another fortnight. Very busy in the office and then dashed out to take old Bob to the blacksmith. When I got back to Holly Trees, what was my amazement to find Poulter sitting in the office, just as if he had never moved since I saw him on Thursday. He was in far better spirits than he has been recently but he knows that he has a bad time before him until the results of the examination are known. If the growth is malignant he will probably lose his voice forever.

Apparently modern surgery is such, and Poulter is so strong, that he can have a throat operation on Friday and walk back to Holly Trees on Saturday. He was not given a general anaesthetic, only a local application of cocaine. As might be expected, he made a great hit with the nurses and has asked six of them to tea at Holly Trees to celebrate his recovery.

January 17 Sunday

Heard on the 9pm news that there was a raid on Berlin last night, so I suppose raids will now begin on London again and will no doubt catch everybody quite unprepared.

January 18 Monday

Just after 4am the sirens sounded. I thought 'surely they won't bomb Colchester to avenge Berlin'. There was a searchlight to the west and I could hear the distant boom of guns. Went into the Castle and put on the Vault lights. Taylor came along, with the old couple from Queen Street, who always appear at every alarm. The guns were firing much nearer now and I could hear a 'plane. A solitary man came down and then a man, a woman and a little girl from East Hill.

The little girl was very nervous and kept saying, 'Mum I can hear a 'plane'. The man said, 'That's alright, that's one of our night fighters', regardless of the fact the each 'plane was being heavily fired on as it crossed over the town. He then said to me, 'She's nervous. She had a packet in London once.' 'All clear' came at a 5.45am and I went up to the 'Oven', thankful to be able to lie down.

There were two more alarms in the afternoon. Nothing came and they lasted only a few minutes. Vague news about damage at London. No less than 12 people killed by AA shells.

January 21 Thursday

Learnt from 'The Times' that there was a terrible attack on London yesterday at lunch time. The alarms were sounded too late and the balloons were not up. A good deal of damage has been done, especially by a direct hit on a London County Council school.

January 24 Sunday

To Holly Trees at 9pm. Poulter was there, in very good humour, his voice rather better I think.

I hate these weekend watches more and more. The whole night through I am in a state of nervous anxiety, yet I went through hundreds of night alarms in 1940 and 1941. Went down to the Muniment Room for 3 or 4 hours, looking through various manuscripts. What neglected treasures we have there. What a tragedy it will be if they are destroyed unread and unappreciated. Over to the Castle at 1.30am in a thin drizzling rain. Very cold.

January 25 Monday

Committee meeting at Birch very much as usual. A good deal of talk about the 1943 Cropping Programme forms, which are unanimously held to be a most absurd waste of time. Farmers are now so 'snowed under' by forms, leaflets and returns of all sorts that they have not the least idea what information is really wanted. The Government officials have gone completely mad on this sort of thing and in 90 per cent of the returns made the information given is wrong.

January 28 Thursday

Had a long letter from Joanna, who says she is expecting a baby in August. Quite sure it will be a boy and is to be called Oliver, her dead brother's name.

January 30 Saturday

Felt depressed by the news that the RAF had raided Berlin in daylight this morning. No doubt this will result in more unpleasant reprisals. We have now reached the stage when we no longer claim we bomb 'military objectives'. This was a 'demonstration' for the people of Berlin. It is a silly, childish effort of no military value whatever.

February 1 Monday

Poulter told me that his medical report is bad and that he has to go to the Royal Free Hospital, London within a few days, where he will be given radium treatment. Poor old man, it is worrying him a great deal but he did his best to make light of it.

February 2 Tuesday

Charlie Baldwin called in this afternoon and we had a talk about horses and wagons. He told me that it was quite true that not more than half a dozen of the Committee's men were able to manage two horses and that none of the young lads took any interest in them at all.

February 3 Wednesday

This afternoon there was a phone call from the Royal Free Hospital, London, to say that Poulter must come at once. The old man bore up well. He expects to be there for three weeks and then for another week later. Poulter then told me that Hull was ill in bed and would not be in for some time. What is to happen to the Museum?

February 4 Thursday

This afternoon poor old Poulter went up to London. He was very cheerful and left with kindly words for everybody. The old man walked down the stairs, across the hall and away up the street, not knowing whether he will ever come back again. We had quite an argument, in his old style, as to whether he ought to take a taxi from Liverpool Street or whether it would cost too much.

February 8 Monday

Saw in the 'Herald' today the first mention I have ever seen in the daily press of the possibility of a revolution. General Sir Arthur Smith, London Area Home Guard, warned his men that their time of testing had not yet come but that it might well come after the war, when they might have to maintain order at a time when discipline had become rather slack. This seems to be a most extraordinary thing to say and I should think hardly likely to be well received by the Home Guards.

February 12 Friday

Got out this morning to meet Matheson [Secretary of the National Trust] and Kenn in the Town Planning Office [about the conservation of Bourne Mill].

Kenn was very rude and gave away his (i.e. the official) attitude to historic monuments in the first few minutes. He said nobody was keener than he to see ancient buildings protected, if they were in their proper place – 'which is not on a car-park, Mr Rudsdale,' referring to the old house destroyed in Culver Street [in 1939, which was dismantled to make a car park]. There is no reply to this attitude of mind. There is nothing one can do.

At another point he agreed that the valley below Bourne Mill would, in the horrible jargon of town planning, be a very good 'lung' but of course the whole of the lovely little water meadows would have to be considerably raised by dumping town refuse on them. Then they could be provided with swings, see-saws etc., for the children.

February 13 Saturday

To my surprise, a few minutes after 9, Poulter walked in – come home for the weekend. He did not look very well and his voice was certainly worse than when he left. He is to go back for further treatment on Monday.

Mother (dear Mother!) gave me £1 for my birthday tomorrow. There is really nothing one can give anybody in these days except money. Bought rations and two books at Smith's – A G Street's 'Thinking Aloud', and Robert Harling's 'Home: A Victorian Vignette'. Big crowds in the bookshop, mostly soldiers buying cheap technical books.

February 14 Sunday

My birthday, 33 years old. It seems a great age, made up of wasted years, sprinkled with good intentions which never come to anything.

Had to go on duty tonight, which I hate, as it makes the Sundays seem very short. Poulter came down and sat and talked in a husky whisper. He said suddenly, 'I've only got about one chance in a hundred, you know.' It does not seem possible that he may be dying, that he will never again potter about in the workshop or build cases for the Museum. I never imagined that a situation such as this would arise. Hull has not been seen and there is no news of him.

February 19 Friday

This afternoon went down to Young's about an account. Slightly shocked to find the usual accounts clerk gone – called up. This sort of thing always gives one a little chill.

Called at Cannock Mill, to see if there was any hay. The mill was working, grinding barley meal. I love to stand inside and feel the whole structure vibrating gently, with the rumble of the stones and the splash of the water over the wheel. If you open a little door you can see the great wooden cogwheels whirling swiftly round, the horizontal one sweeping over your head. I went right upstairs, to the top floor. Even there you can feel the trembling of the structure and the barley in the hopper makes a gently sifting noise as it slowly falls through to the stones below.

Evening papers tonight full of Russian advances and American retreats in Africa. Some people take this retreat very seriously indeed and say it will mean that the Allied offence will have to be cancelled and that the war will last another year.

February 20 Saturday

Went up to Kingswode Hoe, in [Lexden] and had a look in it [for office accommodation for the EWAC]. The housekeeper was extremely garrulous. She said the Americans had been after the place but she was very glad they were not having it – 'You see, I've got a daughter of 16. If we had them here, there's no knowing what might happen between the gates and the house …'

Some soldiers marched past onto Sheepen Fields for drill and she said, 'Ah, there go the boys, training for the Front. They train parachute troops here, you know. They bring a great tall thing on a lorry and the men have to jump off with parachutes. They saw me watching one day, so they stopped and the officer came over and said, "Do you live here alone?" and he made me go in and draw the blinds until they had gone.'

Back to Holly Trees. Poulter walked in, very depressed and said that he was finished, his medical report was bad and that he would undoubtedly lose his voice. He seems to wish to retire almost at once but I did all I could to make him more cheerful. Apparently there has been a great row. The Committee were in the Castle for an hour and a half, everybody trying to make the old Chairman see how bad things were.

I have no idea what will happen now. If only the war would stop. Poor old Poulter, it is terrible for him. He made one attempt to joke – asked me to think of some really striking thing he could say as his last words before his voice is gone forever. What can one do to help him?

February 22 Monday

Benton [Secretary of the Essex Archaeological Society] came [to Holly Trees Museum] this morning. Quite like old times to see him about the place. He has agreed to come until further notice and will look after Holly Trees and receive visitors.

February 23 Tuesday

Rather a startling sight in the High Street today – the Soviet flag, with hammer and sickle, flying from the Town Hall flagstaff. This is in honour of the 25th Anniversary of the founding of the Red Army. How the old 'diehards' must be squirming with fury.

February 24 Wednesday

This week is the 100th anniversary of the opening of the railway to Colchester. The coaching age is now receding further and further into the past.

Councillor Blomfield in today. We talked about the Museum and he asked me to outline a scheme for the post-war reorganisation of the place.

February 25 Thursday

Mr Craig came in this afternoon. He said he had been approached by 'an alderman' to see if the WAC would release me back to the Museum to help them in their present predicament. Mr Craig said very firmly that they would not hear of such a thing. It is really rather heartening to be wanted by two different Committees at once!

As I was writing the above, heavy bombers began to go over so that the house trembled with their incessant roar. Several times I thought one or another seemed to be out of control, when suddenly a piercing scream detached itself from the general roar and came down, louder and louder. I flung myself on the floor by the bed, there was a great red flash which showed through the curtains and the house shook from an explosion. I ran out onto the stairs. Parry called, 'He's dropping something. He's coming down,' and I heard Joy answer from the back door, 'He is down, there's a fire.'

It was as light as day and there was a leaping crimson glare towards the buildings. I ran up the track. People cycled, ran, walked, all going towards the fire. A fire engine with a trailer pump came along from Manningtree, the bell clanging, and I could hear another coming from the Colchester direction. Two policemen cycled by, tall, calm and erect in capes and helmets, silhouetted against the fire. Now I could see a stack flaming, near the railway line and hundreds of little fires all round. Every now and then a red or green flare would shoot up into the sky, glare and go out. Ammunition was exploding rapidly and I wondered where the bullets were going to. There was a group standing by the railway bridge and I could hear scraps of conversation – 'Yes, I heard it coming, thought it was a Jerry …', 'Me and my sister got under the table. We wasn't half scared!' and 'Poor buggers, what a death …'

In the farmyard were two motor-pumps roaring away, sucking water out of the pond. People were hurrying to and fro, their steps unheard amidst the roar of the pumps. Went into the field just beyond the farmyard. Bits of metal all over the place, everywhere you walked you touched them. There were firemen, farm labourers and a policeman searching about the field with torches as the light from the stack was dying down. Fifty yards from the burning mass were two or three bundles, bits of clothing and equipment but nothing recognisable. The policeman began to clear everybody out of the field. Two girls carrying a stretcher and blankets and a grim faced elderly man with another stretcher, all wearing Civil Defence uniforms and hung round with respirators and haversacks, came pushing through the crowd. An ATS girl, the driver of an Army ambulance, said to the policeman, 'Do you think I ought to move up there?' He said, 'No, I shouldn't miss, there's nothing you can do.'

Walked back by way of Hungerdowns. Suddenly, just as I got to Kennel Cottages, there was a violent explosion. Thousands of coloured lights shot up, some bursting high in the air. I stood entranced. It was for all the world like an old-time firework show. Then I heard a heavy piece of metal sighing through the air towards me and flung myself flat on the road. It passed humming over me and fell with a thud behind the cottages. I waited a second or two to see if there was an explosion but nothing happened so I suppose it must have been a case of some sort.

Parry and Joy had gone to bed. I don't think a bomber crashing in their own garden would keep them out of bed five minutes after their accustomed time. Gave them a brief account of what had happened and then to bed myself.

February 26 Friday

No sign of last night's affair as I cycled past the settlement this morning. At lunchtime I heard that the crew were Canadians.

February 27 Saturday

Poulter back again today, much brighter than last week. His doctors have given him a more hopeful report. He is having more intense radium treatment and it is beginning to have an effect.

February 28 Sunday

Saw Poulter tonight. He said, 'You know, I've never been one to worry much but when I was waiting for Maclagan (the surgeon) on Friday night, I sure was worried. When Maclagan gave me a better report and said I was reacting, the relief was wonderful. My word, I've never felt worried like that before.' Poor old man.

March 2 Tuesday

In the office today heard the girls talking about the war. One of them, aged 16, said she could not imagine what it was like without a war on, as she could hardly remember the time before the war started. Daphne hates the war and longs for it to be over. She does not say much but I know she hates it all intensely.

March 3 Wednesday

About 8.15pm heard the sirens. Soon there was gunfire and the horizon was lit by flashes. Several 'planes over, very low above clouds. I heard only one lot of bombs fall, somewhere to the south and it seemed as if this was the reprisal raid on London which had been expected ever since the senseless RAF raid on Berlin.

March 4 Thursday

Joy told me tonight that Lieutenant Smygelski of the Polish Army had been to tea. He hates the Russians far worse than the Germans and spoke a lot about the dispute between the Polish and Russian Governments over the boundary question. He spoke with certainty that before very long we shall be fighting the Russians, not Germans. So here are we, in the most disastrous war ever waged, primarily to rescue Poland, and yet we (and the Poles) are allied to Poland's hated enemy, while the King of England sends hearty congratulations to Stalin, the man who is sworn to abolish all kings.

March 5 Friday

Heard today that in the raid on Wednesday 178 people were killed in a panic at a London tube station. This is the worst disaster of this kind that has happened. The Ministry of Information refused to release the news until late last night.

Bombs fell on the main line near Ingatestone, which is now completely blocked except for one track which is open for goods trains. A passenger train from London to Harwich fell into the crater and the driver and fireman, both Harwich men, were killed. Nothing has been said in the papers about this and there were none of the usual notices on Colchester station regarding delay on the line. This news came from Fisher, who said a man from Manningtree, a platelayer, had been up the line on repair work and had returned last night.

Baker, from the Labour Office, Writtle came in this afternoon. Told me he had been to see a 22 year old tractor driver who may be transferred. The man told him that labour was restive and that they ought to come out on strike. Baker said he thought strikes could be dealt with, whereupon the young man said, 'Ah, but you must remember 90 per cent of us have rifles and ammunition in these days.'

March 10 Wednesday

Long account in the 'Gazette' of a young Quaker being imprisoned for two months for refusing to fire watch. He made a very sensible and reasoned statement, in which he declined to have anything to do with the war at all. He is quite right and I only wish I had his courage. The Chairman of the Bench was Pope, the Co-op Secretary, who had a son killed in the RAF last year. Perhaps an unfortunate choice for a chairman in a case like this.

March 11 Thursday

About 8pm 'planes began to go over, so that the sky was filled with their roaring. A few are still going as I write these words. The papers today made a great deal of the fact that almost every art gallery in Munich has been destroyed and the ancient city of Nuremberg has been terribly damaged. Five more years of war and there will not be a town left in England or on the Continent.

Noticed by the return today that of our 35 girls in the WLA at Peldon only 13 put in a full week last week. All the rest were ill or absent some part of the time.

Saw lambs this morning at Ardleigh Heath, the first I have seen this year. Men and women working in almost every field now.

March 14 Sunday

Up early and got ready to go on a picnic with Mrs Nicholls [from Lawford Hall] and Mrs Belfield. Went up to Lawford Hall and helped harness the pony to the tub-cart and the big old horse to the phaeton. Mrs Nicholls drove the tub, with her two little girls and their German governess. I drove old Kitty. Away we went through Dedham, in great style, people staring, old folks smiling and waving, young hooligans yowling and cat-calling. The valley looked very lovely, the grass extraordinarily green and several willow trees beginning to come out, as well as hawthorn.

Mrs Nicholls thought that Withermarsh Green would be a good place to have lunch, so we stopped and took out the horses. The sun shone, the birds sang, some little children played, in fact it was the most peaceful spot you could imagine. Not a sign of the war anywhere, no tank blocks, no aeroplane traps, nothing. I met the shepherd from the farm and he showed me the lambing pens. He said, 'I'm going to have a lie down in a minute, for I haven't had my clothes off for three days.'

As we were talking we heard two dull, distant booms and he said, 'Listen! There's bombs!' Then, far away, came the wail of a siren. And so even remote Withermarsh Green is in the war, just as is Lawford or Clacton, or Colchester.

Back to Lawford Hall after a most delightful day, the best I have had for a long time.

March 16 Tuesday

[Air raid alarm this morning.] Children were running home from school as lessons had not begun and would not while the alarm was on. One little girl was crying bitterly, while being led by the hands by two others. It is still a firm rule that all school children go into shelters as soon as an alarm is given.

These frequent alarms on fine days are more like the times of 1940. Does this indicate a new German air offensive or are they trying to find signs of big troop movements over here?

Went round by Langham [Aerodrome site] and called on Williamson at Park Farm. The desolation along Park Lane is astounding, one seems to be in a vast moor, crossed by concrete roads. There are a lot of American lorries about and American soldiers in working clothes. Had to see Williamson about one of his men who is to be compulsorily transferred to the Committee, under orders from the Labour Committee. Williamson is furious and no wonder. The man is a tractor driver, yet we shall have to employ him as a labourer. The Labour Committee are setting everybody by the ears on account of their absurd behaviour.

March 22 Monday

Joy says everybody within a certain radius of Langham aerodrome has now been provided with an Anderson shelter.

March 27 Saturday

Joanna came in to see us, home with her husband for 10 days. She looked wonderfully well and said she was busy buying baby clothes for the child she expects in August.

Poulter back from London, voice very much improved and looking very much better.

There is no hay in the town and I have only 2 hundredweight left. If things do not improve I shall have to sell Robin. It is impossible to carry on like this.

March 29 Monday

Saw the morning 'Mail' and was horrified to find there had been a big raid on Berlin on Saturday night. What insanity to waste men and machines in sheer spitefulness, carrying out a raid of no military value whatever. What must be the effect on soldiers in Libya and sailors at sea, who cannot be given adequate air protection, when they hear that hundreds of bombers have spent a night wilfully bombing a large open city?

Evening papers hint at immediate reprisals but it is emphasised that we ought to be glad to have them, firstly, because by the size of the reprisals we shall be able to judge how much we have hurt the Germans and secondly, because it will draw bombers away from the Russian front.

April 4 Sunday

Clocks changed today, giving another hour of daylight. Tonight I could write without a candle at 8.45pm. The farmers hate this 'double Summer time'.

April 9 Friday

This morning drove to Bromley with Robin. The great pylons make it impossible to get lost. You can see them from Colchester, Lawford, Ramsey and Wix and I suppose from further than that on clear days. All round the pylons are the remains of defence points – tangled barbed wire, rotting sandbags, trenches half filled in. They are obviously abandoned, yet we are warned that at any time the Germans may swoop down on these Radio Location Stations, just as the English have done on the Continent.

Another sign that the 'war is over' is that they are now taking down the poles and wires put up to obstruct enemy troop 'planes when landing. Actually they would not have obstructed a child's paper glider but it seems strange to take them down at a time like this. All the papers talk of 'post war' activities of various sorts as if the war was to end this summer.

April 11 Sunday

About 1 o'clock this morning a great number of bombers went out over the coast, just above the clouds. The noise woke me up and I woke again when they came back soon after 3. What will it be like when the aerodromes at Earls Colne, Birch, Wormingford, Langham and Raydon are all finished?

April 13 Tuesday

Much activity in the Castle this morning, putting up a show arranged by the RAF called 'On The Target'. I strongly disapprove and consider it scandalous that such a thing should be put in the Castle.

[Many curators were opposed to the display of propaganda material in museums.]

April 14 Wednesday

Went by Ipswich Road and saw a bus full of Italian prisoners going out to work on Suffolk farms.

April 20 Tuesday

An alarm about 11.30am. After a few minutes heard the sound of a 'plane very high and then firing. Right above the High Street was a vapour trail, at a tremendous height, with little shell-burst clouds all round it. The 'plane was invisible but one could see the trail extending and turning towards the south and then eastwards. Two more vapour trails, like white ribbon unrolling across the sky, came up from the east and turned in pursuit. There was a great crowd in the Park and in the streets. I felt no fear at all, only fascination. Suddenly a tiny gleam of light appeared and some people cheered and clapped. The gleam sank behind some houses and after a few minutes the 'all clear' sounded. Quite unbelievable that we had just been watching at least two young men done to death by two others. Still more unbelievable to read in the evening paper that the whole event took place nearly 7 miles high and that the German 'plane fell into the sea 5 miles off Clacton. The man who shot it down was said to be a Norwegian.

April 21 Wednesday

Going past the Hippodrome in High Street, I noticed the sign 'The Eighth Army – in "Desert Victory"', as one might say 'Charles Laughton in "Henry VIII"'. Very interesting – man's highest ambition – to be on the films.

April 22 Thursday

Dramatic notice issued from Downing Street today, threatening the Germans with poison gas if they use it on the Russian front. All countries are longing to use gas. Mrs Sisson told me long ago that there were enormous stocks in the country.

April 28 Wednesday

This afternoon had tea with Diana Davis [Stage Manager for Colchester Repertory Company]. The Company are doing Emlyn William's 'The Corn is Green' this week, so I decided to go. Diana showed me photos of Welsh towns where they were on tour last year – Carmarthen and Dolgellau. Those little places, with the glorious mountains behind them, looked to me like a far distant unattainable heaven. What bliss to be there now. The show was very good indeed and the company had mastered both the Welsh accent and the language very well.

Slept well last night, 6 hours at least, first time for a week. My nerves are bad and I lie listening for hours.

April 29 Thursday

Went to the office of the Clerk of the Works, where I had an appointment, and found to my surprise that it was not Air Ministry men whom I was to meet but United States Air Force officers. Two of them I had seen at the Holly Trees, a Major Miller and a Lieutenant Walters. Miller looks the typical 'small-town' American one sees in so many films, his worn, lined face surmounted by rimless glasses. Walters was dark and dapper, with an olive complexion. The arrangement was that we all went off in two cars, driven by English girls in a pseudo-American uniform, to inspect sites for a shooting butt. I was supposed to say whether the site was suitable from an agricultural point of view.

As we moved off along the concrete perimeter road, through a desert of derelict farm land, I remarked, 'Well, there has certainly been a change since I was here last. Why, you've changed the whole landscape.' I said this quite innocently but at once Major Miller turned on me and snapped out, 'Well, wouldn't you rather have us here than the Germans? We can't bother about the convenience of a few British farmers, you know.' It was obvious from his manner that he had already had a good deal of criticism since he came to England.

I decided to keep quiet, as I felt sure I should only lose my temper, and the atmosphere in the car became rather strained. Miller was very off-hand with me for the rest of the trip. I was very glad to get away from them.

May 6 Thursday

There was trouble at Layer de la Haye today, with the excavator gang there, because a man had been sent from Writtle to learn to work the machine who turned out to be a conscientious objector and an Italian. He had uncles who were still in Italy. The result was that the whole gang struck work until he was sent away again. Two Land Girls who work with the machine were particularly indignant, as they both have brothers who are prisoners in Italy.

May 7 Friday

Bird-chorus began soon after 6am, when a cuckoo started to call. The other birds joined in and the cool morning air was full of the sound of them. At about 7.20, heard sirens.

The cuckoo stopped calling for a few moments, as if listening. Later heard that at that moment four Focke-Wulfs swooped down on Walton, killed 10 people in their houses and did great damage. All I heard was a very faint thud. Then the cuckoo began to call again and in a few minutes came the 'all clear'.

May 8 Saturday

American flag and the Union Jack flying on the Town Hall today, in honour of the victory in North Africa [over the Axis Forces]. But is the war over? No.

May 9 Sunday

Read Wentworth Day's 'Farming Adventure'. His facts are often utterly and wildly wrong but his Essex dialect and phraseology is very good. He is most unfavourable towards War Agricultural Committees, those in Essex especially. There is something in what he says but it is noticeable that Mr Day rode right through Wigborough, Mersea and Langenhoe and yet makes no mention at all of the vast tracts of land now being farmed by our Committee.

[James Wentworth Day criticised the 'bureaucratic tyranny' of the War Agricultural Committees in his books Farming Adventure *(1943) and* Harvest Adventure *(1946) and led a number of protest meetings against the 'high-handed' methods employed by the War Agricultural Committees.]*

May 14 Friday

Awakened from a light sleep just before 2am by the roar of high flying 'planes and the wailing of sirens. There seemed to be a great number of 'planes overhead and I could see searchlights towards Harwich. Guns began to bang all round and a moment later the whole house shook violently as bombs fell somewhere nearby.

By this time the noise was deafening, guns and bombs in all directions. 'Plane after 'plane came swooping down right over the house and every now and then the Colchester guns went off with a tremendous rumbling roar.

Great relief to see everything normal this morning but it was not until we found that we could not telephone to Chelmsford that we realised where the attack had been. Went out to get a haircut and heard a man in the next chair saying that a good deal of damage had been done.

Sat a long time looking out of my bedroom window tonight, as the landscape slowly faded. Heard the sound of distant motors, birds chattering in their nests, calves lowing, the moon calm and serene, surrounded by pale stars. Felt amazement that we should sit here waiting for bombs to come screaming out of the clear sky. We are all quite mad.

May 15 Saturday

Saw Molly Blomfield who came through from Oxford last night and she says that the damage at Chelmsford is considerable – the YMCA is gone and most of the National [Bus] Garage. Part of the station was hit but trains were running.

At home for lunch and tea and tried to be especially bright to cheer up the parents. Went down to Bourne Mill. Sat on the grass for a time and thought wildly of running away – Wales, Scotland, anywhere.

On duty [tonight]. Sat writing in Holly Trees, when suddenly the sirens went off. Went over and found the two firewatchers standing at the main gate. We heard some dull thumps but whether bombs or guns I don't know. One of the men said, 'Reconnaissance 'plane' and the other, 'More likely a "hit & run".' The sky was clear and bats flitted about. One of the men said, 'All clear on the Western Front' and we went in and shut the main doors. Hope there won't be any more alarms tonight.

May 16 Sunday

A quiet night and a lovely morning. This afternoon saw the Home Guard parading in the Lower Park, several hundred strong. The old men looked tremendously martial, with medal ribbons of the last war.

May 18 Tuesday

At the office this morning, Spencer mentioned the destruction of the Ruhr dams and said, 'Isn't it bloody silly? To keep on this aimless destruction.' Capt Folkard replied, 'Yes, in peacetime, if a thing like this happened, we should open a Lord Mayor's Fund and send relief to Germany. As it is we simply say "Jolly good show". We're like a lot of kids, smashing up each other's sand-castles.' Spencer said, 'You know, this really is a wicked war' and Folkard replied, 'Yes but I suppose we've got to win it somehow.'

May 25 Tuesday

The great news in the morning papers is that 2,000 tons of bombs were dropped in Dortmund between 1am and 2am yesterday. All the usual details of great fires, great explosions, smoke towering 15,000 feet in the air, etc. Thirty-eight bombers are admitted to have been lost. What effect does a raid such as this have on the war? Very little – except to stir up fresh hatreds.

May 26 Wednesday

Had a horrid dream in the early hours of the morning – that our house and the house next to it were demolished by a direct hit. In the dream I felt cold and vague but I began to climb over the rubble. Then I found that underneath was a sort of cellar. Mother and Father were sitting there quite unhurt. Mother said she heard it coming but was only covered with fine plaster.

May 27 Thursday

At Lawford heard that a searchlight is definitely coming into the top meadow by the buildings. A Capt Klitz came today and signed the papers with Parry. Fisher said, 'Now we shall have some bombs – searchlights always attract bombs,' as if they were moths round a candle.

May 28 Friday

Saw Hervey Benham. Much talk about the scandal [about farmers' rights] which is being stirred up by the Rector of Peldon and Wentworth Day, against our Committee. The unanimous opinion in the office (excluding me) is 'Let well alone, let 'em say what they like.' I think this is wrong but cannot move Folkard or any of the others.

May 31 Monday

We heard today, officially, that tank trenches on farm land may be filled in, so apparently 'invasion' is now definitely over. I wonder?

June 2 Wednesday

Was amazed to hear that about 5.30am, when I was still asleep, several 'planes attacked the Bromley radio location place, firing cannon-shells, one of which went clean through a cottage roof and burst between a man and woman in bed, both of whom are very seriously hurt. The 'planes then made off without a shot being fired at them.

June 5 Saturday

Telephoned to Sisson about [a job with] the National Buildings Record. Should be only too pleased to take on full time work for them but doubtful whether the Ministry of Labour would allow me to do so. Godfrey [Director of the NBR] is very keen that I should and wrote to Sisson making a definite suggestion to that effect. Sisson now suggests Molly Blomfield and I quite agree. She is badly in need of work of this nature, which ought to suit her admirably, as she has had a terrible time with illness and her duties at the ambulance depot. Agreed with Sisson that we would both recommend her to Godfrey. Phoned her and arranged to see her when I go to Colchester for duty tomorrow night.

[The National Buildings Record was founded in 1941 to make a photographic record of Britain's historic buildings in case of destruction by bombing. Rudsdale gave copies from his photographic collection to the NBR for their records on Colchester and these photographs can be viewed amongst the NBR's collections at the National Monuments Record Centre in Swindon.]

June 6 Sunday

Had a long talk with Molly Blomfield about the National Buildings Record business. She was quite excited at the prospect. I shall do everything I can to get her the job. She can get a car and petrol will be allowed. The scheme will be for her to work the whole of Essex, parish by parish, with a centre at Colchester.

I feel sure that we can get accurate lists of every building in the county worth photographing and before winter we must try to get all the best ones actually photographed, particularly in Harwich, Colchester and the London suburban districts. The authorities anticipate tremendous raids during next winter and the recording of all good buildings is regarded as a very urgent matter indeed.

Molly is anxious to get useful work. This should be ideal and much as I should like the job myself I am sure she deserves it much more than I do and will do the routine part much better. In my advisory capacity I shall be able to keep in close touch with what goes on.

June 10 Thursday

Much talk at the office about this absurd 'Farm Sunday' which the Minister has ordered to be celebrated all over the country in July. The idea is a typical piece of British Government insanity and ineptitude. Apparently the Bishop of Winchester thought it would be a good thing to revive the ancient custom of blessing the crops and suggested this to the Minister but of course by the time the business had been passed on to the Ministry it had become quite nonsensical. Nobody at the Ministry can be expected to know of either Rogation Days or Harvest Thanksgiving, so they have to invent a special day, in July, on which we shall thank God for the harvest which has not yet been gathered. What could be more absurd? Everybody at the office is against it and says that the WLA girls will refuse to turn out on a Sunday in any case.

Went down to Mersea with [Nott], to see the pea-picking at Cross Lane. Extraordinary sight, quite 100 pickers in the field, Land Girls, Mersea women, old men, etc. Our 'Colchester Gang' men refused to pick on piece work and all sat under a hedge, grumbling and swearing, yet the pay is now 3/- a bag and used to be 6d a few years ago.

Cycled out by Langham Lane tonight and saw the first 'planes on the aerodrome – 16 or 17 twin-engine Marauders, sleek, horrible looking objects. Crowds of small boys swarming all over them, quite unhindered, no sentries visible anywhere.

Decided to call on Ida Hughes-Stanton and found a most charming girl there – Jacqueline Conran, the wife of the Director of Southampton Art Gallery. She is a tiny, delightful little thing, with short, wavy copper-coloured hair, most charming. She used to be a ballet dancer. We had a lot of talk about museums and art galleries. She told me that she had a cottage at Higham and asked me to call.

June 13 Sunday

Went over to Higham, to see if I could find the Conrans' cottage. Found it down a deep dell, not far from the banks of the Brett, the only access being down a steep driftway. Delightfully remote, almost reminiscent of Wales. It is surrounded by tall, dark trees, with a few little sheds and stables nearby.

Jacqueline was there. She seemed glad to see me and showed me all over the house. The period of the place must I imagine be between 1480 and 1500. Wish it was mine.

June 16 Wednesday

To Oxford today. All the way along the line saw crowds of people hoeing and turning haycocks.

At Liverpool Street, as I had my cycle, I went round by London Wall. Great destruction in these parts, acre after acre with nothing but a few stones and bits of girders left, the streets and pavements like a plan on blank paper.

Crowds at Paddington and the train jammed to suffocation. Had to stand in the corridor, wedged between two labourers and a major. The labourers talked in fine cockney about their income-tax problems and one said he was now paying £4 a week in taxes. The major looked glum.

Oxford at last. Found [All Souls' College] went through the gracious gateway into a lovely grass-floored courtyard. Found the National Buildings Record offices – three dark rooms, with thick stone walls, lined with large red photograph files, bearing the names of the towns and counties. No file for Colchester, which is included under 'Essex'.

Mr Godfrey was very pleasant. Talked over the whole matter and told him how sorry I am not to be able to undertake the Essex survey myself. Told him that I considered Molly Blomfield very suitable. She is to begin at the end of the month.

Looked over photographs. Wonderful series from Wisbech, taken 1853-57, excellent prints from the original negatives. Have never been to Wisbech but Penrose took a great deal of interest in it. Must go sometime and see these magnificent Georgian houses.

Cycled back along Abingdon Road and saw lots of undergraduates going on fire watching duties at the Colleges and wardens going to their various posts. The city has been wonderfully fortunate as there has never been a bomb here yet, in spite of the Cowley works being so near.

June 17 Thursday

[Back] to All Souls. Godfrey gave me a War Damage Permit to enable me to go into any bomb-damaged buildings or into prohibited areas to see if any antiquities have been damaged. This should be very useful.

June 18 Friday

Went home to find poor little Mother had fallen on the stairs and had given herself a bad shaking. Poor little thing looked very sorry for herself but had had a lot of enjoyment out of telling all the friends and neighbours about it. Father looked rather worried but I think she is alright.

June 19 Saturday

Delighted to see in the papers that the Bishop of Lichfield, Dr Woods, has boldly expressed his disapproval of the destruction which is being carried out by the RAF.

June 22 Tuesday

This afternoon went down to Bourne Mill and found Sisson there, making a survey. Sisson is convinced that this building was never intended as a mill when it was put up in 1591 but was designed as a 'water-pavilion', where dinner-parties might be held overlooking the pleasant mere. This had never occurred to me before but without doubt there is a lot in favour of the idea.

June 28 Monday

At Lawford saw the searchlight has come as I feared – some tents, a lorry and a small projector. Nobody here likes it, especially as the one just across the railway was bombed 3 years ago.

June 30 Wednesday

News today that Cologne Cathedral has been destroyed by the English and Eden promises to bomb Rome as hard as possible.

July 1 Thursday

Had to go to Birch aerodrome this afternoon, to enquire into some sites they want. Dreadful mess and desolation all the way – unbelievable that so short a while ago this was all good farm land.

Layer Wood is cut up by concrete roads, full of huts and cooking-places. Lorries, cars and jeeps all over the place. Major Anderson of USAAF arrived in a big car, driven by a girl in US uniform. He was very affable. I'd met him before when he had been in the office. Gardiner Church [EWAC District Committee Member] and the Air Ministry man also came. Major Anderson looked at the lay-out plan and said, 'This is a mean site, I guess this is the meanest site I've ever seen.' Then we went into various details and their final requirements were not unreasonable. At first they wanted to pull down Shemmings Farm but Gardiner Church talked them out of that idea very firmly. We rode all over the site in two jeeps – old Church was very tickled and said, 'These are the things for farming, boy! I'm going to have one o'they after the war!'

We got a memo this morning from Writtle about the Farm Sunday celebrations. The Ministry of Agriculture and the Church have issued a joint statement, to be circulated to WACs, which speaks of 'The harvest is the fruit of man's co-operation with God. In this time of war, the duty of developing that co-operation to the utmost is evident and urgent.' One feels that God must have been sent a memo about it. Anyway, nothing whatever is being done in Colchester as neither Bishop, Dean nor Mayor is available on that day.

July 5 Monday

This evening had to go [to Langham Aerodrome] to see a man who we are taking on at Hill Farm, Layer. He was living in a cottage near Langham Lodge. Had no trouble to get onto the site, the sentry passing me in without comment. This man is now living in frightful misery, with bomb-dumps a few yards away and 'planes swooping over the cottage roof every 10 seconds. The noise is frightful. He has to leave within 2 days, or the cottage will be pulled down over him. Arranged for him to go into one of the cottages at Hill Farm, which fortunately happens to be vacant.

July 10 Saturday

Lot of business today about office re-organisation. Writtle have all sorts of crack-brained schemes to complicate wage-paying and are now contemplating an entirely new schedule of rates of pay. Our wage-bill is now somewhere around £1,000 a week – it was just over £100 when I began in 1941.

Duty at the Castle tonight but funked it – felt nervous and just did not want to go. Went to the Sissons' instead and met the younger brother of the famous T E Lawrence, a most charming man. Much very interesting talk and discussion about the possibility of a Ministry of Works 'flying-squad', to go anywhere it may be required to save historic buildings damaged by bombs. I suggested a similar arrangement to the Museums Association in 1940, to enable trained people to be sent to bombed museums to help salvage work but they would not consider it.

July 11 Sunday

Went to Higham, Jacquie was there. This evening she suddenly suggested that I should hire the cottage next October when she goes back to Portsmouth and I at once agreed to do so – delightfully lonely place in which to spend the winter. Don't want to leave Lawford, where I am treated with such kindness but feel that it would be an imposition to stay much longer. Am to go over next week to meet Conran, who will be home on leave.

July 12 Monday

Went to Benham's to arrange for him to attend a press conference which Sadler is holding in the Holly Trees, at which he is going to state the Executive Committee's case about this business in the papers about the Peldon farmers' [complaints against the EWAC].

Went into Hervey's office and he said, 'Wait a minute, there's somebody in with the old man I'd like you to meet,' and went through into Sir Gurney's office. When he came back he had with him a bespectacled man with a moustache, who he introduced as 'Mr Wentworth Day – meet the Secretary of the War Agricultural Committee!' We both looked a bit blank and then I said to Hervey, 'Well, what are we supposed to do now? Shoot each other?' Wentworth Day laughed and said no, he didn't think that was necessary and that he was glad of a chance to talk to anybody on the WAC. I said that at any rate he'd written enough about us, so he might as well hear what we had to say. Then we started in and had a real good chatter. He went off about 'British justice', 'Gestapo', 'German methods', and all that sort of thing and blackguarded most of the members of the Committee individually and quite wrongly. Then I went over various cases one by one and he had to admit that most of the complainants were utter scoundrels anyway.

However, after a while we all got very friendly and he suggested we should have a drink in the 'Red Lion', so we went there. Pointed out to him that now he had something else to write about – how WAC officials spent most of their time in pubs. He laughed.

We had some drinks and he told several good stories in excellent Essex dialect. Finally Day, Benham and I were all telling yarns in the broadest Essex to the great astonishment of the customers in the bar. Had to leave quickly, parting on the best of terms and hurried back to the office. Committee at Birch. Told Chairman about Day but he only said, 'Damned scoundrel, ought to be shot'.

July 14 Wednesday

There was an attack just after midnight. The guns were firing towards Harwich and I saw a red flare falling. Some searchlights came on and I heard the voices of the men up by the buildings, then the shout of 'Lights!' and the beam flashed and strained out over the house towards the east. Far away a bomb fell and the dogs began to bark.

There was another alarm about 4am. The Colchester guns fired an ineffective salvo, like thunder. Several 'planes came over, twisting and diving. Felt very nervous, as there was no way of knowing whether they had dropped their bombs or not [owing to the noise]. Joy told me at breakfast that she had felt very frightened too, as the 'planes seemed so low. Parrington had slept through the whole business. Such is now the blessing of deafness.

Called at home. Poor Mother had been up twice during the night. She says that even if she slept downstairs she would always get up and dress for a siren, so there is not much point in her moving down.

Back to Lawford. Fed calves. Calm lovely evening. Birds singing. Night-jars in the coppice beyond the buildings. Hope for a quiet night, very tired.

July 17 Saturday

Press conference in the Holly Trees drawing room at 9.30am. Sadler came, very cocksure of himself, and five press-men [including two from the] 'Essex Chronicle' and the 'Essex Weekly News', both of which papers have been very hostile to us. Sadler was not very good and the reporters were not by any means convinced. They all wanted details of the individual cases of hardship in this district but Sadler said he was not allowed to discuss them and would only talk in vague and general terms on the policy of the Ministry and the EWAC. It was not at all satisfactory and after an hour of this they were taken off to see the land-in-possession. Should have liked to have heard Sadler's story when he got down to Wigborough but have too much to do on a Saturday.

Went to Higham for the night. Conran and Jacquie both very pleased to see me. Discussed the possibility of my hiring the cottage, which seems very likely. Then to bed at midnight, in a lovely little room in the gable end, with ballet photos and Jacquie's ballet skirts and shoes hanging on the walls.

July 18 Sunday

Wonderful night, soft bed, deep silence. Woke about 8 and heard Doyle-Jones' cowman coming up to milk. Lay thinking about the difficulties of living here – 8 and a half miles to Holly Trees. Can I do it all through the winter? Mean to try, anyway. Shall make this little bedroom mine.

July 19 Monday

News-placards tonight shriek delightedly ROME BOMBED TODAY. News says briefly that the Americans bombed railway yards 'on the outskirts of Rome'.

July 20 Tuesday

Papers say little about Rome raid. The Italians say one church, San Lorenzo, badly damaged. Nott said this morning: 'You know where you ought to have been yesterday?' I said, 'No, where?' 'Why in Rome. I'll bet there were some old Roman pennies and things flying about.'

Heard a lot today about robbery of peas from trains going to London. Most thefts take place at night, when the trains are in sidings near Romford. We have lost 15 bags of the Committee's peas and Frank Warren has lost over 50.

July 21 Wednesday

Lot of talk today about getting another combine harvester for use at Wigborough. The previous one we had was no good, anyway. Can't see that these things are any use but Nott and Folkard are so worried about the shortage of binders that they feel anything is better than nothing. Agricultural machinery is in a terrible state.

July 22 Thursday

Letter from the Pope in the papers today on the bombing of Rome. It is a quiet, dignified protest. His Holiness proposes to move into a palace in the centre of Rome if any other attacks are made.

July 23 Friday

Got Bob round to the blacksmith's from where Clayton took him over to Ardleigh for his girl to ride. Hope to God they look after him well.

July 25 Sunday

To Dedham and found Mrs Sisson at home. She said that Joy would like me to stay at Dedham for about 10 days while the harvest is on to make room for extra helpers.

July 26 Monday

Startling news in 'The Times'. Mussolini has resigned. Great emphasis that the war with Italy still goes on, yet England's war aim was stated to be the crushing of Hitler and Mussolini.

Committee at Birch. One matter that came up was an application from Ward, the cattle carter of Birch, to have a phone at his new premises. It was agreed that he must have one. When I was young it was still usual to drive cattle 10 or even 15 miles but during the last 20 years it has become the practice to put them in lorries even to go from market to station or from one Committee farm to another. Parrington relies entirely on motors, even to take a bull a couple of miles to Ardleigh. Often greater energy is expended and more time taken to get the beasts loaded and unloaded than to drive them by road.

July 31 Saturday

To Dedham. The Sissons made me very welcome and gave me a dear little room right at the top of the house, with one tiny window looking onto Spearing's red roofs next door and another looking out over the Stour Valley to Stratford and Higham.

August 1 Sunday

Met Nott at the office and went off with him to Abbott's Wick to pay the Land Club workers. The Land Club effort was pathetic. They were supposed to be traving but nobody was there to show them how, as none of our foremen will turn out on Sundays.

There were a dozen women, mostly members of the local Communist party, and three men – one civilian, one English sergeant and one American sergeant. The pay was an awful bother – there were different rates for men and women and different again according to age. Paid out in all £4.10.0, and as the lorry will come to about 30/- the Government will have today paid £6 for no work at all.

[Land Club members were full-time workers who offered their time and labour at weekends to undertake farm work.]

August 2 Monday (Bank Holiday)

This afternoon went over to Higham to see Jacquie. She was very pleased to see me. Spent the afternoon listening to the radio. An American called Trigg came in, quite a nice chap. Then another Yank came, with a lorry and Jacquie went off for a ride. They had just been into Colchester to collect 'a bunch o' dames' for an officers' dance at Raydon.

August 4 Wednesday

Very busy day. Sun came out by 10am and the harvest is going well, except that the men won't work. Nothing will induce them to do overtime, they say they pay enough Income Tax already.

Spent a pleasant evening, reading and writing. Mrs Sisson began drawing me in pastels. Many 'planes flying from Langham all evening, dreadful noise.

In the café at lunch today an old Jew woman who keeps a vegetable stall said to Winnie 'The Yanks get paid today. They're awful drunk,' and Winnie replied, 'Yes, they scare me at night, I'm always afraid they'll break the door down when I've locked up.'

August 5 Thursday

Rain fell very heavily this morning. Don't want it now, especially at Wigborough. Two WLA gangs struck work altogether. A new woman Labour Officer has just begun, a Mrs Allen, who used to be a teacher. She seems very capable.

August 6 Friday

Rain, rather cold. All our harvest carting stopped and of course the combine stopped too.

August 7 Saturday

Called on Hervey Benham today. He told me there had been a meeting at the Regional Commissioner's office at Cambridge, to which press, church and chapel representatives were invited, together with American officers, to discuss the American attitude to young women in this country. The police and social welfare people are all very worried and there was a lot of talk about the transporting of young girls into American camps in Army trucks (referred to as 'passion wagons'). The American authorities approve of this, as they say they would rather have women in the camps than have their 'boys' wandering all over the country looking for them. The church people say this is nothing but organised prostitution but apparently there is no action that the English authorities can take, as they have to avoid giving offence to the Americans.

Ought to have stayed to do duty tonight but felt quite worn out, so left for Dedham at 6pm and spent a delightful evening reading, then to bed at 11.

August 9 Monday

Cycled in early. Poulter warned me that trouble might be expected. [Hull] knew I was not in the Castle on Saturday night and has made a report to the Fire Guard Officer.

August 10 Tuesday

This afternoon out with the District Officer and Poulter to take photos of the harvest. First to Layer Marney Hall and drove down into the fields below the buildings. They have put up the biggest straw stacks I have ever seen. The engine and drum were there threshing, beside a mound of fat sacks of corn.

Poulter took three photos and then we drove over the fields to the top of the hill. Lovely view, with hundreds of acres of traved corn in every direction. Such a sight has not been seen here for a century I should think and once the war is over will never be seen again. *[See Image 23]*

Down to Abbott's Wick. Two more stacks were going up near the buildings, with my lovely wagon and one of Polley's carts in use. On to Abbott's Hall. Corn all the way. We went through nearly 200 acres of barley, which they are just beginning to cut, right down to Marsh Barn, where the combine was working, or rather should have been working had it not (as usual) broken down. However, we put some men on it to act as if they were really using it and took several photos, so as to be able to advertise the marvels of mechanised farming.

August 11 Wednesday

My portrait is now finished – I look very noble, rather like T E Lawrence done by Kennington.

August 12 Thursday

Heard two or three waves of aircraft go out and tonight Sisson heard a report that this was an attack by the Americans on the ancient university city of Bonn. Apparently great damage has been done and Beethoven's birthplace has been destroyed. Sisson is very depressed and says, 'We are destroying everything worth having in Europe and nobody cares.'

Saw Mrs Stuart Rose this morning and have arranged to go over to Boxted for a few days at the end of this week.

August 14 Saturday

Very busy all morning, having a lot of trouble with labour. Out of 14 men in one gang, only 2 went to work this morning, with the result that the threshing machine was idle.

Home to lunch, changed and rushed out to meet Jacquie at the Regal. The news showed the actual bombing of Hamburg. This must be the first time in history that people seated in comfort in vast palatial halls can actually watch the destruction of a city. It is said that 24,000 were killed in this one raid on Hamburg.

It has been announced on the midnight news – Rome is declared an open city. The Pope, whom future generations will praise, has apparently been using great influence.

August 18 Wednesday

[Stayed at Boxted tonight.] Awakened by bombs nearby, the house shaking – an attack on the aerodrome. Within a few minutes 6 or 7 loads of bombs came screaming down, one lot seemingly quite near. The moon was brilliant and somewhere to the left a 'plane went into a steep dive. Went outside, just in time to hear Colchester sirens braying to the moon, a little late as usual. Shells bursting somewhere beyond the town and three more lots of bombs came down.

Could hear the 'loud-hailers' on the aerodrome bellowing orders – a lot of these Yanks were experiencing their first raid. Ducked inside the door as another 'plane came in, vaguely chased by a few shells. The bombs seemed to fall in the orchards.

Nothing else happened and after a few minutes I could hear nothing but a 'plane or two far away. Then there were footsteps in the lane and a shadowy figure stood by the gate. It was old King, from the cottage below.

I said: 'Something about this morning, eh Mr King?'

He replied: 'That's right, master, there is.'

'Where do you reckon they were?'

'I don't rightly know, but that's brought down a bit o' plaster in my cottage.'

'Go on? Are you and the missus alright?'

'Oh, ah, we're alright, but the woman what slep' in that room come a-busting out pretty slippy. That come right through the roof, that did.'

Just at that moment the sirens wailed the 'all clear' so I suggested we should go down to see if anything was wanted at the cottage. We walked down in the now quiet moonlight and the old man shut the garden gate, remarking: 'I'll shet that, now they're gone, then you can go back through the garden,' as if for some reason the presence of German aircraft in the sky necessitated the front gate being kept open.

A youngish woman came out of the house, followed by Granny King and a little boy. I suddenly remembered I was wearing only the top half of my pyjamas and corduroy trousers.

The old man got a torch, went upstairs and came down again. The plaster had only been shaken down and nothing had come through the roof after all – 'I reckon some o'them slates is shifted, though – I heard 'em rattle a bit.'

The little boy said: 'Coo, that'll let the water in, that will!'

Said goodnight and walked back to Little Rivers through the raspberry canes. Undressed and wrote these notes. In this ancient room there is not the slightest sign of what has just happened, nor any sign of the million things which must have happened in it during the last 500 years. Only the mice are scratching under the floorboards as they did centuries ago.

Office at 9am. Molly Blomfield phoned from Ardleigh to say Bob had had a narrow escape – bombs in the next field had killed a heifer.

Cycled out tonight by Langham Lane and saw bomb holes and windows broken. Some of the aerodrome huts smashed and twisted and it is said several men killed.

Received a most extraordinary letter from Hull, accusing me of dereliction of duty etc. and threatening all sorts of penalties. Feel too ill tonight to worry about it, anyway.

August 19 Thursday

Quiet night. Felt very ill and decided to see Dr Rowland. He told me I ought to have a holiday, which he thought was 'long overdue' and gave a certificate to excuse all fire watching and night duty until further notice. I think he guessed a good deal but did not say much.

August 20 Friday

Got some sleeping-tablets tonight from the chemist, on Rowland's prescription. Have never taken anything in the way of bromides before and have great hopes from them. Am wondering whether to apply for leave, so as to be able to go to Wales or Scotland.

Back to Lawford tonight, lovely to be back with all my books, papers and journals about me. The harvest all done right through Ardleigh and Lawford.

August 22 Sunday

Drafted the synopsis of a story to be called 'Chadborough Farm', a story of our wartime farming at Wigborough.

Had tea at the Dedham café. Two Czechs sitting at a table and when they left two Americans took it. How many of these strange foreigners will ever see their homes again?

August 23 Monday

Had a ghastly night, tablets no good at all. A big raid began to go out as soon as I got to bed, flying very low. Some seemed to be struggling along with great difficulty and about 11.30pm a brilliant red glow lit up the room, followed by a dull explosion. Looked out and saw a huge cloud of black smoke showing dimly against the stars.

Committee today and had to have it in the Town Hall because Joanna is 'near her time' at Birch. One of the tractor drivers wants to leave and set up his own farm and it was very noticeable how everybody, especially Folkard, was much against the idea and thought he was mad to think of it. No man, they say, can keep himself on a 30 acre holding.

August 24 Tuesday

Wakened by gunfire but no alarm. About 10am, Mrs Round phoned to say Joanna had a baby boy while the guns were firing. Everybody overjoyed. No baby has been born at the Hall since Joanna's youngest brother and perhaps no baby will be born there again.

Went home. Horrified to find that Dr Penry Rowland had been there and had told the old folks that I was very unwell. What a fool. I was furious. Mother said: 'The doctor said you ought to have a holiday but there's nowhere to go except the Midlands and the raids are just as bad there.'

August 25 Wednesday

Decided to go over to Higham. Found pretty little Jacquie Conran in the Higham pub on her way to see Ida. Went back with her and after a talk decided to take the cottage on 15th of next month. This gives me a chance to have a short holiday in Wales first. Felt happier than I have done for weeks.

August 26 Thursday

To Lawford and told Joy about the cottage. She said she would be glad to have the room this winter as they want to get a Land Girl to live in.

August 28 Saturday

This afternoon went with Molly Blomfield in her car on a National Buildings Record tour to St Osyth. Went through Great Clacton and the Hollands. How dreary and desolate everything looks. No raid damage noticeable but the whole scene looks weird and unreal – road after road of empty houses and shuttered shops and garages, as if some plague had struck the place. There has been no painting for years and a lot of the property seemed to be crumbling gently away. Noted a few buildings worth a photo, went across the lonely Holland Gap and back to Weeley.

September 1 Wednesday

Managed to get a word with Folkard and he agreed, not very enthusiastically, to let me have a fortnight's leave.

September 3 Friday

News today that Italy has been invaded so that we may now expect the victorious allied armies to rush madly up the peninsula, driving all before them and leaving behind a trail of smashed cathedrals, museums, palaces and monuments. What will happen to Pompeii? Poulter seems to think 'the end is in sight' and can't understand why the papers are talking about the war going on until 1945.

September 5 Sunday

Spent the day writing and clearing things up. Took my belongings over to Higham. Am very sorry to leave this cosy little room [at Sherbourne], where I have been very happy, but the cottage will be nice. The place is so remote, so utterly away from everything, that it might be in another country. True the 'planes still go over but being sunk in this valley the noise does not seem so bad.

[Rudsdale left Essex the following day and visited Scotland, Wales and Oxford.]

September 21 Tuesday

Home at lunch time. Both the old folks very well and glad to see me. Told them all about Wales and cheered them up.

September 27 Monday

It is now practically settled that we shall move into new offices in Military Road before long.

October 11 Monday

Poulter came in and said, 'Sir Gurney Benham's had a slight stroke'. Is this the end?

Saw lights on at Ida [Hughes-Stanton's] so called and stayed there talking and reading the typescript of her new book, which deals with a girls' school in the last war. It seemed to me to be very good indeed.

We had supper and then two boys came in, Lucien, the grandson of Freud, and a fellow called Craxton, son of the pianist. They were on holiday, both about 19, and had been to Ipswich. They brought fish and Ida cooked it. Both boys had some rather good drawings in the modern style.

October 13 Wednesday

Poulter came in and said that Sir Gurney has resigned all offices. Most unexpected. I never thought he would.

October 16 Saturday

I ought to be on duty [tonight] but as the Holly Trees man has been moved to the Castle at Poulter's request, Poulter tells me I need not go any more. This is a great relief. I hope I never have to take duty at the Castle again.

October 19 Tuesday

Announced on the news this morning that 5,000 men are being sent home from Germany. This has been talked about for some time and Ida is convinced that Blair Hughes-Stanton will be among them.

Museum Committee today at which the Chairman's resignation was received and so he leaves the Committee after sitting on it since 1892.

October 20 Wednesday

Bought a book – 'Fanny by Gaslight' for Mother's birthday and took it home. Put £1 inside it. She was very pleased and had had several little gifts from the family.

October 26 Tuesday

Woke very late, did not get away until nearly 9. Got a tow on a lorry, the driver of which tried hard to shake me off by swinging into the verge and out again but I stuck on until we reached the Borough boundary.

Heard from Air Ministry that Harvey's Farm, Wormingford is to be demolished.

Rushed home to tea, Mother out shopping. Wonderful how she gets about.

In the café, at lunch time, the news was giving an account of the latest Russian victories, which are undoubtedly outstanding successes. Winnie said to a customer, nodding her head towards the radio, 'I always take this sort of thing with a pinch of salt, don't you?' The man replied, 'Rather! I expect next week they'll be telling us the Germans are in Moscow.'

Tonight called at Sisson's about Harvey's Farm. He agreed to come and see it.

October 29 Friday

This morning went to Wormingford with Sisson and Poulter. Had quite a trouble to get onto the flying ground owing to the deep mud.

Sisson was most impressed with Harvey's Farm and we made a thorough examination. He said the ceiling was remarkably good and I suggested that if we can get it out safely it might be stored over at his place at Hadleigh.

How desolate the place looked today, so recently prosperous farmlands. The stables still have much in them and the cow chains hang rusting, in the milking shed.

October 31 Sunday

Spent the usual lazy day, household chores, radio, reading and writing. Almost 2 years since I was de-reserved, yet I am still at liberty. I wonder whether they will get me now?

Radio faded at 10pm and at about 10.30 bombs and gunfire. The fading of the London station is a better warning than sirens. A few 'planes to the south, where I could see a fire burning. Harwich guns fired long and loud and two searchlights swept the sky.

November 1 Monday

We are finally moving out of Holly Trees tomorrow. I wonder if I shall ever work in the place again? Poulter seems, at the last, quite sorry that we are going. The girls have arranged a farewell tea tomorrow to which everybody is to go.

November 2 Tuesday

Great excitement, as we were moving the office today. The whole thing went very well and by 10.30am we were well established. So I come back to New Town, where I really belong, where I was born and spent my whole life. The house is on the corner of New Town Road, a pleasant place about 40 years old.

This afternoon we had the grand farewell party at the Holly Trees. Poulter and the attendants were all there and it was a tremendous feed – sandwiches, cakes, apples, jellies, blancmanges, all done wonderfully. Folkard came and about 20 sat down. The girls loved it, Folkard made a speech and Daphne answered. Well, that is the end of that! Poulter asked me to keep my key as I should 'always be popping in'.

A funny thing happened just as we were about to begin. A phone call came through from Writtle to ask if it was true I had left last month? Said I was still very much here but talk of leaving made me feel strange. Such extraordinary things go on at Writtle, one never knows what will happen next.

November 3 Wednesday

Got in in good time and was getting well into my work when one of the girls brought me a letter addressed 'Mr Eric Rudsdale'. I recognised the writing as Miss Ralling's. The note was brief:

Winnock Lodge, 3.11.43

Dear Eric,

Miss Horwood has just phoned Dr Rowland, as your little mother is not well. Run home and see her as soon as you can.

Annie R Ralling

I felt quite cold. I hurried down the road, went in the house. Father was sitting in his old chair, doing the inevitable crossword. I went upstairs. She was on Father's side of the bed, her face pinched. Her right hand clutched mine and she said, 'Oh Eric dear, I've had a fall', her voice was thick and there were tears in her eyes. I saw at once what had happened – a stroke, her left hand and leg were quite dead. She kept saying, 'I can't get up, I can't get up' and hung onto my hand.

It had taken her suddenly, her leg gave way and she fell down. Father, terrified, had hobbled over to Nurse Horwood's. Dr Rowland came in. He said her blood-pressure was enormous and there was nothing to be done but to keep her quiet and hope.

What happened this afternoon I have only hazy recollections. I rushed round, got a nurse and got a woman to come in. The great worry is to get a permanent housekeeper. There was an advert in 'The Gazette' from a woman at Boxted, so I thought I would go over and interview her.

I felt sure there must be a raid and at 6.40pm the sirens wailed out. More and more 'planes came over from the east and heavy firing began, hundreds of shells bursting in little pinpoints of fire. Thought of poor Mother and the poor devils who must have been killed tonight. Oh if only the war would end.

Saw the woman but she refused to take a job in Colchester 'because of the raids'. Who can blame her? Back home. Mother sleeping. What is to become of us?

November 5 Friday

Mother asleep, made tea for Father and went to work. As soon as I went into my office everything seemed better – the sun was struggling through the clouds, horses and carts went up and down Military Road, soldiers marched past. Then every now and then waves of depression came over me, as I realised what was happening and what the future must be.

Went out at 12, bought soft sweets and soda water for Mother and took them back to her. She was very grateful and said, 'You are good dear, you are kind', which, alas, is just what I'm not. Then she said, 'Your hands are like ice, you ought to wear your gloves.'

Went to Higham and was alarmed to find an extraordinary sort of red searchlight in the derelict field near the cottage. It appeared to be some sort of signalling device, flashing on and off. Even here they find me out. My last place of peace. Could hear the shouting of American voices.

The Chairman came in this morning. When he went out he noticed a fox skin in the back of Culley's [the Pests Officer] car. He was furious and said, 'Don't let me see a thing like that again. I know it has to be done but don't let me see it. If there's one thing I love it's a fox.' Charles James Round, Esq, JP, MFH – he meant every word he said.

I still can't realise that in a few days or even hours I may have no mother. If only I had got them both away from Colchester this might not have happened. The Doctor agrees that it must have been largely brought on by worry about air raids. Poor little Mother.

November 7 Sunday

At home found Father in a cheerful mood – Mother had improved slightly. I believe Mother has really improved.

November 8 Monday

A quiet night but news of a terrible disaster in London – hundreds killed in a dance hall, struck by a bomb.

Mother decidedly better but by no means the same. I think things are a little more hopeful. Walked to Bourne Mill, thinking what I can do for her if she gets better.

November 9 Tuesday

Mother decidedly talkative. Went to the Food Office and got extra milk permit for her.

Phone call from [Writtle] to speak about my deferment. What irony if I am taken now, after four years. Heard today that Shaw, the Jew farmer at Ardleigh has been taken, in spite of all appeals by Writtle and the National Farmers Union. Poor little wretch.

Called at Stratford, Blair Hughes-Stanton home from Germany. Looks well, but thin.

November 10 Wednesday

Called at home at midday. Mother lay with her eyes open and spoke in a whisper. Went away feeling bad. No woman came today and the District Nurse did not come. Father looking very peaky. He cried in bed last night, poor old man and said he wished he was dead.

Phoned Rowland and he advised Mother being sent to the Infirmary, as it was obviously no good trying to carry on without proper help. Reluctantly, I agreed. Poor darling Mother, how she would hate it but what else is to be done?

November 11 Thursday

Called at Penry Rowland's. He urged the necessity of getting Mother in at once and said he was convinced Father was on the verge of collapse. Went to the Infirmary. It is a pity that although the status of the old Poor Law Infirmary has been changed to a public hospital, the old staff remain. The atmosphere was dreadful – dark green and brown paint, huge offices, tall wide corridors, the institution smell prevailing everywhere. Signed papers, agreeing to pay all charges myself. Then, endless walking through cold dark passages, along which paupers trudged to their tasks, carrying coals, laundry, crockery. I felt terribly depressed. At last found the place and there was Mother, tiny and frail, in a little iron cot, so different from her old bed at home. Mother knew me. I said, 'Are you alright?' and she said, 'Yes, I hope I can go home soon.'

To Rallings' at Winnock Lodge and found Father [there] smiling and comfortable, as he said, 'happy for the first time for a week'. Poor dear old man.

November 12 Friday

Went to hospital – Mother very bad. She did not know me. Held her hand but she only murmured. Nurses very pessimistic. I said, 'Is she really sinking?' They would not say. Nothing of her seemed alive but her right hand and a pulse beating violently in her neck.

Went to Winnock Lodge. Rowland had been to see Father and advised him not to visit Mother for a day or two. The Rallings, God bless them, say he can stop on [with them] willingly. I can never repay them for what they have done.

In the evening papers, the RAF has raided the defenceless seaside town of Cannes. Also a good deal of gloomy talk about a renewed German air offensive against England.

Well it looks as if Mother will never know these nights of terror again.

November 13 Saturday

I was writing last night until after 2am and just about the time I dropped off to sleep, my little Mother slipped gently away into eternity.

Went to the Infirmary and the Sister said, 'She passed away very peacefully. She was unconscious for some time.'

I left and cycled round to regain my composure but still had the worst of all before me – telling Father. Cycled to Winnock Lodge. When I went into the room Father looked at me and his face puckered up like a baby. We clung together, weeping and suffering. He said, 'Has she gone? Has she gone? Poor little Dot,' and sobbed like a child. When I could at last speak I said, 'Oh don't, daddy, don't.' He quieted a little and I said, 'Would you like a cup of tea?' He shook his head but I said, 'Well I would, so you have one as well.' Annie Ralling made one in a minute and we both drank it, sweet and boiling and became more composed.

Back to the Infirmary and collected Mother's little things. Among them was her gas mask case, the mask having been sent back to ARP headquarters.

November 14 Sunday

Lay thinking about Mother. It seems quite incredible, unbelievable, that I shall never see her again, never hear her beg me to wear warmer clothes or eat more food.

November 16 Tuesday

Folkard told me today that he had heard from Writtle that I had never been deferred and that application must now be made. How this extraordinary position arises I don't know, considering I have worked for the Committee for almost 3 years. Folkard told them I could be regarded as 'technical' which was very good of him. Actually I don't care very much whether they take me or not.

November 17 Wednesday

My Mother's funeral. Just as we got to Magdalene Church the old cracked bell clanged out. The little procession formed. The parson began to read very quietly and between the clangs of the bell I heard the words 'I am the Resurrection and the Life'. The service was short. I could not follow it at all. Every few minutes tears welled into my eyes. Noticed Poulter in the congregation. Good of him to come.

And so into the Cemetery and there just beyond the Chapel, by a Cypress tree, was the grave. Two 'planes swooped and turned high in the sky and the sun was beginning to sink behind the fir trees. There she lay. 'Agnes Rudsdale, died November 13 1943, aged 76,' engraved on a shining brass plate. I said to myself 'Goodnight, darling dear.' And we went away and left her, lying on the right hand of her mother and father.

November 20 Saturday

Went to see Father this afternoon. Suddenly he said, 'Did you find Mother's birth certifi-cate?' I said, 'No'. 'Then how did you know she was 76?' I thought quickly and did not want to say I heard it from Nurse Horwood, a stranger, so said, 'Uncle Frank [Webb] told me.' Actually Frank did not know himself.

'Ah well,' said Father, 'I never knew how old she was.' And they had been married nearly 40 years.

November 23 Tuesday

The weather still fine. It has really been an extraordinary season so far and a tremendous amount of winter corn has been got in.

Had letters of sympathy from Col Round and Joanna and one from the Executive Officer himself. Thought when I read them how Mother would enjoy reading them and had a vague feeling that I must take them to show her at teatime. Still not used to her not being there.

Went out to Higham at 6.30, called at Ida's, found her with Blair, sitting by the fire, very domesticated. Strange to think he has lived among Germans for 2 years. He did not speak about it. Looked very well.

November 25 Thursday

My Father shocked me badly this afternoon when I saw him. He asked if I knew where 'our boys' went last night. I said, 'No', although the papers suggest another Berlin raid. 'Well,' he said, 'I hope they have another good go at Berlin tonight.' And this is my dear gentle old father. I am glad I have never discussed the war with him in any way.

December 1 Wednesday

This evening went to Rallings to see a Miss Payne as a prospective housekeeper. She seemed a kindly, capable woman, of about 60. I think she should be fairly suitable but it is an awful responsibility to choose a woman who is to be almost another wife to Father. I introduced Miss Payne to him and he seemed quite favourably impressed.

December 4 Saturday

Went to draw rations and find I am a week wrong now. I don't seem to be able to manage on sugar, jam or margarine, even though I have meals in Colchester.

December 6 Monday

We have all been watching, with considerable amusement, the establishment of a brothel in a house opposite the office. There appears to be 5 or 6 girls there, all very young and several babies. The upstairs windows are curtained all day long and two or three times a day American soldiers go in and out of the house. Last Friday we watched two walk up and down for a long while and finally go away without tasting the delights within. Everybody in the office, down to the youngest girl, knows what is going on.

December 9 Thursday

Very ill. Cannot read or write more than a few words. Jacquie and Ida arrived about 4pm. Too weak and exhausted to move. Cannot stop coughing. Jacquie gave me 4 'M & B' tablets [for soar throats and pneumonia]. Don't know whether they will do any good

December 10 Friday

Felt better but ached all over. Just as we were settling down for a quiet evening, there was a tremendous commotion at the door and in came Jacquie's mother. All peace gone, rushing about at her behest while her crying plaintive voice went on and on, reciting disasters and misadventures which had pursued her right across England, ending with having her suitcase stolen at Colchester station.

In the middle of this, heavy firing began and when I looked out the sky was a mass of bursting shells. A lot of 'planes came over and the noise was tremendous. Somewhere fairly near at hand the guns went into action and the cottage shook violently whenever they fired. The noise died away in about half an hour but the 'all clears' did not sound until nearly 9pm.

December 11 Saturday

I had forgotten all about last night's raid until I was going up East Hill [Colchester] when I noticed two broken windows in a shop and another in the next house, which was displaying little Union Jacks from every window. From there saw that dozens of windows were out, piles of plaster in the gutters, several roofs almost stripped, glass and slates all over the place and the Park locked with 'Unexploded Bomb' on the gate. Found all the Park gates locked but Holly Trees and the Castle standing complete and unhurt.

Then to the Library to see if there was a Casualty Board and found with relief there was only one name – a man called Willis, injured. (Hear that he was in the 'Sun', when the siren went and, in trying to get out in a great hurry, fell and broke his leg. Poor old man.)

Made enquiries and soon heard that the unexploded bomb is only 12 feet from the back of the Castle, those bombs which burst being on the other side of the Ramparts. There were people in the Vaults at the time.

And so after all these years and all the nights I have waited there for this to happen, it does at last happen when I am safely 8 miles away.

December 13 Monday

Got out at 12 to go to Holly Trees. Went in the Park and met Poulter. The bomb is only feet away from the north wall of the Castle. There are 87 panes of glass broken at Holly Trees.

December 15 Wednesday

Called at Holly Trees. Several policemen at the Park Gates, a crowd of soldiers, two lorries standing inside the gates in the dusk. A policeman let me in and said , 'Tell Mr Poulter to keep his windows and doors open, they're just drawing the fuse out.' Down the east side of the Castle I could see one or two motionless figures and hurried on expecting to be knocked flat by an explosion any minute. Poulter was sitting with his feet on the desk, every door and window open and an icy draught sweeping through the building.

Shortly after a phone call came through from the police to say the fuse was out but the bomb would be left there until morning.

December 16 Thursday

Went to the Castle and Poulter came out and showed me all the bomb holes. Two small ones on the Bowling Green and just inside Holly Trees Meadow showed nothing and that in the Meadow had smashed every pane of glass in the greenhouses. The big crater near the Bandstand shows part of the [Roman] Street and many fragments of road metal. There is considerable damage to the Refreshment Room.

The other big bomb, which fortunately failed to explode, was about 20 feet from the north wall of the Castle and can only have missed the top of the building by a few feet as it fell. It was about 30 feet from the emergency exit out of the Vaults, where I always look out during raids. What an amazing thing.

[Rudsdale's sketch and notes on this site record that the remains of a tiled Roman drain were found underneath the unexploded bomb when it was removed.]

[See Image 24]

December 21 Tuesday

Went to the cinema with Diana Davis. We were watching an absurd film about the Amazon when the alarm notice was flashed on the screen. She made a little clutch at my hand, so took the opportunity to hold it for the rest of the performance. Nobody in the audience moved when the alarm was on. The days when doughty ARP men rushed away to their posts are now far behind. Came out soon after 9pm and went to have a drink in the Grosvenor. I was quite enjoying myself, as I have not had an evening out with a girl for a good many months.

Diana then suggested supper at her lodgings. She sat beside me on the sofa and I put my arm round her and stroked her hair. Thus we sat until midnight struck and later. At last I said I must go, so kissed her and went out into the dark. Fell into bed half-dressed at 1.20am. A very pleasant evening although I feel really too old for this sort of thing.

December 22 Wednesday

Christmas is almost on us again. Streets and shops full, even a few cards for sale but I bought none again this year. I used to enjoy buying cards a lot in the old days.

December 23 Thursday

To Dedham and collected a toy vegetable stall for the Roses' baby, paid Mrs Sisson £1. A lovely little thing. The beacon on at Higham but no 'planes. How I hate that thing.

December 24 Friday

Went to Boxted, called at the Roses' and gave them the vegetable stall. They were both genuinely delighted, even the baby, although she is only a year old. She had been crying all day with stomach ache but stopped as soon as she saw the toy vegetables and flowers being unpacked. Then on to Colchester. Hundreds of 'planes streaming back from the coast, some in formation, some straggling along alone.

To Winnock Lodge for tea. Gave Father a quarter of a pound of tobacco.

Heard on the news that the Allies had celebrated Christmas Eve with a heavy raid on Berlin at 4am (hence the beacon last night) and by sending 1,300 'planes to bomb places near Calais today. It was these I saw coming back. Suggested that their objectives were the 'rocket guns' which the Germans are said to be building to bombard London from France. Wonder if they could reach Colchester? The distance is very little further.

The first Christmas without Mother. She always loved Christmas.

December 25 Saturday

Felt happy on the assumption that this, the fifth Christmas of the war, would be as peaceful as its predecessors. At the Sissons' found Major Inde also invited – Mrs Sisson had taken compassion on two lonely bachelors. Magnificent lunch – chicken, plum-pudding, black-currant pudding, raisins, apples and nuts, sherry and beer, coffee. Not being used to such rich food recently, felt very ill.

The Pentons came just before tea. Jack bought his recorder and played duets with Mrs Sisson, Sisson accompanying them on the piano. They played 'Stille Nacht, Heilige Nacht', 'Three Ships,' 'Wenceslas' and the candles in the Christmas tree were lit. It was very lovely.

The Pentons went at 8 in their car and were caught at the very door by PC Wiggins, who accused them of illegally using petrol and made a great to-do, upsetting Mrs Penton, who is very ill. An unpleasant little episode on Christmas night.

December 27 Monday

Listened to radio and heard that the 'Scharnhorst' is sunk. The destruction of a great battleship is terrible. This was far away in the Arctic Seas in darkness. Who survived?

December 29 Wednesday

I must get somewhere [else to live] as the light was on again tonight and I could not sleep for nervousness and anxiety. Sat listening to radio until 2 in the morning. The English midnight news said that Germany had announced there had just been a raid on Berlin.

December 31 Friday

So ends 1943, bloodshed, terror, wild aimless destruction, and so we rush on into 1944, with the promise from our leaders that we shall have more of it. Some people in Colchester all rather alarmed to find that the town is only about 90 miles from Calais so that if the new 'rocket shells' can reach 125 miles we may have something else to worry about.

Chapter 6

❧ 1944 ❧

January 1 Saturday

New Year's Day, the fifth of the war. There is much to be thankful for. Although the war has been on for nearly four and a half years, I have never had a medical examination, never had to join the Home Guard and have avoided doing any fire watching since last August. Few people under 34 can have had such extraordinary luck.

Made arrangements to meet our new housekeeper on Monday. Father will move back into the old house by the end of the week. Went over there myself and even now I cannot believe that Mother will never again sit in her chair, drinking her tea.

January 3 Monday

Went out to [Wormingford] Aerodrome and called at the forge there, where Emmison began work today. As I approached I could hear the clink of the hammer on the anvil, a sound not heard there for many years. He was shoeing the first horse as I walked in – an old grey gelding. The fire blazed cheerfully and the smith looked just as cheerful and just as hot. It was a good thing to see and this is the first time in my life I have known a forge, once closed, to re-open. While I was there old Mrs Partridge, widow of the last smith and owner of the forge, looked in over the half door, delighted to see the fire and smell singed horn again.

What an amazing sight this [aerodrome] is. To think that only 2 years ago this vast 'town' was open farm land. Saw a group of Americans playing American-style football. Noticed that nowhere is there any sign of protection – no guns, no sandbags, only a few shallow trenches near the huts. How sure we are of ourselves now.

January 4 Tuesday

Masses of seagulls at East Bridge, wheeling and crying round the mill, the first time I have seen them inland this winter. A great mass of birds in flight, tumbling and hovering, is a very beautiful sight. As I was going over the bridge into Nayland yesterday evening, a flock of rooks, to the number of several hundred, went over, sailing before the wind like black feathers blowing out of a pillow, crying and cawing and making the most lovely patterns against the grey stormy clouds.

Called at Winnock Lodge. Miss Payne has made a very favourable impression, even Father likes her but says pathetically, 'She talks too much'.

The evening papers say: 'Russians Enter Poland'.

Bought a tin of treacle at the grocer's today, the first treacle I have had since 1940.

January 5 Wednesday

Got to Higham tonight and found the beacon alight. It seems to work every Wednesday and Sunday. Cannot force myself to go to bed when the beacon is on so I curled up to sleep in the dining room, listening to the radio.

January 8 Saturday

This afternoon bought a new jacket and a pair of trousers for 65/- and 20 coupons. The jacket is not very good and would not have cost more than 30/- before the war.

Out at 5, in broad daylight into the crowded streets – country people, Americans, negroes, sailors, ATS girls, Land Girls, all pushing and crowding on the pavements.

January 10 Monday

To Birch this afternoon, for the 78th meeting since I attended my first one 3 years ago almost to the day. Out of the 78 I have missed only 2, last September. Capt Folkard has not missed one since the beginning in September 1939.

Went to Dedham, to the Sissons'. Molly Blomfield had been there recently, bringing Mr Merton, the National Buildings Record photographer. Apparently all Essex coast photos must be done at once, as no photography will be allowed in coastal districts after this month. Sounds very sinister.

January 11 Tuesday

Went down to Mersea with Nott to number the Committee's horses. Heated the iron with a blow-lamp and stamped them on the off-fore hoof. I have never seen a finer lot. The names are pure poetry – Dodman, Blossom, Sprightly, Prince, Jolly, Joe, Short, Captain, Boxer, Arco. It is fine to see how the horsemen fondle these huge animals and talk to them as if they were tame cats or dogs.

It was now dinner time, so we went to the Wigborough 'King's Head'. There was an old man in the bar called Foakes. It was coming on to rain and Nott said, 'No drilling on this land now.' Foakes said, 'Ah, master, that'd puzzle you to dib an acre of beans in a day, wouldn't it? Five we used to put in every hole –

"One for the mice,
One for the crow,
Two to rot
And one to grow."'

January 13 Thursday

Called at Dedham about moving the ceiling [from Harvey's Farm, Wormingford] on Saturday. Sisson told me that a large quantity of anti-gas powder has been brought into Dedham. Noticed that ATS girls carry gas masks on some occasions now. Have not seen mine for months.

January 15 Saturday

Thick fog this morning and bitterly cold. At [Wormingford Aerodrome] found the old farm house quite demolished – only a few of the buildings remaining. For a long while we could not find the lorry, the fog was so thick, but at last it turned up and we got busy loading the moulded ceiling timbers, with the help of three Land Girls. The driver ventured onto the mud, against my advice and soon the lorry was stuck fast, so that no amount of tugging could release it. Took one of the Land Girls (the prettiest) and went off to see if we could get any help. It was very strange to wander about among 'planes and lorries in the thick fog, hearing the accents of America and Ireland intermingled as we passed groups of mechanics or labourers. Found the big hangar, which thrilled the Land Girl a good deal – 'Well,' she said, 'I never thought I should see the inside of a hangar.' Neither did I.

Here we found several first-class sergeants with a motor truck, who, at the sight of the Land Girl, at once sprang to our aid, truck and all, in fact we got the idea we could have had an aeroplane had we wanted it. Away we went in the truck with six sergeants. The Yankees fell to on our wreck with great enthusiasm but in a short time, having broken our tow-rope twice, they had their own truck bogged as well.

It was quite clear that the only thing likely to help us was a tractor and as I had seen one towing an aeroplane I suggested that we might borrow that. The sergeant in charge could not do enough for us and within a matter of minutes the enormous tractor, clouds of smoke belching from its exhaust, was ploughing through the mud towards us. It had a wire Hauser wound on a drum, which was driven by the motor. The wire was attached to the lorry's front axle, the motor raced, and out she came, with a sucking noise like a cork coming out of a bottle, leaving behind four pits almost as big as graves where the wheels had been.

Set off back to Colchester, collecting one of the Land Girls from the pilot's seat of a nearby 'plane, where a sergeant was showing her the controls. The fog was as thick as a wall. I don't mind if it stays like this for a month if it keeps the Germans away.

Went home to tea. Father and Miss Payne seem to be quite settled and he seems happy.

January 19 Wednesday

This morning we had a call from the BBC, asking Capt Folkard to make a recording for a Colchester broadcast on Friday. Folkard and Alec Craig are to hold a conversation on farming matters.

January 23 Sunday

Worked hard all the morning cleaning the house ready for Jacquie to come back. About 10pm she turned up with a very pleasant young artillery captain, called Brown, who had driven her from Stratford in an Army lorry. He stayed talking until after midnight. Talked about the chances of an invasion of the Continent during the next few weeks and said he did not believe they would go straight to France, although all his men had been issued with 1-inch French maps and a 1939 Michelin guide. He thinks it is a bluff and that the real attack will be made elsewhere.

January 27 Thursday

Old Tabakoff came in complaining about his land which we have taken. While he was there the sirens sounded, the first alarm in daylight for several months. The old man shook his fist and said, 'That 'itler, 'e can do nothin' now, 'e is buggered.'

January 31 Monday

Hervey Benham told me an amusing story today. He sent a telephone message to a Home Guard officer at Aldham to say that there would be a radio test as follows: 'Testing at 10.30 on ten kilocycles, word – "holiday".' This was eventually delivered as 'Ten motor cyclists will be going on holiday at 10.30.'

February 1 Tuesday

Sat up nearly all night, writing, preparing selections from my wartime journals for Hervey Benham.

The 'Colchester' broadcast was on the radio tonight, being sent out for the Forces abroad. Folkard and the Chairman came through well, the Chairman being especially good. Hervey Benham spoke well, too.

Saw Hervey Benham [this afternoon] and got talking about the BBC broadcast. He mentioned some of the extraordinary regulations which the BBC enforces. He was forbidden to mention the work done by canteens in the town as this would indicate the presence of troops. When he suggested that perhaps by now the Germans may be aware that Colchester is a garrison town, the BBC producer agreed but said that to mention soldiers in Colchester would make Colchester soldiers abroad anxious about their wives. He was also forbidden to mention that several of the Aldermen and Councillors had died in recent years, as this might make the men depressed.

February 4 Friday

Went home for a cup of tea. Father not down and Miss Payne gave me a letter from the Ministry of Labour, to attend for a medical examination on Thursday next. Felt a moment of panic but nothing like so bad as I felt when I got a similar notice in September 1941. What a long time ago that seems. Don't believe I really care what happens now. Of course, Writtle may make a strong appeal to retain me, although the Manpower Board is not likely to take much notice of that. Wish I knew what medical grade I am. Glad that Father did not see the letter.

This afternoon took Hervey Benham the journal extracts and started on some more tonight.

February 5 Saturday

Hervey Benham phoned this morning to say that the journal extracts are good and that he wants to publish some of them forthwith and wants to buy the publishing rights to the whole thing. Felt quite excited but don't think I can agree, as I had never intended to have anything published until 50 years after my death.

February 7 Monday

Called at Little Rivers. Dodo Rose seems to believe that if an invasion of Europe is attempted it will have the same effect here as a German attack on England – food supplies will fail, transport will be cut off, some places will have to be evacuated on account of enemy counter attacks. All work will have to stop, as the Home Guard will be mustered. All very extraordinary.

February 9 Wednesday

People are now talking about the position in Italy and some think that the Allied forces will soon be driven into the sea. As there is now a very serious danger of Rome being totally destroyed during the Allies' attempts to 'liberate' the Italians, a few protests against indiscriminate bombing have been published in 'The Times' and on the news tonight we hear that the Bishop of Chichester has made a spirited attack in the Lords today.

Less than 10 hours to go [to medical examination].

February 10 Thursday

[Got to Colchester] and turned into the Wesleyan Church forecourt, following signs which read 'Medical Board Room and Recruiting Centre'. Tried to remember to keep my face quite expressionless, whatever happened.

The waiting room was small, on one side two-dozen chairs and on the other, two desks with Ministry of Labour officials. I went in, falling over a brick which was used to keep the door shut. There were a dozen men and boys sitting on the chairs, some in Air Training Corps uniform, one Home Guard and a Sea Cadet and three men of my age or rather older. Handed in my papers and registration card to a pleasant man who received them courteously but insisted on referring to me as a 'lad' when speaking to the other clerk.

Then we all sat and waited, staring at the dirty ceiling and the green-painted walls. The men never spoke but the ATC boys whispered and giggled amongst themselves. They were nothing but children, yet I suppose in two or three years they will be flying over Germany or Japan.

At 10am the four oldest men were called outside – our hour had come. We were each given a cubicle and told to undress, leaving only jacket and trousers. Then into a big room, under bright lights. I did not feel very self conscious or nervous. I seemed to be acting a part all the time.

First we were each asked to retire behind a screen and pass a sample of urine. Then, stripped of our coats, we were weighed and measured, after which the real ordeal began. There were five doctors, sitting in large screened cubicles, and one was sent from one to another, right round the room.

The first, short, dark, rather bald, with glasses, began to ask me the most searching questions – Was I afraid of the dark? Did I think people followed me in the dark? Was I sick at the sight of blood? Had I any nervous illnesses? His manner was so persistent and compelling that I had to admit to some of my more nervous fears but muttered something about having spent too many nights in the Castle. He laughed and said, 'I know all about that.' How did he know? Perhaps Dr Rowland told him.

The next doctor tested my reflexes and looked at my teeth. Then he asked me to read some illuminated letters across the room but I could only manage two lines and found that my left eye was worse than my right. Then my ears, which are good.

The next doctor took my blood-pressure and my pulse. He prodded my stomach all over and found various tender spots, then sounded my heart and lungs, entered up the details on my dossier and handed me on to the last man, who looked it over very carefully and then sounded my heart and lungs again. I murmured something about heart pains and he said, 'Naturally, your heart's sound, but with a synodrome ...' I think that was the word. What is a 'synodrome'?

The fifth doctor sat at a centre table and asked me to be seated while he wrote out a medical card, which he handed to me to sign. As I did so, I caught sight of 'Grade: 3 III', and a feeling of relief came over me but I thought I must do nothing to show it.

Even now I was not sure what would happen to me but I was not very surprised when the clerk said, 'Grade 3, so you won't be called up unless they reclassify you.' I thanked him without emotion, collected my card and walked out into Culver Street. It was 11 o'clock and I was free and had a life in front of me. I believe the other three men of my age were all passed as Grade I.

February 11 Friday

Cannot yet believe my luck. A memo from Writtle to say that they do not intend to apply for a deferment for me – no need to now. Am I really ill? When I was handed my card yesterday I laughed and said, 'Not a very high grade, is it?' and the clerk said, 'No, you can't go much lower without being dead.' Yet I feel no worse than I did ten years ago. Went to the Library to find a medical dictionary but there did not seem to be one there and I did not like to ask any of the girls, so have not yet found what a 'synodrome' is (if anything).

More protests in the press against British bombing and very many letters in favour of it, the writers of which blackguard the Bishop of Chichester as much as they dare.

Had some difficult orders to serve today but had difficulty to concentrate – as if I had another life and feel I ought to do something about it. Told Folkard today [about my medical grade]. He seemed rather surprised.

February 14 Monday

My birthday – 34. Father gave me a stick of shaving soap and some blades, so difficult to get in these days and Miss Payne gave me two new handkerchiefs, just as Mother used to do.

February 15 Tuesday

Capt Skinner, the Land Commissioner, came in this morning and gave Capt Folkard a confidential report from the Minister on the way in which an invasion of the Continent may affect farmers. For one thing, it is thought that there will be no Scotch Seed Potatoes this year, as the Admiralty will take over all the coastal shipping. Also suggested that all road and rail traffic will stop and farmers will have to make do as best they can.

On the 9 o'clock news it was announced, with great satisfaction, that the sacred monastery of Monte Cassino has been destroyed by American bombers. The building contained most of the treasures from Naples Museum and about 2,000 civilian refugees who had gone there for safety. In several papers Monte Cassino has been compared to Coventry Cathedral.

February 16 Wednesday

In the evening papers, announcements of another raid on Berlin last night – the 'biggest of the war'. Every raid on Berlin is the 'biggest'. Papers say that thousands were killed.

February 19 Saturday

Surprised to hear on the radio that there had been a heavy raid on London during the night. Apparently it was mostly incendiary bombs. There was a fire near Boxted and a greengrocer said several houses were down.

February 22 Tuesday

The papers today admit that the raids on London are serious. Churchill has been out to see the ruins and said that it reminded him of the old days. On the radio tonight an account was given of his speech in the House today, in which he prophesised bloody events.

Coming out tonight noticed that signposts have suddenly been replaced on the main road, from which they were removed in 1940. No doubt this is to help military transport. I hear that the railways are now refusing to bring goods to Colchester, with the exception of foodstuffs. This is all preparatory to the invasion of the Continent.

Just before midnight the radio faded out and at once I heard gunfire to the east. Went out to look and saw cone after cone of searchlights. One 'plane began to dive and there was a great cluster of shell-bursts just over Higham. The firing kept on intermittently until just after 1am but there did not seem to be so many 'planes as usual. While I was waiting for the firing to stop, I thought of all the places in the British Isles where the nights are quiet, where you can rest in bed from 11pm until 8am.

February 23 Wednesday

At Gun Hill met a procession of 30 NFS fire-pumps, coming from the direction of Colchester and began to wonder what had happened. When I got into the town there was a smell of burning, firemen walking about, rolls of hose-pipe across High Street from the Park.

Went along Culver Street, walking, because of broken glass on the road. Winnie was at the door of the café, sweeping dirt into the road, the glass panels shattered and a hole in the ceiling where an incendiary had come through. The Medical Aid Depot opposite was burnt out with charred remains of medical appliances on the pavement.

Hosepipes all the way, crowds of people, NFS cars parked both sides, dense clouds of smoke at the bottom of St Botolph's Street. Strange police on duty and could not get through. Went round to St John's Green, where I could see the full majesty of the ruin for the first time – Hollington's factory gone and Leaning's on Mersea Road, Griffin's depository in Osborne Street and many shops. Everywhere a tremendous smell of burning and great columns of white steam and smoke going up from Hollington's and Griffin's. Amazed to see American military police, armed with revolvers, stopping civilians.

On the bus park were twenty or thirty fire-pumps, a mobile canteen serving tea and two or three hundred firemen standing about. The furniture depository was still burning, right up to the wall of the electricity offices and I noticed the inscription painted on the side: 'H L Griffin & Co. Removals and Storage. Heated repository.'

A steam-roller was being used to pull over dangerous ruined walls. As I watched, the façade of Blomfield's furniture shop came crashing down and brick rubble streamed across the roadway. Noticed that a lot of the roof of the Britannia [Engineering] Works had been burnt off.

Heard from several people that in all this vast holocaust, there was only one casualty – a poor old woman of 70 in Vineyard Street, who was actually struck by an incendiary bomb as she lay in bed and was very badly burnt.

The whole thing seems to have been caused by two or three canisters of incendiaries. So after hundreds of explosive bombs have been dropped on the town with very little effect, one 'plane drops sufficient firebombs to destroy two factories, a furniture store, part of an engineering works and about 30 shops and other premises.

[See Image 25]

February 24 Thursday

Demolitions have been going on all day at the ruins and we could often hear the roar of falling brickwork. Smoke still rises from several cellars and the firemen are still playing water on the timbers.

Huge red notices put up all over the town – USE WATER SPARINGLY. Apparently the whole of the available water was pumped onto the fire last night. They even ran pipes down to Bourne Pond. Everybody expected the petrol in St Botolph's Station yard to go up.

Felt dreadfully ill, with agonising pains in the face and head and bad stomach ache this evening.

February 27 Sunday

Notice that Mr Malcolm MacDonald, MP, has been speaking in Canada to the effect that the British have had the unspeakable joy of being bombed, which has so improved their character. How well this sounds when spoken in Canada, 3,000 miles from the nearest bomb-hole.

February 29 Tuesday

Had a coffee at the Milk Bar, packed with girls and Americans. Pleasant ride to Dedham in the dusk, a lot of young factory girls on the back seats singing and laughing, talking about 'dates' and parties.

March 2 Thursday

On the way up town, called in at Rose's Café and ordered a coffee. Only the waitress there. I said, 'Where's Miss Browne?' She replied, 'Didn't you know? She was married yesterday and she's at Torquay on her honeymoon.'

I walked out and left the coffee standing on the table. My sensations were terrible. My Rose should creep away and marry without even telling me. Spent the afternoon idling in the office, no willpower to do anything.

March 3 Friday

Yet another brilliant cold morning. Not the slightest sign of rain which we need so badly. Everybody anxious to get ahead with spring drilling soon. Can't be helped if the seed doesn't come up, it must be sown.

All day long we see platoons of recruits, wearing heavy boots, shorts and shirts, running down Military Road under the orders of physical training instructors. Some are young boys, loping along cheerfully, others are men of 40, bald and short of wind, struggling along in the rear. Today, a young man in one batch was very distressed and clung to the fence outside the office heaving and panting. One of the instructors grabbed him by the arm and said, 'Come on, run, quick now, run' and thrust him into the road but the wretched man could only stagger a few yards and then sat down on the pavement, his head in his hands. At last he got up from the curb stone and walked towards the barracks. He looked terribly humiliated.

Tea with Diana tonight, which made me feel better. Suddenly thought that even now I have no idea who she has married.

March 5 Sunday

Had a clean-up at the cottage. I am really very sorry to leave the place. Had it not been for the wretched light I should have had another month here.

March 7 Tuesday

Mrs Sisson phoned, asking me to call. Heard that an American officer had been there, claiming to be a descendant of General Sherman and had wanted to buy the house. When the offer was politely declined he said, 'Well, can I buy those candlesticks?' pointing to a pair on the shelf.

March 10 Friday

Cycled by Bromley Road to Colliers Wood Farm to see the Lyons about them having Bob. Very nice people and seemed keen to have him, so I agreed.

March 11 Saturday

Had a pleasant surprise today. Went to the Bank and found I had more money than I had thought. Makes me determined to go away to Wales.

March 14 Tuesday

About 10.30pm [heard] sirens and heavy gunfire. 'Planes came over very low and were back within an hour so apparently another raid on London. Felt terribly nervous, more so than usual and lay on the floor for a long time. Wish I were anywhere but here.

March 15 Wednesday

From the evening papers it is obvious that there was a very big raid last night, quite 200 or 300 'planes over and, as usual, very few brought down.

In the advertisement column of the same paper, saw a notice offering furnished room and attendance. Found this to be a Miss Bentley, at Woodside, Boxted, a house on the edge of Spratt's Marsh, about 1.5 miles from the aerodrome. This is rather closer than I should wish to be but I rang the number and arranged an interview. Must get somewhere within the next few days.

March 16 Thursday

Heavy bombers coming back about 7.30am and 'planes warming up at Langham. More going out all morning and news in the papers that 1,000 were over Europe last night. At the office heard that two bombs fell at Copt Hall, one within 10 feet of the stable where Robin was, but it failed to explode. The other made a huge crater two fields away.

Went out to Woodside, Boxted. Found a very charming lady, Miss Bentley. Agreed to go there for 30/- a week, starting Saturday. It is a nice house, about 50 years old, brick built, with a set of rather dilapidated buildings adjoining. Seems very comfortable and was offered a nice little room at the back.

March 18 Saturday

Enormous flight of 'planes began to go over [this evening] as I went into Boxted so I did not go into Woodside until they had all gone. Wish we were further from the aerodrome but it seems very pleasant. Miss Bentley got me a nice meal and I went to bed, very tired.

March 21 Tuesday

Big formations going over all day. Quite unable to concentrate on work and spent most of the day thinking about going away. Hinted to Father that I may be going this week. Intended to speak to Folkard but had no chance as he was out all day.

Cough very bad today, especially early this morning, when I literally coughed myself sick. Simply cannot go on like this much longer.

March 22 Wednesday

Heard guns during the night, about 2am I should think but blocked my ears and refused to listen. Apparently another big raid on London.

Am now quite determined to go. No chance to say anything to Folkard, as he was out again. Worked hard all day and got everything cleared up. Nobody at the office has the slightest idea what I intend to do. Dealt with everybody just as if I should be here tomorrow.

It has just been announced that a huge area of the coast is to be a restricted area from April 1, all the way from the Wash to Land's End and including Colchester, Ipswich and Chelmsford.

March 23 Thursday

Ran away.

[Rudsdale spent the next week in North Wales.]

April 2 Sunday

Back to Colchester for lunch at the old home. Got there late and had it alone with Father. He seemed pleased.

Feel worried about going to the office tomorrow. Don't know how I shall be received.

Back to the old routine now, of laying out boots, trousers near to hand, when going to bed and remembering where the matches have been put.

April 3 Monday

Folkard came at 10am and was very cold and distant, obviously furious at what I had done. Felt dreadfully ashamed at having upset him. Admitted freely that I was no longer up to my work and suggested that I should clear up all outstanding jobs and then leave. He agreed, with some show of reluctance. Shortly after he began to treat me quite normally and although he had at first ordered me not to attend the Committee today he changed his mind and said I had better get ready after all.

On the way to Birch, Folkard astounded and confused me by saying that he too had recently considered throwing up the work, being so depressed at the inanity of the whole thing. I did not know what to say. He went in ahead of me at Birch Hall to see the Chairman about this and in Committee the whole matter was thrashed out at great length. It is obvious that there is very bad feeling between Writtle and this District, particularly on labour matters. It was finally decided to form a special labour sub-committee, to deal with recalcitrant labour (I had the grace to feel guilty), with the Chairman at its head. The idea is that if men or girls absent themselves from work (we have an average of about 50 absentees every day) they will be ordered to appear before this sub-committee. It did not appear to occur to anyone that (a) such a sub-committee has no powers whatever to punish such cases, by stoppage of pay or other means and (b) that most girls would refuse to come before it in any case.

How the WAC work has changed since I began in 1941. Then we at least felt that we knew what we were doing, as the urgent need to grow food overrode everything else. Now we are beginning to think far more about money than food. The Ministry almost go into hysterics if farmer's accounts are unpaid and utter all manner of threats. Writtle send back officer's travelling claims on the slightest pretext and haggle over 1/6 for a bus fare. It cannot be wondered that everyone is becoming very depressed and dispirited. We heard today that the Land Commissioner is actually beginning to discuss whether such-and-such a farm is 'worth' farming, whether it would not be cheaper to let it go derelict again?

If the Government is taking this attitude already, what will it be like when the war is over? And, in view of such an attitude, can they really believe that the war is likely to last another 2 or 3 years?

April 4 Tuesday

Went to the Holly Trees. Poulter full of all sorts of news. He went up to the Royal Free Hospital last week and was given a clean bill regarding his health. Maclagan told him that a year ago he was not expected to recover.

April 5 Wednesday

Busy day, getting everything cleared up with the idea that I shall be going soon, although nothing more has been said.

There has been no raid for nearly a week.

April 11 Tuesday

Got to Boxted tonight and saw a light gleaming on a pole in Spratt's Marsh, then saw others, strung across the fields. I suppose this means night flying at Langham. What an infernal nuisance. No matter where I go, this sort of thing seems to follow me about. The wood was full of lorries and soldiers but whether American or English I don't know. Feel dreadfully nervous and only hope that the lights will be put out if there is an attack but I rather doubt it.

April 12 Wednesday

Telephoned Spivy at the Labour Exchange, to see if he can get me into the Royal Observer Corps (ROC). I feel I could work at one of the outposts.

April 13 Thursday

Went up town and met Hervey Benham. The old Alderman is breaking up now and will not be coming to the office any more. He has at last stopped writing his 'Colchester and County Notes' [for the *Essex County Standard*] after 60 years of it, all but a few months.

Felt exceptionally nervous as something seems to be going on in the district. All the Americans were restricted to their camps tonight, in fact all day, and large numbers left in lorries this morning. One of the girls at the office said she thought they were going to Maidstone. The town looked quite empty this evening, no Americans in the streets except a couple of police and no jeeps or lorries on the car parks.

April 14 Friday

More WLA troubles today. Four more girls walked off the threshing machine and came to the office to make a complaint about their ill treatment. They did not think it at all fair that they should be put on the threshing drum for 2 or 3 weeks at a stretch. The ringleader was a tall, dark girl. She did all the talking so that Capt Folkard, who was supposed to be reprimanding them, could scarcely get a word in edgeways. She told us that she had her rights and that [Foreman] Cutting had spoken rudely to her – he told her to clear out if she didn't want to do the work [and had] suggested that girls only joined the WLA so as to get out of munitions or the ATS. Capt Folkard simply told them to clear off back to Wigborough and get on with their work. These girls are as foreign to Cutting and Baldwin as if they were Chinese.

A few Americans about today and in the streets tonight saw a negro policeman. He had a truncheon but no revolver such as the white police carry. Also saw two RAF police, the first I have seen in Colchester.

April 15 Saturday

Folkard was at Writtle yesterday and spoke very pessimistically today of what is happening up there. They are interested in 'paper' results only. Nothing matters, crops, efficiency, amount of work done, so long as regular returns are sent in. Very depressing.

April 19 Wednesday

Telephone from ROC this morning, for me to see one of the officers, Claydon. Went up there. The whole place was very much in the RAF tradition. Endless girls rushing about, all in ROC uniforms, obviously enjoying every minute of it. Claydon was very pleasant and gave me numerous forms to complete and sign and made me swear to secrecy. Suddenly felt very dreary about the whole affair and know I can't possibly make a success of it.

April 20 Thursday

Felt oddly nervous tonight so went off to wander about as long as I could. 'Planes were going over in hundreds but as there was no firing I suppose they were RAF. The noise was terrible. Wandered about the Plantation, listening to the nightingales, which were singing clear and sweet it seemed on almost every tree. Sat on a stile and listened for half an hour. Far away in Suffolk heard an alarm and the signal lights flickered madly. Had a vague idea of spending the night in the wood and lay in a ditch full of dry leaves for some time until at last cold drove me into the house, at nearly 3 in the morning. So tired I fell asleep almost at once.

April 21 Friday

Papers full of the London bus strike and the gas-works strikes at Manchester. The Government have sent Army lorries into London and everybody thinks it's a fine joke.

This morning heard the first cuckoos calling in the Plantation. The radio says enemy activity over the East Coast during the night but apparently they were mostly reconnaissance 'planes looking for invasion stuff and not much damage was done.

Folkard told me in the course of conversation today that even now, under war conditions, it would be impossible for a farmer to make a living off one of the Committee's heavy-land farms, if he farmed it properly. That is, if he grew a good acreage of wheat, he would lose on it at present prices, and if he grew fodder crops on the rest of his land to fatten cattle, he would find it impossible to make a profit out of them either.

April 22 Saturday

Called at Collier's Wood to see old Bob, who looks fine, twice the horse he was at Clayton's. A cart horse had just pushed him into a deep ditch and he was wet through and very bad tempered.

April 23 Sunday

Noise of aircraft ear-splitting. Papers full of 'invasion' alarms and back at the old business: 'What will the Germans do next?'

Great activity on the aerodrome, piles of bombs everywhere, 'planes landing, 'planes taking off, 'planes taxiing up to the butt and testing their guns with a stuttering roar. Behind the butt is a great pit dug to provide material for it, which has now become full of water and two airmen were sailing on it in a rubber boat out of one of the 'planes. There were people standing all along the hedges in the lane, watching each 'plane soar away with its bomb hanging beneath it.

April 24 Monday

Tea at Last's. Hervey Benham came in full of gloom. Says the 'next 10 days' is the time and obviously anticipates a tremendous disaster. As we were talking, little Last came up and said, 'For your information, gentlemen, the sirens are now sounding, so if you would like to go down into the cellar and finish your tea there …' We both laughed and Last laughed. He went on to speak of the early days of the war, when all alarms were announced very loudly and several people did used to go downstairs. Apparently these cellar-trips were stopped because the waitresses refused to serve some of the younger men there.

April 25 Tuesday

Press getting more and more alarming about invasions and seems unable to make up its mind who is going to invade who. The Home Guard are expected to be called out at any moment.

Folkard is to go to Writtle tomorrow to interview a man called Maidstone, from Sussex, who is to be 'Deputy District Officer', a new appointment. Feel that he will more or less supersede me, so I might as well go at any time.

April 29 Saturday

These wretched American 'planes begin to fly over as soon as it is light, making sleep quite impossible. How many more years must this go on?

There seems to be a sort of wave of optimism going through people now. All big towns are absolutely packed with folks who have returned from the country, yet frightful and devastating air raids are a certainty unless the war is stopped within the next few months.

April 30 Sunday

Lovely warm summer day. The Boxted orchards are a wonderful sight, a mass of blossom.

Went to Sisson's. Major Inde called and a Sergeant Merrill of the US Army, whom Sisson had met in the 'Sun'. The Sergeant was particularly keen to discuss amusements for what he called 'the masses' and thought that the very apex of civilisation was a radio in every room and an 'ice-box'. Told him I have never owned a car, never lived in a house with electric light and should not have cared if the radio had never been invented.

May 5 Friday

Can't understand why I have heard nothing from the Royal Observer Corps. It is now a week since I sent in the papers.

At lunch, everybody at my table was complaining about the behaviour of the Americans and longing for the day when they will at last go. Several people mentioned that most of the British Army vehicles have now been painted over with the American star.

May 7 Sunday

Saw a big American convoy sweeping along the By-Pass this evening, while a dour looking man stood on the pavement holding a banner inscribed 'Prepare to Meet Thy God'.

May 9 Tuesday

'Planes going out in hundreds but still no sign of a major attack. Heard this morning that the cook at the Layer Marney Hostel was murdered by an American near Heynes Green on Friday night. He had been out with Americans all evening and had then gone off alone with this one. Something went wrong, there was a quarrel and the American strangled him after a terrific fight. He has since been arrested.

Great-to-do this morning because one of the Land Girls has been discovered canvassing for the Transport and General Workers Union among the other girls. Capt Folkard and Mrs Allen were in a great way, Mrs Allen wanting to send a report to Writtle at once, to ask for the girl's dismissal. Capt Folkard very wisely thought that perhaps this would not be very well received by socialist-inclined men at Writtle and suggested that she confined herself to speaking to the girl instead.

Had tea with Hervey Benham. He is now of the opinion that an invasion of the Continent has been postponed indefinitely on the advice of General Montgomery and was very despondent. He says that the rumour is that if there is a great public outcry because there is no invasion the blame is to be thrown on the miners and they will be blackguarded as 'Trotskyists', 'defeatists' and 'quislings'.

Afterwards Hervey took me in to see the Ballet Rambert. This is the first time I have ever seen ballet danced and I enjoyed it immensely in spite of the limitations of the very small stage at the Albert Hall and the fact that the music was provided by two pianos only. There were no seats but I stood throughout the whole performance. They danced the classic 'Les Sylphides' just as I have always imagined it would be done. Madame Marie Rambert came in and stood alongside me for a few minutes. She is quite tiny, with fine features and a beautiful long black skirt, about 35 I should think. Robert Digby [the theatre manager] says she works her company very hard.

May 11 Thursday

Saw Father. He has not been very well lately and has had heart pains. Saw Dr Rowland tonight who confirms that this is serious and may carry him off at any time. He gave me some tablets for him, to stop the pain when it comes. Poor old Dad. It is terrible for old people to suffer.

May 13 Saturday

Poulter telephoned to say that Gurney Benham had died last night. This is the end of the great days of the Colchester Museum. He worked literally to the very end and actually presided at a Board Meeting of the Gas Company a few hours before his death.

He was born in 1859 when men wore 'stove-pipe' hats and increased trousers, women the widest of crinoline skirts and the streets, still cobbled, had no perambulators or bicycles in them, yet he lived until today, when the stench of petrol and the roar of engines is inescapable.

He was always very kind to me during the 17 years that I knew him and it was through him that I was first appointed to the Museum. In all he served on that Committee continuously for 43 years and was Chairman of it for 25 years. An incredible record.

May 16 Tuesday

Met Frank Warren to go to Ipswich. It was a pleasure to me to see the place again, as I had not been for so long. The markets were crowded for the fair, over 900 cattle in Bond's pens and a fine lot of horses in Spurling and Hempson's. The horses made good prices, especially cobs. A decent bay cob, said to be 6, a good set of harness and a London built trolley came to 100gns. An old cob, with very awkward action, only warranted 'sound on day of sale', started at 40gns and went up to 50gns.

Saw the cattle which Frank Warren had bought for the Committee. One lot were a nice bunch of Hereford steers, the others shorthorns and polled. Raining hard by now and the market seemed dirty and depressing. I have come to feel more and more the brutality of these markets – the pushing, jostling cattle in the narrow pens, the bellowing of the animals crushed against the rails, the crashes as they fall on the slippery concrete, the shrieks and yells of the drover boys and the ceaseless thud of their sticks on skulls, rumps and fetlocks. It is all so unnecessary and could be done with a quarter of the suffering if only the auctioneers took a little interest in anything besides the actual selling of the beasts.

May 19 Friday

This afternoon, looking out of the office window, saw two little boys pushing an aeroplane petrol tank on a perambulator. They took it up into the yard, sawed it into two halves, thus providing themselves with two little canoes. These they then balanced on their shoulders, for all the world like little coracle men and set off in the direction of Bourne Pond.

May 20 Saturday

Called at Seymour's and found Jeffrey Saunders there, just back from Russia, where he has been in Murmansk for 6 months. Hates the Russians and the Soviet system. Says the whole population are starving.

Papers today are full of the shooting of 47 RAF men who escaped with 30 others from a prison camp. [Great indignaton being worked up [about] 'reprisals after the war'.

May 21 Sunday

Sunday papers full of an account of a vision of 'Christ in Glory' seen at Ipswich last month. Nobody seems to know whether this portends the Second Coming or the Second Front.

May 22 Monday

Labour Sub-Committee this afternoon in the office. The Chairman presided and had several Land Girls up before him for striking and being absent without leave. One girl said, 'You don't know anything about farm work, you know.' The old gentleman was too flabbergasted to make any reply. Three other girls came dressed in their ordinary clothes and it was discovered that as they had been told to be at the Colchester office at 2.30pm they had taken the whole day off from work to get ready. One girl never came at all.

May 23 Tuesday

Several hundred 'planes went out between 2am and 7am. Heard on radio that there had been very heavy raids on France and Germany and raids over here last night on the south and east coasts.

Called to see Poulter. He told me that there had been an amusing set-to about the 'secret' place at the North-East Postern. Duncan Clark had brought up the matter of repairs to the Roman Gate fabric and Poulter told him that nothing could be done there owing to the existence of the 'secret chamber'. Duncan Clark calmly brings this forward in the Museum Committee today and after much enquiry found an officer in the garrison who knew about it. He, poor man, is now shaken to the roots to find that his 'secret' is known to dozens of people and is, in fact, no secret at all. Apparently the real purpose of the place is as a store of explosives, to be used by 'saboteurs' after Colchester had been occupied by the Germans. The Army were going to leave some picked men behind to do this work. The fact that each subsequent explosion would result in the summary execution of several of the inhabitants of the town would worry no one (except the persons executed).

Noticed that most of the guns seem to have gone, only a few left on the Abbey Field and the battery in Severalls Lane has gone.

May 29 Monday

To Little Rivers and heard that an American 'plane had crashed today near Kersey's Farm [Boxted], and had burnt out. The crew of 7 came down safely by parachutes. The explosion and fire was tremendous.

May 30 Tuesday

Observer Corps phoned today and told me to report to Horkesley on Thursday.

Heard this about the Americans – There's three things wrong with them, they're over paid, over sexed and over here.

June 1 Thursday

Cycled over to the Observer Post at Boxted to report there. The Post is on the road from Boxted to Horkesley Causeway, not far from Kersey's Farm. It is a small brick-built platform, about 4ft from the ground, surrounded by a brick parapet about 5ft high. On the west side is a roofed extension, making a tiny room not more than 8ft by 3ft, with a fireplace, an old desk, the seat out of a motor bus, two rifles, some shelves holding boxes of ammunition and official books, a noticeboard with a rota and the 'Post procedure' and notices about rations and clothing coupons.

In the centre of the Post is the 'instrument' and the plotting table, marked off in numbered squares. The instrument is a curious thing of brass, showing heights in hundreds of feet, fitted with a sighting piece and various adjusting screws.

The place had something of the appearance of a block-house on some remote frontier, the short drain-pipe chimney smoking and the telephone wires on little makeshift poles running away towards civilisation.

Had to explain my presence, as the Centre had quite forgotten to tell anybody I was coming. However, I made myself known to the men on duty, one of whom was Minter, Alec Page's tractor driver. They were very kind and explained the whole business very lucidly, although I had not been there five minutes before I realised that I was quite out of my depth. I had no idea how much depended on the ability of the individual Observer, as I had always believed there was some sort of instrument which automatically located enemy aircraft and registered their height. On the contrary, all this has to be done by the Observer himself, and I have not the slightest idea how high a 'plane may be.

However, I stayed an hour and heard them plotting a good many 'planes. This Post is 'F1', spoken as 'Fox One' (just as 'C' posts are 'Charlie', 'E' posts 'Easy' etc.) The three 'Foxes' are linked together and can hear each other speaking. 'Fox 2' is near Earls Colne and can see the aerodromes at Colne and Wormingford, while 'Fox 3' is south of Sudbury and reports Acton aerodrome, where the Flying Fortresses are stationed.

While I was there an American soldier was in the Post. He was supposed to be guarding the wreck of the 'plane which crashed near Kerseys on Whit Monday but seemed to spend most of his time talking to the Observers. Most of the talk was about baseball and football. Then they started talking about the big raids of 1940 and said that on many occasions they plotted as many as 600 'planes coming in. This was never admitted at the time. 'And never a shot fired at them.'

June 4 Sunday

To Horkesley at 5, to the Post. Found 'Ginger' Pawsey in charge. Haven't seen him since I was at school. Many 'planes going out and spent a very uncomfortable 4 hours. Heard Pawsey say that an American officer had told him that the invasion of the Continent begins at 12 tonight. It is alleged to have been postponed from last night. Apparently a lot of American officers have been talking about this during the weekend. Heard the midnight news – the Allies are entering Rome. No mention of any damage.

The 'plane wreck at Kersey's, having been guarded for a week, was buried by RAF men today.

June 5 Monday

The new Assistant District Officer came – Maidstone. Seems quite a decent chap, about 30.

Saw Stuart Rose and he told me that on Saturday afternoon the road between Wormingford and Fordham running through the aerodrome was closed by the Americans. They suddenly erected barriers at about 5.30pm, shutting in about 200 people, labourers, canteen girls and stray passers-by. Soon after lunch, Hugh Gray phoned from Fordham to say the same thing and told us that no milk could be got out from the farms. I tried to phone the aerodrome but all the phones were dead and could get no reply at all. Must be something very big in the wind, perhaps what Pawsey was saying last night.

June 6 Tuesday

About 2am heard the sound of many 'planes warming up at Wormingford but soon went to sleep. Woke soon after 3 to a tremendous roar and looked out to see the whole sky filled with 'planes, all carrying their navigation lights, dropping red and green flares in every direction. Just before 4 the [Langham]-Boxted aerodrome lights came on and all the Thunderbolts took off in pairs in a series of shattering roars, coming up over the house and flashing away to the south-west. The sky was just a mass of gleaming lights of all colours and the house trembled with the vibration of thousands of engines. Have never known the Americans to take off before dawn, so guessed this must be something big and was not surprised to hear on the 8 o'clock news that there had been heavy raids on Calais and Dunkirk and that British naval forces were off Le Havre, while the Germans had announced that landings were being attempted both by sea and air.

And so comes what we were promised was to be the great climax of the whole war, when the great Allied armies are to storm 'Hitler's fortress' and 'liberate starving Europe'. But where is the excitement we were promised? And the hardships? We were told that on 'D-Day' every road would be shut, all trains stopped, no buses and everybody living under siege conditions. Yet all is just as it was yesterday – buses running, trains running, soldiers marching out to training, little children going to school. At the office, hardly a mention of this great final battle, except to remark on the noise of 'planes during the night and say wisely, 'Ah! As soon as I heard them, I knew it was the invasion.'

At lunch, people were almost quiet when the news came on though, for once. One girl looked pale and worried and her hands shook. Perhaps she has a friend or a brother out there. Troops are landing near Caen and Bayeux.

In the midst of all this a great row boiled up with Writtle, about our Labour Officer, Mrs Allen. Engledow came from Writtle to say he had decided, for no particular reason, to dismiss her. Folkard was livid and there was a blazing row. Mrs Allen was terribly upset and wept all over the place. This sort of thing is absolutely intolerable. The Chairman is taking up the matter very strongly.

Went out to Horkesley at 6pm, to see the sugar beet competition. There was a good show in a field at Potter's Farm belonging to Alec Page. Twelve Borough Police came in two police cars, with Chief Inspector Clear and another inspector. In spite of threatened retaliation raids from the Germans, they apparently felt justified in leaving Colchester. Only 5 Land Girls came, although 30 had been told to report, and only 1 man from the Committee labour, so that he had a special lorry to bring him all by himself.

Work began at 7 and went very well while bombers and Thunderbolts roared overhead on their way to Normandy. When it was all over we went into the farmhouse and had beer and whisky, after which the Chairman gave the prizes and made a rousing speech, all about what a great day this was, etc.

Went along to the Post at 9, for another 4 hours training. Am doing very badly. Wondered if there was likely to be a raid tonight. The weather got worse but still 'planes came back from France and the aerodrome lights were on.

Heard the King's speech on the radio. He seemed very tense and harsh. News at midnight said that Rome was quite safe, so we have something to be thankful for.

June 7 Wednesday

More row about Mrs Allen today. The WLA supervisors came in and told Capt Folkard that they would stand by her and would resign if she were dismissed. Nott said the WLA girls are terribly depressed about the invasion and feel that now there will be a great disaster in which their brothers and husbands will be killed. A rather different attitude from that we were told to expect at this great climax. Radio news today rather vague.

June 8 Thursday

News of the invasion not very good and a faint rumour spreading that something has gone wrong. Papers full of glowing accounts of the wonderful treatment given to the wounded – nothing else. Cloud coming up again and rain beginning as I went to Boxted. Conditions must be terrible in Normandy.

June 11 Sunday

Cycled to Lawford this afternoon. Commander Richardson was there to tea and was talking about the precautions taken at Harwich before the invasion began. No men were allowed ashore on any pretext whatever and, when a case of appendicitis occurred on one ship, the man was sent to hospital ashore under armed guard.

June 16 Friday

Two alarms during the night, one about 4am and the other after 6am. Most unusual to have one so late. During the first, heard what seemed to be the scream of a falling 'plane and a heavy thud. When I got to the office, Capt Folkard told me that this was one of the long-expected 'rocket 'planes', sent over from France and that it crashed in a field near Baker's Hall, Bures, passing over Fordham.

All talk at lunch about the 'rocket'. Everybody seemed to have heard it and to know all the details. Now rumoured that these things have been coming over for about three days.

If these new 'planes really work it means that the Germans will be able to launch heavy attacks on England no matter what the weather and without risking a single man. What will happen to us in the winter? Perhaps the Allies will have occupied all France by then. It is not clear at the moment whether these things are controlled by radio or whether they are simply directed on a set course. At night they show a brilliant orange flame, which ought to make them easy to shoot down.

[Went to Writtle for a Committee Secretaries Meeting.] Sadler gave a most extraordinary résumé of the Minister's talk to Chairmen of Advisory Committees last week. He spoke of the plans now proposed for the next four years and stated that further plans to cover up to 1954 were under consideration. Was ever such nonsense talked? Felt more and more gloomy. If they imagine that I'm staying in this wretched job for another 10 years they are sadly mistaken.

According to Sadler, the Minister has announced that the whole future of British farming lies in – wheat! Providing that the British farmer can produce wheat at 12/- per hundredweight, there is no reason why we should not compete in the world market. Mr Hudson has been assured by 'leading farmers' that wheat can be produced at this price. As for cattle, the Minister sees no hope whatever. Milk – even worse prospects, as we shall find it much cheaper to get all our milk dried in tins from America. As regards beef, we simply cannot hope to compete with the Argentine. Do these fools ever stop to think what their words mean?

At last got away. Back in Chelmsford there were news placards out – 'Rocket 'Planes over Southern England'.

The Government have announced that all steps are being taken to prevent information being given as to where these things fall, in order to confuse the enemy. This will, no doubt, cause a certain amount of confusion among the English as well but that, of course, is of small moment.

Heard the 9 o'clock news, with a special announcement about these 'rockets'. Very alarming. We seem to be in considerable danger and it is hinted that 'serious' damage and casualties are being caused.

June 18 Sunday

Miss Bentley telephoned to her sister at Brighton, to ask how she was and was told that 'rocket 'planes' were coming in day and night. The press is full of descriptions of these bombs, saying how difficult it is to shoot them down. They have apparently decided to call them 'flying bombs'. Everybody round here busy looking up their atlases and being alarmed to find that Calais is nearer to Colchester than it is to London.

[The V1 flying bombs became more generally known as 'doodlebugs' or 'buzz bombs'. However, Rudsdale mostly refers to them as 'divers', the term used by the Royal Observer Corps.]

June 19 Monday

Maidstone came back from Chessington this morning, very worried. Says conditions in South London are terrible, a flying bomb coming in every 15 minutes day and night. The damage and casualties are enormous. Maidstone says he saw men playing cricket wearing steel helmets. So far there have been no bombs in the City or in North London. Mrs Maidstone is due to have a baby in October and he is very anxious to get her away from Chessington.

June 21 Wednesday

Heard that a flying bomb fell at Frinton last night and this morning there was one at Freston, near Ipswich.

Maidstone had news this morning that his home at Chessington has been badly damaged so that he must get his wife away at once. He went off this morning to attend to things.

As I passed the station tonight saw crowds of business men coming off the London train, several carrying steel helmets.

June 24 Saturday

Two books displayed in Poyser's [bookshop] window have the following titles:
'Get to know the Americans'
'Self-defence for Women and Girls'

Evening papers say heavy attacks have been made on the Pas de Calais area but there is no slackening of the attacks by the flying bombs. The papers are full of obituaries, 'due to enemy action'. Extraordinary that at a time like this the Allies still think it worth while to make futile attacks on Berlin. Some say that it is done only to stimulate the Londoners' morale.

June 28 Wednesday

Took little Daphne to see [the film] 'Jane Eyre', very well done indeed. In the news-film a flying bomb was shown. The people laughed and hissed.

June 29 Thursday

Wakened by sirens at 5am. Went to the window, heard a diver for a moment before it cut out, then a tremendous crash accompanied by a blast of air. Thought it must be about Mile End but heard later that it fell near Baker's Lane [Braiswick].

To the Post tonight. Lovely evening, with high light clouds and a few 'planes about, circling for height, looking like little tadpoles swimming in a bowl. As the sun sank there were great bars of golden light to the west and dark clouds piled up like endless mountain ranges.

Did very badly this evening, not a thing right but enjoyed myself watching a lark hovering above the Post. Very quiet evening. Studied every detail of the Stour Valley through the glasses – Stoke Church, majestic on the horizon, rising from the green woods by Tendring Hall, the village roofs, brown or grey, Nayland Church below, a green bus moving slowly along the road into the village. The hills behind, dotted with little farms and, in the foreground, flat, dark green water meadows, with cattle and horses, the river a black streak among reeded banks and, nearer still waving corn, oats and barley, coming right up to the Post itself. On the Boxted side, some of Mr Page's men were still at work, hoeing sugar-beet behind Holly Lodge.

The other man on with me was a middle-aged fellow called New. He is an 'A' class man [a full-time Observer] and gets paid 1/10 an hour. He was quite pleasant but seemed very reluctant to let me have the phones at all, not without good cause.

June 30 Friday

Went to the Food Office this morning and had not been inside two minutes when the sirens sounded. Immediately all the little girls began calling 'Sirens, Mr Newbourne!' 'Sirens, Mr Potter!' and these two gentlemen started to shepherd their little flocks down into the basement. Have never seen anything like this done since the days of 1940 but there were no divers and no explosions.

July 1 Saturday

Felt very nervous all day with the ever-present danger of flying bombs. Maidstone said that he tried to telephone friends in London last night but was told that there was no chance whatever of getting through. Nobody knows what is happening up there.

Listening to dance music on the radio from Hammersmith Palais de Danse tonight and heard the wail of sirens in London coming over the air – quite uncanny. Set off for the Post soon after midnight.

July 2 Sunday

Cycled slowly so as not to get to the Post too early. Suddenly saw, in the gloom, what appeared to be a man hanging from a tree. It was so real that I was quite convinced it was a suicide and approached cautiously to touch his feet, only to find they were made of wood. It was a wooden figure put up to draw attention to Boxted 'Salute the Soldier' week. As more money is contributed, the man is hauled up higher.

It was a long four hours. No divers came our way, though they were constantly coming in over Kent and we could hear some of the girls at the Centre, who were looking at the long distance board, saying 'Coo! Look at that!' 'Poor old Bromley' 'There's another – north of Maidstone!' A lot of 'planes came in between 2am and 3am, perhaps from bombing around Calais.

July 5 Wednesday

Cycled out to the Post. Old Diaper was on tonight. Nothing much about but about 10pm some Thunderbolts took off from Langham and came right over us. As they passed over Holly Lodge, one dropped its extra petrol tank, which fell just like a bomb, bursting in a great cloud of petrol vapour. We reported this and very soon the police sent a constable round to see if there was any damage. He came along to the Post afterwards just in time to get a cup of tea.

July 8 Saturday

Lots of Americans going past the house on cycles on their way from the aerodrome to the pubs at Gt Horkesley. Most pubs can now only open on alternate days owing to the shortage of beer. A lot of the big breweries are in the London area and have been damaged by the divers.

July 10 Monday

Three alarms during the night. Maidstone says that three divers went past Layer Marney, towards Tiptree, apparently coming from the east. Can't understand this, as it would mean that they were being launched from the Belgian coast or even from Holland rather than the Pas de Calais. Should not have thought that they would be able to send them so far. Of course, the Government don't admit that there are launching places anywhere except the Calais area but probably there are many others besides this.

July 11 Tuesday

Got to the Post at 9pm, young John Page on with me. Heard on the phones that they had 67 [divers] over Kent this afternoon and that 27 had been brought down short of London. A lot of chattering on the phones tonight, girls at Centre making arrangements for pictures and dancing. A quiet watch and young Page and I talked about religion and ghosts most of the time.

July 12 Wednesday

Went to Peldon on my cycle to see the new cattle. We brought up some heifers and steers to the yards, where they were sorted for the markets on Friday and Saturday. It was great fun, everybody shouting, yelling, waving sticks and generally behaving like small boys at a cattle market. Enjoyed myself immensely.

   Then I went on to Copt Hall, found some Land Girls and took them down to the lower marshes to bring up all the bullocks. These girls are all from Durham and have only been here a week. None of them had ever seen cattle except out of a train window, yet they made no bones about driving them. I asked one how she liked them and she said, 'They're alright, but they're bigger than I thought.' Two of the girls said they would like to be trained to look after the stock but I did not tell them they have little chance here of being trained to do anything.

July 13 Thursday

The papers tonight are now alleging that the bombs are being sent over from Holland and Belgium. Seems hardly possible, as there is nearly 100 miles of sea to cross.

July 17 Monday

Had a letter from Mary Tovell, to say they are having a terrible time at Erith, hospital very busy. Poor little Mary.

Feel tired tonight but have to be at the Post again at 1am.

July 18 Tuesday

When we got in they said there had been no divers for 16 hours, said to be the longest break since the things started over a month ago. However, there was an alarm at 2.15am and in a few minutes we could hear that there were 16 on the board at one time. Only three of these were brought down. Alarm lasted about an hour and, when divers at last went off, I was so tired I fell asleep sitting in the corner of the Post, only waking when the relief cycled into the yard at 5 o'clock. Home and slept until 9am. Office, 9.45am, could see Capt Folkard was furious but really there was nothing I could do about it.

Fine, hot and sunny. A shame to be indoors. We all of us ought to be out in the harvest fields – oats have begun to be cut.

July 20 Thursday

Happened to look out about 11am and saw the road quite full of horses and carts and not a car in sight. Saw a company of soldiers march up towards the barracks, in full kit, streaming with sweat and was much amused to see half a dozen more jump off a bus, on which they had ridden up from the ranges and form up with the rest before marching into barracks.

July 23 Sunday

Got to the Post before 1am. A few minutes later a huge mass of bombers came in, back from a raid. After the 'planes had gone all was quiet for more than 3 hours, hardly a thing about. Centre shut off and went to supper. We had our tea and sandwiches and old Diaper (who was on with me) had just gone out to wash up. I had the phones on, when suddenly Centre came through to say that 2 divers were crossing the coast at Bradwell. The controller said: 'Fox One and Two, you may be able to see them. They're going west.' I called Diaper and we looked through the glasses and saw two little golden balls, far away to the south as if they were crawling along the ground. Suddenly heard a voice at Centre say: 'My God, look! There's another one there, heading straight at us!' And another voice said: 'No, it's turning – it's over Jig 3 now, more towards Horkesley.' Then a third voice: 'That's the one that came in over Walton.' A pause, then the first voice called: 'Look out! Fox One! There's a diver coming up to the east of you!' I said: 'OK, Centre.'

Looked east and saw a big light, like a comet, leap over a tree apparently half a mile away, I said into the phones: 'Christ, here it comes, Centre, south of the Post, on 47, about 500 feet, going west.' It sailed by us, slightly south-west now, with a steady glow and a deep low roar, which seemed to follow some little way behind the light. I logged it across our circle. It did not seem to be moving very fast, in fact dear old Diaper remarked: 'That don't seem to move no quicker'n a fast trot,' and passed out of sight towards Fordham.

I stood on the coping of the Post, with a slight feeling of bewilderment and a sort of wonder that we were still all there.

Our relief arrived, full of excitement about the 'doodle bug' – 'Went right over ours', he said. 'My wife said: "There's a doodle-bug!" and there that was!' Heard no explosion but Centre said it had crashed about 35 miles away, somewhere in the direction of Brentwood. Although it sailed right over Langham and Wormingford aerodromes, not a shot was fired at it. Perhaps the Americans were too surprised to move.

'All clear' went as I cycled back to Woodside. Bed at 5.30am, very thoughtful about this latest development. The thing must have been sent from somewhere near the Hague. Feel that we are facing the worst winter of the whole war and that by Christmas life here will be intolerable.

July 24 Monday

Several people in the café talking about the divers all cursing the Germans for using such a 'wicked thing'. There is now guarded talk going around about another sort of rocket, very much larger, which is shot up into the stratosphere to a height of 70 miles. Who dare say whether or not some mad scientist may not have invented such a thing?

July 28 Friday

Felt very depressed this evening and decided I could not bear to go to bed, so collected my blankets and crept out to the ditch by the edge of the wood. Lay for some time thinking of the idiotic insanity of my life, then dozed off peacefully, listening to heavy drops of rain falling on the trees and things rustling in the leaves. Woke suddenly and a few minutes later the sirens sounded and there was the distant hum of a diver. A bunch of searchlights flashed up and there it was, a glowing ball, chased by bursts of AA fire. It grew larger and louder and the gunfire came nearer. It passed over, well towards the west. The sound gradually died away and a few moments later a dull boom came drifting down from some spot in Suffolk.

Curled up again. Could not sleep and watched the sky go pale and the stars fade. Heard Mile End Church strike 5am and the jays began to shriek in the wood.

August 2 Wednesday

A fair going on in the Holly Trees grounds. Mechanical music screaming out behind the house but not a soul dancing on the lawn. A tall, striking looking girl walking across the street, very fair, thick wavy hair, dressed in long green slacks. She walked slowly into the Park ignoring the squeaks and yelps of American soldiers. American baseball match in the Lower Park, with much shouting, arms raised, the batsman slogging left-handed.

Midnight news quite cheerful – war seems to be moving on faster.

August 5 Saturday

To Post before 1am, feeling dreadful. Could hardly move. Great pain everywhere. Found it very hard to carry on for 4 hours with pain and sickness. Never so glad to see the dawn and thankful to crawl into bed at 5.30am. Slept like a log until 3pm!

August 8 Tuesday

At office found a very alarming letter from Mary Tovell, to say she is threatened with tuberculosis, no doubt brought about by the conditions under which she had to work at Erith Hospital during the heavy raids. Sounds very bad.

Felt very depressed tonight, longing to get away from Colchester. Feel I must give up the Observer Corps work, as I am genuinely so bad at it. At first, it did not seem to matter very much but recently I have become conscious that the other men resent my inefficiency. Also, am becoming quite worn out with the continual duties, although so often I prefer to be out of doors rather than in.

August 9 Wednesday

Curious that there has been no alarm today. Evening papers say that nobody was killed by flying bombs last night for the first time for weeks.

Bed at 11pm, determined to get sleep somehow. What a curious life this is – the night watches make some days seem as if they were really two. Cannot keep on any longer and have today written to Centre suggesting my resignation on grounds of ill health – cannot bring myself to claim utter incompetence.

August 10 Thursday

Walked through the Park this evening. Some sort of concert going on at the bandstand, by local children, something to do with these 'Holidays at Home' affairs. From the Castle Ramparts one could hear the shrill voices squeaking 'When Shall I Have a Banana Again?' followed by frenzied clapping by friends and relations.

The sun was westering, sending a great beam of warm orange light into the north wall of the Castle and across the grass beneath the trees, while the east wall was dark in cool shadow and there was a dark green cavern under the elm trees.

Miss Bentley's sister came from Brighton today, prohibited area not withstanding, as things are so bad there. Not much damage but too nerve wracking for her to continue.

August 11 Friday

Evening paper headlines – 'Americans Fifty Miles from Paris'. But no sign of divers slackening.

To the Post at 9. Heard over the phones that 36 divers were destroyed today.

August 12 Saturday

Wakened by another alarm at 7am, followed by a tremendous explosion, shaking the windows.

This evening went to Higham [and called at Henry] Rushbury's [the artist's home]. Mrs Rushbury said that a scientist told her that the Government was working day and night on plans to 'sink' Japan by means of an artificial earthquake. They think that as Japan is in an area prone to earthquakes, if they can create a big enough explosion, it might start an earth movement which would destroy a large part of the country. Said this seemed utter madness but she assured me that she knew it to be a scientific possibility. Apparently no thought is given for the countless non-combatants in the country, nor the many thousands of our own men who are prisoners, by those who have conceived this incredible and wicked scheme.

August 15 Tuesday

Most of the morning spent in rows – first Downes, the threshing engine driver who struck for more pay and got it. Then Nott came in and was very unpleasant about two new WLA girls sent down yesterday. I had told them to get a lift in Baldwin's van but Nott had made them walk to the hostel carrying their kit. Came very near to losing my temper over this. He does everything he can to upset the workers.

At lunch heard on the radio that new landings had been made on the South of France. Normandy news rather depressing as the Germans appear to be withdrawing their men and material successfully. Rumours of rockets weighing 90 tons are steadily circulating and we are almost beginning to believe that some have landed in Essex.

Most of the corn is now carted at Boxted, each holding making its little stack. Chicken huts have been moved out into the stubbles and the hens were industriously gleaning.

August 16 Wednesday

Went down to St Botolph's Corner, where a deep trench has been dug across the street. From the hole came a small urn of black polished ware with a double band of rouletting on the body, 6 inches high. It is quite complete except for a small piece out of the base. There were a few other Roman sherds but nothing else.

Just as I was paying the finder of the pot 2/6, there was an alarm and at once we heard the chugging of a bomb. In an instant it came into sight rattling along under the clear blue sky. We had a fine view of the thing, with its short little wings, plump body and the curious tail erection with a red exhaust flame spurting behind.

As we gazed open mouthed it disappeared out of sight to the north and for a few seconds more we heard the motor, then sudden silence and a low rumbling bang. 'Christ!' said the workman, in tones of the greatest astonishment, 'That's down!' And pocketing the half-crown he hurried off saying 'Must see to my missus.'

August 21 Monday

Left at 10pm, a dark, wet, windy night. Felt strangely confident and looked forward eagerly to a night at the Post. Heard the midnight news – Americans are across the Seine.

Young Carter was on with me and we spent the dark wet hours telling stories of ghosts and witchcraft. Diver warnings on and off all night but nothing came on our side of the Thames.

August 22 Tuesday

In the papers, Montgomery says 'The end is in sight'. We wonder and turn the page, to read that Churchill (in Italy) says 'No sign of the end yet'. How helpful are our leaders. What confidence we have in them.

August 23 Wednesday

At Northgate [this morning] noticed a small excavation on the pavement, on the east side of the street and, looking into it, as is always my habit, was amazed to see the side and curved front of the Roman Gate itself, the masonry lying just under the paving slabs. It was an Electric Light job and, fortunately, Jones was there, whom I know well, so I at once told him how important the find was.

Rushed to the office and saw Folkard the moment he came in. Told him what had happened, begged an hour off, which he most generously gave, although with a good show of grumbling, to keep me and archaeology in our proper places.

Then back to Northgate and began a quick plan and sketch. Gate is obviously of the same type as the North-East Postern, with rounded outer angles and a simple return with a recess in which the leaf of the gate itself was hung. Of course, there was probably a central pier and even perhaps an arched footway on the west side of the street, similar to the Newport Gate at Lincoln.

Rang the Holly Trees but no sign of Hull. Poulter unwilling to take any action, saying that whatever was done would be wrong and warning me that I shall undoubtedly find myself in trouble for this 'interference'. Asked him what he would have done, had he happened to have discovered the North Gate, to which he replied, 'Pretended I was Nelson!'

This is the third of the Roman town gates which we can plot with accuracy. Telephoned to Sam Blomfield, to let him know about this discovery. He was delighted.

[The remaining walls of the Roman North Gate had been demolished in 1823.]

[See Image 26]

August 24 Thursday

News this morning about advances onto Paris and Marseilles and news too that the Germans are pulling out of Romania.

August 28 Monday

News in the midday papers that British forces are advancing fast over the sites of the diver bases and that the end of the menace is definitely in sight. Unfortunately most of today's papers threaten us with the huge rockets any time now.

August 29 Tuesday

Poulter now thinks something ought to be done about the North Gate to make quite sure of all the details. So I rushed down to the site, saw Jones the foreman, and he agreed to make quite sure that the south return of the gate is where it ought to be.

Went down to the Gate this afternoon and found that Jones's man was hard at it – he had already uncovered a beautifully preserved panel in Roman brick, with the rebate where the leaf of the gate folded back, standing 3 feet high. Most interesting.

Went down again after tea and found that the corner of the return had been safely located. Hull suddenly appeared and was most affable. Rang Alderman Sam Blomfield tonight and told him what had been done. Thanked me for all the work I had put in. Must tell Poulter to go down and tip the men tomorrow. Cannot help feeling a bit pleased with myself, for had it not been for my efforts this great find would never have been known at all.

August 30 Wednesday

See in the papers today that the order for the immobilisation of cars and boats is now at an end. Headlines scream – 'Patten's Drive on Belgium'. Is part of the war really over? Yet the HG is still maintained at full strength and men are still being drafted into it. The Civil Defence people are still hard at it, new recruits are being trained in fire fighting and there is a great ARP rehearsal at the Castle on Thursday. How the CD people do enjoy themselves and how sad they will be when it is all over. Incredible to believe that in a few months? weeks? we may never hear a siren again, or at least not for another 20 years. How strange to sleep quietly in bed. Yet neither Father, Mother or myself have ever slept in a shelter, nor even an Anderson or Morrison.

Set off for the Post for the 1am watch. Nothing happened the whole watch until 4.40am, when we suddenly heard Colchester sirens and diver was in operation a few minutes later. Almost at once Centre came through calling: 'Fox 1, Fox 3, look out for divers'. 'Where from?' I asked. 'The east.' Took the glasses and climbed onto the brick wall and began to search the eastern sky, where traces of dawn were already beginning to show. Almost immediately saw three stars glowing red, then another, widely spaced, between Boxted village and Potter's Farm. Two suddenly vanished but there were no flashes or explosions, so they may have fallen in the sea. Pawsey had the phones and was plotting steadily.

Then another diver disappeared in a flash and a roar. 'Crashed in 38' said Pawsey. We saw a distant flash towards Hadleigh and another towards Bromley pylons. Pawsey said that Centre seemed to be getting very rattled and he could not hear where any of the explosions were.

Nothing else was to be seen, so I hastily washed up but Centre reported more on the way, so the cups got only a brief rinse. The reliefs came at 5am and Pawsey took me back in the car. Once we heard an engine and opened the car door to listen but it was only a Mosquito. Pawsey suddenly said, 'The first few minutes of a raid I'm always windy as hell, but then I'm alright'. Maintained a discrete silence. 'All clear' as I went into Woodside. Miss Bentley called out from her room as I crept upstairs, to ask if it was now alright? She said that while the attack was on, the Horkesley police had twice got her as a wrong number, asking heatedly for the Boxted Head Warden. They must have been expecting trouble.

August 31 Thursday

Poulter talked of his leaving as he is due to retire next year. We both agree that it is high time that I made some move to get back to the Museum before he goes and he wants me to see Sam Blomfield as soon as possible and suggests that I ought to aim to be back by next January. Am not sure whether Folkard would allow me to go but I think he would if I approached him properly. Must do all I can to get back into the Museum.

September 2 Saturday

A few showers during the day. Not good harvest weather and we have another 100 stacks to get up yet. The Chairman worries himself almost ill over labour shortage, possibilities of crops being spoilt and so forth.

Heard on the 1 o'clock news that a new kind of 'device' was used last night – a 'glider' bomb, apparently consisting of an old bomber-plane full of explosive, launched towards the English coast and left to glide in by itself.

To Post at 5pm and heavy rain began and the wind rose to half a gale. What a harvest, hundreds of acres of corn not yet carted. Terrible.

Spent 10 minutes watching a kestrel through glasses, hunting mice in the stubbles.

Just occurred to me that the view due north from the Post, to Stoke by Nayland, is almost the same as Constable's view in the painting in the National Gallery ['The Cornfield']. He must have sat in the fields somewhere below the Post.

[Rudsdale's identification of this site as a possible location for Constable's painting 'The Cornfield' is under investigation. After the war, Rudsdale went on to identify the location of a hitherto unknown sketch by Constable (in the Victoria & Albert Museum) as being a rare depiction of the remains of the Roman East Gate in Colchester in 1813.]

[See Images 27, 28 and 29]

September 4 Monday

Heavy rain nearly all day. Can't understand why farmers don't shoot themselves. Our best wheat all in, however.

To Birch. Long, tedious meeting. Stanley Webb was there talking about the future and he said, 'Let all the Committee land you can this Michaelmas, even to poor farmers. Within 12 months all confidence in farming will be gone and you won't be able to give the stuff away.' Is he possibly right? Everybody filled with gloom.

On news tonight, Brussels [liberated]. Can it really be that we are to sleep in peace again?

September 5 Tuesday

Peace is not yet. Wakened by sirens at 5am, heralding the biggest diver attack we have ever had. Heard about 2 dozen go over and 4 or 5 crash. No firing at them in this district. All hopes that the launching bases are overrun shattered.

Went home to see Father. Told him I should be having a holiday in about a fortnight or three weeks and that I hoped to go to York for a few days and also see the Whitby people. He was pleased.

September 7 Thursday

The 8am news tells of the continued advance into Germany but not so fast as before. Advance into Holland halted. The HG is to be 'stood down' and a lot of men released from Civil Defence.

Got soaking on the way in. Everybody very depressed about the weather. WLA girls phoning all day long to know if they could go home out of the wet.

Heard a very odd story at the Post last night. It is alleged that some of the pigeon fanciers in Colchester are lending their birds to the Army, to be sent to France by 'plane and then dropped by parachute. They are picked up by the French [Resistance], messages attached to them and are then released for home, whereupon they fly rapidly to the cotes in the back streets of Colchester. How odd that in this most modern of wars such an ancient method of sending messages is used.

Another Writtle man came today – Walsh of the Land Agency. He told me that quite definitely food production is no longer regarded as a No. 1 priority.

September 8 Friday

The press today now tells us definitely that the danger from divers ought to end within a fortnight. Find it very hard to believe. Allied advance is being slowed down but quite a lot of people think the war will end in October or November. How curious if it should end while I am on holiday.

September 9 Saturday

Saw Hervey Benham this morning, lent him the Journal extracts from 1938 and 1939 again, for his proposed work 'Essex at War' which he wants to get out next year. Urged him to wait but he is full of impatience and must have it on the bookstalls the moment the last 'all clear' has sounded.

I heard that in Tuesday's attack one diver blasted Blackbrook Farm on Ipswich Road and another fell near Godfreys, Langham, without much harm.

September 10 Sunday

Went by Blackbrook Farm. The diver dropped on the edge of the road, about 30 yards east of the house, which is a total loss. Walls cracked from top to bottom, every window and door gone, all the tiles off the roof. Fortunately, empty, so nobody hurt. Curious how ruins look so old already.

There were several large pieces of the bomb casing on both sides of the road, some nearly 100 yards away. An American came by, looked at a sheet of twisted metal and said, 'My, think what that'd do to you if it hit you.'

To Post at 9pm, on with young Carter. Not much about but a tremendous explosion away to the south-west just before 10. Perhaps a 'plane crashed. The four hours passed quickly and pleasantly, talking ghosts and witchcraft. He told me three excellent stories. They sounded well with a background of a sheep coughing somewhere in the darkness like an asthmatical old man and a distant dog howling mournfully.

September 11 Monday

Bright, sunny, cold, with white frost on the grass at dawn. This weather ought to save the harvest yet but it will be a near thing.

Lord Dudley, in the press today, warns the public to expect a mysterious missile called 'V2', due to arrive at any moment. It is like a huge shell. Tonight Miss Bentley told me she had a phone call from London, from which she learnt that there was a tremendous explosion there last night. Perhaps this, and the unidentified explosions we have heard on the Post recently, are caused by this 'V2', and perhaps Lord Dudley's warning really means that a new attack has already begun.

September 13 Wednesday

Heavy explosions between 11 and 12, shaking the building. These rockets fall so fast they can't be heard until after they strike. There is no means of preventing them. A man named Bevis, who stays at Woodside told me that 3 rockets have hit London, one at Chiswick, last Friday. The whole matter is to be kept deadly secret, the Observer Corps have not had a word about it.

In spite of all the alarm that is being caused, there is one advantage to the victims – there can be no warning, no sirens, and nothing whatever is required to be done about it. Whatever are we to do about these new attacks? At any moment, without the slightest warning, we may all disappear without a trace. There will be real terror in London if these things become as common as the divers are.

September 15 Friday

Up early, to the sound of a threshing machine in the yard outside my window. Looked out to see WLA girls beginning on a stack. These will be our Committee girls, who travel round with each set. They hate threshing more than anything else.

Felt ill today – throat bad and a bad pain in the stomach. Have had this intermittently for years, and always feared appendix or duodenal ulcer. Yet it always goes off.

To the Post at 9pm. Nothing whatever known or heard officially of rockets. The policeman from Horkesley came in for an hour and said he thought it was nothing but rumours and said no official warning had been given to the police at all.

September 16 Saturday

This afternoon to Holly Trees and had a long talk with Poulter about my going back to the Museum. He is very anxious that I should. This evening talked to Alderman Sam Blomfield. He too wants me back, the proper course being that the Committee shall apply to the WAC for my release. Feel sure that this can be arranged, without too great a difficulty but of course the Ministry of Labour must also agree.

Felt very happy indeed. Am practically certain to be back in the Museum by the New Year and who knows, the war might be over by then? The matter of pay is very difficult. Pointed out to Sam Blomfield that I am getting roughly £5 a week, whereas I was only getting £3 at the Museum in 1940. Told him I could not go back for less than I am now receiving – I would though, I'd go back for 50/- a week if I had the chance.

September 17 Sunday

Tremendous noise shortly before noon and went out to see a vast fleet of Fortresses, Liberators and Dakotas, nearly all towing gliders – there must have been 300 at the very least, all heading due east. It was obvious that a major operation was under way, doubtless the occupation of North Holland. It was an extraordinary sight, this vast mass of machines and men sailing to war. Quite incredible. There were hundreds of fighters in escort.

To the Post at 1pm. By 2 o'clock, the huge armada were coming back, hundreds and hundreds, sailing along, very low. Some of them had the doors open, where the last men had dropped out. At 3.45pm the radio made a special announcement that the Allies had landed in North Holland.

In the evening cycled up towards Stoke and saw a group of Italian prisoners near Tendring Hall, laughing and talking with local girls. The Italians are quite irrepressible, whatever their circumstances.

September 18 Monday

Rang Spivy [at the Ministry of Labour] and slipped out to see him. He was most affable, heard my story, looked up my dossier and told me that there was no reason whatever why I should not go back to the Museum as soon as the Museum Committee like to apply for my return. I was quite delighted.

[Later on] called at Holly Trees and Poulter told me an infuriating story. Alderman Sam had got cold feet and got Poulter to go to Spivy. Poulter then came back with the exact opposite to what Spivy told me. He says Spivy made it very clear that it was entirely my responsibility – that I must give notice to leave the WAC, become out-of-work, report to the Labour Exchange, who might then direct me back to the Museum, or, alternatively, I can apply to the Museum Committee to have my old job back. This I would not do under any circumstances whatever, the post is still mine and I have never left the employment of the Corporation. It is scandalous that I should be treated in this way after all I have done for the Museum. If Sir Gurney were alive it would not have happened.

To Boxted, darkness growing, flooding the road with light from my un-obscured lamp, for the first time since 1939. The Government have at last decided that perhaps bicycle lamps are not such guides to bombers after all, particularly when there are no bombers.

Went up to the Post early. Minter was on with me, talking about rockets. He thinks they may be launched from aircraft flying in the stratosphere.

We spent a quiet night, talking about farming and listening to the girls at the Centre reading fortunes to the men on the Easys until 4am, when there was a sudden cry of 'Diver!' Sirens at Colchester were 5 minutes later and Centre told us and the other two Foxes to look out for a diver on one-four, coming straight at us. We could hear it plainly coming along the valley, over Dedham and Stratford. I had the phones and Minter was plotting.

Centre said, 'Can you see it Fox One?' and I answered, 'No, only hear it, clouds are too low.'

She then said, 'Has it cut out yet?'

'No my God, and it's heading straight for us by the sound.'

Immediately it did cut out, apparently right above us. I shouted: 'Christ! Look out! It's right on us!'

Both Minter and I crouched against the Tower wall.

Centre came through, calmly and said, 'What's that? What did you say?'

'It's cut off, it's going to crash somewhere here' – yet there was nothing but a gently swishing noise among the clouds, while we waited and waited, and the infernal thing floated away to the west until I heard Easy 3 report it crashed on 1951, somewhere the other side of Braintree. Yet sometimes, as soon as the engine cuts, they fall like a stone.

September 20 Wednesday

Office at 9. Asked Folkard for a week's leave next week. He agreed grudgingly. Yet he is not a hard master. It is simply that his boundless energy makes him incapable of seeing when somebody else is quite worn out.

September 21 Thursday

Daphne has gone to Manchester, to try for a job as a teacher. Can't blame her but shall miss her.

Called at home, Father very well and then to Holly Trees, where Poulter told me with much laughing that the famous 'secret place' which the Army dug 3 years ago by Duncan's Gate has been found, broken into and some hand-grenades stolen.

Poulter told the police, who had forgotten all about the place, and they told the Army, who had never heard of it – the people who dug it and stocked it with explosives having long since disappeared. Apparently it was full of bombs and ammunition, to be used by saboteurs after the Germans had occupied the town but nobody knows how much there was, nor how much is stolen. A heap of Army blankets shows that somebody has been sleeping there.

September 23 Saturday

The last day. Worked hard all the morning.

To Post at 9pm. A clear, starlight night and not very cold. Thought the quiet too good to last and diver came on before 10, before we had had any tea.

A few Mosquitoes came around and then we saw a diver to the north-east, over Dedham way, in a cone of searchlights. It seemed to track along the river, over Stoke Church, at great speed but not very high, its light huge and flickering. One of the Mosquitoes suddenly dived from about 3,000ft, with lights on, tracer squirting. We both cheered. Nothing happened. The 'plane did it again and had another shot. Still the diver went on steadily, until it suddenly flared up into a great ball of fire, tongues of flame shooting out all round. The 'plane still fired and the diver still went on, by now about over Nayland. It seemed hours before the flame finally went out and then another few seconds passed before the diver crashed on the marshes, a wave of scarlet flame flecked with silver flowing up behind the trees. There was a tremendous explosion and the Post shook so that the flame of the lamp ducked down. 'Well' said old Diaper, 'That was a piece, I must say!' Then he reported the thing out – 'Fox One, diver crashed on 3547, about 3 miles north-west of the Post.' We were breathing again until Diaper heard over the phones that another diver was coming up on the same line as the first. We saw it, a third behind it. Both rushed by, about a mile north of us and disappeared from view like twin comets.

Diaper, still on the phones, suddenly said, 'Christ! They've got Easy One!' and told me he had heard Easy One say the third diver had cut out to his east almost above him and then his voice shouting, 'We're baling out, Centre!' after which his line was silent and did not answer to repeated calls from Centre and the other two Easys. We were both very shaken and saw in imagination two little figures dropping over the wall of the post and running away across the wet fields, lit by the flame of the explosion. 'Ah well,' said Diaper, 'maybe they're alright. P'raps it's just brought the wires down, so they can't talk.' We said nothing more about it but we were both thinking 'it might be us'.

There were two more flashes far away, beyond Hadleigh, and then diver was off and the first 'all clears' came through. 'Good,' I said, 'now we can have a cupper char. Reckon we deserve some,' and old Diaper replied, 'Kettle's on the boil.' So we sat drinking out of the big mugs (tea too strong as usual), staring at the notices on the brick wall in front of us, about Gas and Recognition tests and so forth, both still thinking about that shout of 'We're baling out, Centre'.

At last 1 o'clock came round and I got away, happy in the knowledge that I shall not see the Post again for a fortnight.

[Rudsdale left for York the following day and visited Whitby, Inverness, Edinburgh and Berkshire. However, illness and anxiety about the ongoing V1 and V2 rocket attacks on Essex delayed his return to Colchester until November.]

November 29 Wednesday

Strange to open this book again, after more than 8 weeks. Dear Father welcomed me just as if I had been away 8 days instead of 8 weeks. Told the old man a few jokes, described York and Whitby and pleased him.

Went out to Boxted and called at Little Rivers. Mr and Mrs Rose were very kind and welcoming. Told me all the chatter of the WAC and the local war news. There is now hardly a parish in Essex or Suffolk which has not had a diver in it.

Left at 11, under a brilliant moon. Not a 'plane in the sky. Kettle simmering at Woodside and made tea and ate cake. How kind of Miss Bentley. Then to the old familiar bedroom.

November 30 Thursday

Felt bad today – head, belly, legs. Am I really ill?

A few distant explosions of rockets from time to time. Wonder what the Germans are thinking up next. All hope of the war ending is now given up. It may last another year or more.

Went up to Holly Trees to see Poulter. Very little said about my absence – hardly asked me how I felt and made me wonder if I really looked changed. Asked him – 'What about my coming back?' He told me it was entirely up to me and that neither Sam nor Hull will make any move on my behalf. All my gloomiest prophecies are coming true.

December 2 Saturday

Called at Holly Trees. Saw in the 'Museums Journal' that there is a vacancy for a Curator at Wisbech in the Fens. Feel I must try for it. Simply must do something. Have never been there but have heard much about the place from Penrose. There are many fine Georgian houses there and the Peckovers, Penrose's people, are the great family.

December 4 Monday

In the early hours of this morning decided to apply [for the post at Wisbech Museum] and shall go over and see the place on Friday. As soon as I got up, wrote a letter to that effect and posted it in Colchester.

Went home and found a letter there from Folkard, asking me to call and see him. Felt glad I had written to Wisbech. Rang him up. Felt terribly bad while I did it but he sounded friendly. Told Father I was after Wisbech. He seemed genuinely glad and wished me the best of luck.

To Holly Trees and told Poulter what I intended to do. He was completely taken aback and told me I was absolutely potty. How, he demanded did I think Colchester would get on? Did I not know he had stayed on only to 'keep the place warm for me?' Had I no sense of responsibility? Calmed him down and pointed out that I was only going to look at the place and had by no means got it. He said: 'Of course you'll get it.'

There is now a 'dim out' in Colchester and windows give a faint glow for the first time for more than 5 years. Nobody seems to mind streams of light pouring out of doorways, either.

Rang the Sissons and told them about Wisbech. Sisson knows the place and recommended it as a delightful little town.

December 6 Wednesday

[Went] to see Capt Folkard. Felt very nervous but he was extremely pleasant. He let me down lightly, said he had seen Col Round (who is very ill) and it was suggested that I might resign as Secretary and then undertake part-time work for a while until quite fit again. Thanked him and agreed to the suggestion, although everything depends on what happens at Wisbech.

December 8 Friday

Wisbech
Am writing this in Room No 6 of the White Lion Hotel on South Brink, looking out onto the muddy swirling Nene under the darkening sky, to the lovely row of Georgian façades on the opposite bank. Street lamps glow on the water's edge, reflecting on the rushing tide and there is a distant harsh murmur of voices with sometimes the clatter of wooden soled boots on the pavements. Feel that I have today made an irrevocable decision.

This morning's train journey ran over the endless Fens, across canals and dykes, the landscape a huge flat disk, dotted with groups of Italians working in the sugar beet, Percheron horses tailing across the black peaty wastes and a few gangs of Land Girls. Long wait at March and the rain came swooping across the dykes and muddy fields, bitterly cold. Off at last, through a tiny station called Coldham and so to Wisbech.

Found the church, with the Museum on the far side of it, facing a neat little square of Georgian houses. It is a large plain yellow brick building, approached up a flight of steps, with columned façade and MUSEUM cut deep on the lintel. General appearance pleasing and delightfully old-fashioned. *[See Image 30]*

Went up the steps and was greeted by a gaunt sad faced man, with a very red nose, who was accompanied by an equally sad looking parson. This was Curtis Edwards, the Curator, and Canon Stalland, the Vicar, who is one of the Trustees. They were both very kind and showed me over the Museum and Library, which is a really delightful surprise. The place is well-built, beautifully clean and quite well arranged. A little shaken to find that it apparently wishes to emulate the Fitzwilliam Museum – 'object d'art', Greek pottery, Egyptian urns, etc. with hardly any local archaeology at all but if I came here I can soon alter this.

On the opposite side of the building is a magnificent Library, quite 70 feet long. It is said to contain 12,000 books, including many first editions. Curtis Edwards said the whole lot was almost destroyed by the ARP authorities in the early part of the war, when they requisitioned the premises. They are still occupying part of the basement, where there was formerly another Library, the 'Town Library', which was ruthlessly bundled into sacks and taken to the Workhouse, where it is still stored, despite every effort on the part of the Town Clerk to send it for waste paper!

The finances are mostly from endowments and seem to vary a good deal. Anyway, there seems to be ample to pay the not very high salary of £225.

Quite fell in love with the whole place and thought of how I would spend long hours in the Library, surrounded by my books and papers.

The variety of the exhibits is quite astounding. Among other things there is the original manuscript of 'Great Expectations', at present kept at the Bank. There is no catalogue of the Museum and the Library. Poor old Curtis Edwards said sadly: 'I often meant to tackle it but never did.' He has been there for 22 years. Gave me a cold little chill to think that I might be saying something like that in 1966.

This place has great possibilities, in spite of Curtis Edwards's cautious pessimism about the lack of local interest. He said that only since the war had there been any school-parties, the London schools evacuated to the town expecting a museum service similar to that enjoyed in London. Local schools never came. It seems to me that the educational side of the place might be worked up a good deal, which would in itself create local interest and support.

If I come here, this must be the leading Museum of the Fens, illustrating every aspect of Fen-history and Fen-life. At present there is not a single example of agricultural tools.

Curtis Edwards asked me to go home with him for tea. Mrs Edwards, elderly, slight and very pleasant, made me most welcome. After tea, we met the senior Vice-President of the Committee, Mr Guy Pearson, a charming old Yorkshireman, who has been here for 40 years and still retains his Yorkshire accent. He is in charge of the management of the Committee. The President of the Institution is the Hon Alexandrina Peckover, who is aunt of Lionel Penrose. Penrose's brother, Alexander, is a member of the Committee.

Back to Hotel at 9.30pm and settled down in the bedroom to write this. Am quite determined to come here if I can.

December 9 Saturday

Back to Museum and saw Curtis Edwards once again. He had obviously made up his mind that I am to have the post but don't know what his influence with the Committee may be worth. I don't think I ever wanted anything as much as this in my life. War has been unknown here for a couple of years or more and it is unlikely that the place will ever be attacked again, unless the Germans get the idea of sending divers over the Wash. The place seems utterly remote and yet actually only some 70 miles north of Colchester.

Tonight lay thinking about Colchester – the last thing I want to do, but in view of Sam's attitude, Hull's attitude, the impossible war conditions and so forth, what alternative is there?

December 10 Sunday

Whilst waiting for the Colchester train met a very pretty girl [from] Fletcher's Farm, Fordham. Told her I was with the WAC and she laughed and said, 'Father waits for you chaps with a gun!'

Got to North Station and as I walked down the station slope, under the grey skies, there was the dull roar and rumble of a rocket a long way off and I knew I was back in Colchester.

Saw Poulter and told him all. He was quite shaken and said if this comes off it is certainly 'the end'. The poor old man kept saying, 'I never thought you'd go.' Argued with him, as to whether he would take a firm stand with Sam? But he said it was useless. If I am to go back to the Museum, it is to be on a fresh application from myself. I said what about Sir Gurney Benham's agreement that I was 'lent' to the WAC? What about the fact that I was still legally employed by the Corporation and paid through their Borough Treasurer? The old man said: 'Look, laddie, you just don't understand – Gurney's dead, the Doc's dead, and you've got no standing with Sam.' Then he said, 'Look, why don't you apply at the next meeting to come back?' But I won't. I did that in 1928 but I'll never do it again. If Colchester Museum want me they can ask for me.

December 11 Monday

Told Father all about Wisbech. He was very excited and seems to hope I shall be successful. If he really feels this, it will make it easier for me to leave him.

Wrote out my official application, addressing it to Curtis Edwards. Felt much better when this was done.

December 13 Wednesday

Hard frost. On these cold nights the Americans often keep their 'plane engines running all night to avoid the danger of having them immobilised by freezing. Many 'planes going out this morning and frequent, though distant, explosions of rockets. It is now admitted that rockets and divers killed 700 last month.

December 14 Thursday

Called on Hervey Benham and talked to him about my plans. He was completely taken aback.

Still no word at all from Wisbech. I understood from Curtis Edwards that the matter was regarded as urgent by them, as his health is so bad that he cannot continue in the New Year – he certainly looked very ill.

December 15 Friday

Letter from Wisbech – I have been appointed Curator and Librarian. Delighted. Went at once to see Spivy at the Ministry of Labour, who agreed that there was no reason against my accepting the post. Wrote to the Town Clerk and formally resigned from my post in the Museum, which I have occupied since April 1928.

Wrote to Wisbech and accepted the offer with almost indecent haste. To Holly Trees and saw Poulter. He was quite horrified and said, 'Boy, boy, you'll regret it, you're a fool to go.'

Father is really delighted and is genuinely glad that I have got a place of my own at last.

Tremendous amount of things to do – arrange to go to Wisbech again, write to Hull, write to Sam.

December 19 Tuesday

Wisbech
Spent the whole time in the Museum, going through the collections and particularly the Library, which quite staggers me. What joy working through this stuff! Am just a little apprehensive of the caretaker, Miss Thompson, who looks as if she could be very troublesome and I gather from Edwards that on occasion she is.

Back to the hotel for 'supper' as they call it, served in the Northern way at 6 o'clock. They have quite a lot of north country habits here.

December 20 Wednesday

Set off from Wisbech in a bitter raw fog. Near Welney, a party of young Germans were lined up outside a Norfolk County Police Station, nobody apparently in charge of them. They wore kepis and long brown over-coats or ground sheets. Further along two Italians were working silent and glum in a wet ditch.

Finally got to Colchester, then to see Poulter. While we were talking a rocket fell in the distance and Poulter said that early on Monday morning a rocket fell on Hoffman's Works at Chelmsford killing over 200 people. Miss Bentley had also heard the rocket story and said that about the same time 18 divers were sent south of Colchester, with many more rockets. Looks like a concentrated bombardment.

December 21 Thursday

This afternoon went round to the WAC office and saw Capt Folkard, who was very kind. He gave me a hint that he is leaving in about a month and old Spencer is off at the end of the week. The family is breaking up.

Home to tea. Rockets fell occasionally but always a long way off. How I want to get away from this. Father and Miss Payne well and excited at my description of the treasures of Wisbech Museum. Told the old man he would have to make the effort to come over there to see it. He grunted unbelievingly but I think he might.

Listened to 9pm news, very bad. The latest German attack has broken the Americans and on Tuesday the advance was only 5 miles from the French border. Great alarm as to whether they will take Antwerp? It is admitted that the Allied High Command was caught unprepared as no attack was suspected. Hints in the press that Germany may still win, even now. In August, the war was to end in November, in October – at Christmas. In November – next Easter. And now? End of 1945? Or 1946?

December 22 Friday

News of battles in Belgium very bad. German Army quite unchecked and likely to gain the Channel coast again. They are already past Liège. Fog is holding up the Allied air offensive but the RAF manage to spare men and machines to bomb Trier and Bonn, which are being systematically destroyed. Some talk as to whether Eisenhower will be dismissed as well as Montgomery.

Letter this morning from the Town Clerk, accepting my resignation, thanking me very briefly for my 'active interest' for 17 years and releasing me on December 30. So that's that.

Enormous crowds in the town but practically nothing in the shops. This is the first war Christmas when the lack of goods has been so very noticeable – no Christmas cards, a few calendars at 2/6 or 4/-, no lamp batteries. Plenty of women's clothes but nobody has the coupons for them. No puddings, hardly any turkeys, no poultry but a few skinny old chickens at 35/- or £2 each. But the lights streaming out of shop doors looked bright and cheerful and give a sort of memory of 'before the war'.

Lots of motors rushing about, people carrying bundles of holly and mistletoe, laughing girls, drunken Americans, not quite so drunk Canadians. Impossible to believe that less than 150 miles away the Germans advance irresistibly, over the very ground from which they retreated 3 months ago. People now talking about an election in May or perhaps in October.

The 9pm news was gloomy – another quarter of a million men to be called up. What a terrible shock this must be to thousands of families this Christmas time.

Paragraphs about my going in the 'Standard' and 'Telegraph' tonight and several people stopped me in the streets today to congratulate me.

I hear from various people that the rocket on Hoffman's killed 50 not 200 people but there is tremendous damage. The rocket fell just clear of the works and brought down most of the remaining houses in Henry Road, where so much damage was done in a raid in 1942. Chelmsford has suffered much more than Colchester so far.

December 23 Saturday

To the stables and gave Hampshire some tobacco for Christmas. 'Boy,' he said, 'I can't believe as you're a going! That don't seem right to have these stables here without you!' So if my absence is never even noticed in Colchester Museum, I'll be missed in the long dark evenings and the bright summer days when the stables are cleaned out and the ponies are groomed in Port Lane.

December 24 Sunday

Spent most of the day writing and preparing stuff to take to Wisbech – I travel tomorrow week. Big explosions during the day but always far off. People wondering whether the Germans, being hard-pressed, will respect the old custom of the 'Christmas truce'. There have been no raids on Christmas Day since the beginning of the war.

A grim, but not unexpected, bit of news on the radio – a big diver attack has been made against the North of England. By bringing air-borne flying bombs to within a few miles of the East Coast, they can be sent easily right across the country to places like Manchester, Widnes, Leeds or Sheffield.

December 25 Monday

Hundreds of aircraft went out so there is no truce on the American side anyway.

Went into Colchester for Christmas dinner at home. Miss Payne laid on a royal spread and obviously meant to show me that she could keep up Mother's standard, which she certainly did. There was chicken and plum pudding and custard and fruit and all the old china was in use, just as it always had been. She kissed me fondly, gave me a pair of woollen gloves (most acceptable) and talked incessantly.

Then went down to the stables and was horrified at the amount of rubbish to be dealt with this week. Robin goes to Fisher at Boxted on Saturday, I shall not see him again. Bob is still at Ardleigh and likely to stay there, Hampshire's pony is sold and only the little jennet remains, all alone in the stable. She was filthy dirty so cleaned her down and bedded her.

Back home to a real Christmas tea and then went up to the Castle to see about my bed and blankets. First time I had been in there for months. The 'Oven' looked forlorn and desolate, just as I had left it. How frightened I have been in that horrible little room. Decided to put on the Vault lights and look round below.

The place was damp, great globes of fungus hanging from the wood frames of the bunks. Suddenly thought – how odd if the sirens should sound now, the last time I am here and immediately they did sound. Rushed back upstairs and before I could open the main door someone was banging on it. It was old Butcher, arrived for the evening fire watch. He was pretty startled to see me and said grimly: 'Good long time since you were here for an alert.'

It was a brilliant moonlight night but before we could begin to wonder what was happening the 'all clear' sounded, so no doubt a false alarm but the record of no alarms at Christmas was broken.

Could not find my own blankets anywhere. Mother's deck chairs, which were used 3 years ago by the roof watchers, have gone, no doubt for firewood.

December 26 Tuesday

Went to the Castle, through streets almost as deserted as they were yesterday. Went all over the place perhaps for the last time. Everywhere dirt and neglect, odd exhibits left all over the place, quite regardless as to where their fellows may be. The Great Hall looks like a railway luggage office at the end of a busy day. My beloved agricultural tools are all battered and broken and their labels destroyed.

Went up onto the roof and walked around thinking of those hundreds of nights up there, the searchlights, the flares, the guns, the night of the fire at the 'George'. There will no doubt be many more worse nights but I shall not be there.

In the old office, in the Great Hall, the case-keys were in confusion all over the desk. My letter files are still there. In the letter basket are pages which I left there 4 years ago.

Loaded my bed and what remains of my other belongings on the hand-truck and wheeled it home. Had tea with Father. He asked me, how often I should be able to get back from Wisbech? Told him, 'Perhaps once a month.' He said quietly, 'Well, I'll be very glad to see you whenever you come.' I could have rushed out and sent a telegram to Wisbech cancelling the whole thing.

Took the handcart back to the Castle, locked up for the last time and took the keys back to Holly Trees.

Heard one or two distant thumps tonight, rockets falling near London. Midnight news reported that the Germans are nearly on the Manse again and that the situation is 'very delicate'. At this critical juncture, Churchill and Eden have gone to Greece to organise a little war of extermination against the Greek Socialists. I wonder what their cabinet colleagues, Bevin and Attlee, think of this?

December 27 Wednesday

Papers very full of the flying bombs in the North last Saturday. No hint as to what towns were hit but some say Manchester. Thirty people are dead in various places. A 'mining village' is mentioned. 'Weather conditions made observation difficult', or in other words nobody knew a thing until the divers crashed into their towns. How loathsome are these vile, official phrases. Some papers emphasise that the towns hit were full of evacuees who had gone there to escape the danger of London. There were few shelters, most of them having been sent to the South and the Civil Defence had been almost disbanded. The German news-agencies claim V-2 attacks on Manchester.

Saw Mary Ralling and asked her to keep an eye on Father. The dear good woman wished me well but wished more so that I was not leaving. 'Whatever will the Museum do now?' she said.

Evening papers are full of Churchill in Athens. Poulter thinks he has done a wonderful thing and has taught the Socialists in the country a good lesson. He thinks he will win the election as nobody has ever won it before.

December 30 Saturday

The whole day at the stables and at Bourne Mill. Have got things pretty tidy now but sad work. Never again shall I see Bob, with his mane flying, cantering round the paddock under the willow trees.

Walked up the street for the sake of seeing Colchester 'of a S'addy afternoon' once more. To Holly Trees, Poulter in the depths of gloom. At last had to go and said goodbye, as there will be no time to see him tomorrow. He said, as I went out of the gate, 'Don't forget us altogether. Write and let us know what you're up to.'

As I cycled along the Boxted Road in the moonlight, rockets fell all around in every direction, some near enough (although miles away) to make the ground tremble gently, the roaring of their passage through the air sounding like so many distant Underground trains.

December 31 Sunday

Last day. Rushed around all morning and then cycled in to say goodbye to Father. He did not seem very depressed at my going, in fact if anything rather pleased at my success.

Cycled slowly up the town. Holly Trees and the Castle in deep darkness.

Decided to go out to Little Rivers to say goodbye to the Roses but found deep depression there as the baby is again desperately ill. Dodo said that early this evening she collapsed completely and she thought it was all over. The doctor does not seem to know what the matter is. During the evening, rockets fell occasionally. Dodo hates them and was visibly affected.

Got back to Woodside. Settled up with Miss Bentley for everything. She has been very kind to me and seems as sorry that I am leaving as I am to go. She went off to bed and I went outside a minute or two before 12. Faintly and far off came the sound of singing and cheering in the town, then a lot of shouting and a fusillade of shots at the aerodrome where the Yankees were 'making whoopee'. Then all was silent and 1944 ended and with it the 'Colchester Journal'. How strange never again to begin a clean book with those familiar words. Now must begin the 'Wisbech Journal'.

And so closes another year of war and sorrow, with the prospect of yet another before us. The war, far from being over, seems to have begun again from the beginning.

Chapter 7

❧ 1945 ☙

January 1 Monday

Got away just after 6. Found the right train. We pulled out and the fog was so thick across the valley that I saw nothing of Colchester but the derelict sheds of the old brickyard.

At Wisbech went straight to the Museum. Poor old Edwards looking like a lost sheep, seeming surprised that I was there at all and equally surprised that I hadn't got there earlier. My journal boxes and kitbag arrived at the same moment that I did, which was a great relief.

Found it difficult to realise that I am now the Curator and Librarian of this place. Edwards said there would be a Committee meeting at 12, so rushed to the hotel and changed into my blue suit.

The meeting was held in the office. Mr Girling was in the chair and five others came. Mr Levers, Second-Master of the Grammar School, Mr Hastings, an elderly man with a real Fenland accent, old Mr Wotton, a lawyer, Mr Southwell, another lawyer and Mrs Woodgate. Mr Girling quickly ran through what little business there was. I was then welcomed by the Committee. Thanked them and was instructed to make enquiries about a cocoanut mat for outside the door. Made my brief notes for the minutes and the meeting ended.

Rather staggered to find that my salary is paid quarterly instead of monthly, so must really be more careful about money.

Old Edwards came in again after lunch, wandering sadly about. Poor old man, it must be terrible to see one's life's work handed over to another. I went back to tea with him and was most kindly welcomed by Mrs Edwards. She said rather pathetically that she hoped I would not mind his coming into the Museum whenever he could as it was the only interest that would keep him going.

About 2.30pm a telegram came to say 'Happy New Year. Love – Father.' What a dear old man. Sat down and wrote to him at once.

I am a citizen of Wisbech and Colchester is another world.

January 2 Tuesday

To the Museum at half past 9, the caretaker saying, 'Oh, I didn't expect you so early. Mr Edwards never got here until 10.'

And so at last I sit in my own office, back to the fire, in a high pleasant room, with two big windows, one looking out into quiet little Museum Square and the other onto the grey-green churchyard, where the west wall of the church fills almost all the window-space. Felt completely vague, as if I did not know what to do or why I was there but routine habits are strong, even after a break of four years, and I soon began to arrange the place more or less as my old office at the Castle.

Wrote a few letters, then poor old Edwards came doddering in again. Sat writing in the office, the sun shining and the church bell tolling solemnly for a funeral. Eight or nine visitors came in today and twenty-six yesterday. They all seem quiet and intelligent and genuinely interested in the collections. Quite a number of quiet studious-looking schoolboys came in but Edwards warns me solemnly about 'evacuees', who he says are 'the very worst types'.

Spent an hour or two in the Library moving the books. This Library is fascinating and I cannot yet realise that I am in sole charge of it. Reminds me of a dream I had sometime last summer in which I was working in a great library. There is a wonderful collection of early maps and atlases and I hope to have a special exhibition of them in the summer.

In the local section found the Colchester Museum Reports. Some were still in the envelopes in which they had been sent, addressed in my handwriting. Never for a moment dreamt how I should see them again, twelve and fourteen years later.

January 3 Wednesday

Spent busy morning. Found some Roman sherds, including parts of a curious vase in the form of a head, similar to one found in Colchester in 1932. The fragments we have are from Friday Bridge, which seems to be the main Roman site in the district. They had not previously been identified.

Tonight just before 7pm – sirens. Felt too dulled with misery to be really surprised. I was in the lounge and everybody had to say 'Hark! Sirens!', 'Well, I'm blessed, fancy that.' 'Wandering doodle-bug I expect.' Went out just in time to hear the familiar roar and then saw the wretched flickering light of the thing, dashing through the rain, heading in the direction of Peterborough. In about 5 minutes there was a distant heavy explosion.

Cannot say what I felt. Have realised all along that there is nothing to stop divers being sent in over the Wash. My only surprise is that they have not been sent up this way before. Last year at the height of the diver attacks, somebody wrote an amusing article on them called 'So They Follow You Around, Too?' and that is how I feel now. The defences are almost nil. All the available guns are on the coast of Suffolk and Essex and we know from bitter experience that it takes at least a month to move guns to a fresh site.

January 4 Thursday

Busy all day mending Roman pottery. Have not enjoyed myself so much for years. The Elm district seems to be thick with Roman sites, according to labels, and I must get down there as soon as the weather improves. Old Edwards came in for a few minutes, obviously most unwell. Asked his advice on a few points, which seemed to please him.

Heard people saying that the diver which was seen last night fell some four miles beyond Peterborough. The evening paper says 'No casualties' from these divers and 'many shot down'.

January 7 Sunday

Cycled out to Leverington to see the church. Magnificent. Wonder if these glorious churches could be used as they were in olden days, as the social centres of the parishes, perhaps reserving only the chancels or aisles for religious worship. It seems so wrong that such vast glorious buildings should not be used.

To Museum all afternoon. Worked all evening and got several letters done. Had a letter from Poulter yesterday, full of beans but seems to miss me. Poor old man must be very lonely.

January 8 Monday

Levers came in and talked about education and school visits. Very nice man and I think will be most helpful.

Quiet tonight and snow falling gently, glistening in the light of the gas-lamps in the Crescent.

Received a letter from Mary Tovell to say that she is now a State Registered Nurse and is going into midwifery at Kingston Hospital. Her fiancé is receiving treatment for tuberculosis.

January 9 Tuesday

This afternoon to the Food Office and changed my ration-book and identity card. The usual alarming inquisition about one's age, occupation, last address, etc.

The Germans still advancing towards France.

January 10 Wednesday

Old Warby from Friday Bridge came in this morning. A most entertaining old chap. He apparently has a large collection of Roman pottery from the Fens between Elm and March. Warby has been collecting for more than 20 years but nobody has taken the slightest interest in the work he has done. He tells me that he always had the greatest difficulty in getting stuff preserved when discovered and says that in many cases complete pots have been broken up as soon as found and the pieces carefully buried.

January 13 Saturday

To the Museum and saw Miss Ellis, the science mistress at the Grammar School, pretty, blonde and plump, not more than 21 or 22. She wants to bring school-parties in and to use the Library. Excellent idea and should be encouraged.

Crowds in the Market Place, much shouting and pushing about. A tall, hawk-nosed man, wearing a scarlet tam o'shanter, riding breeches and gum-boots and selling cabbages, was shouting at a young boy in soldier's uniform, 'Ah! Got ye at last, have they?' The boy, scarlet and furious, moved away. A convoy of American trucks came roaring through, spattering everybody with mud.

January 14 Sunday

Went over to the Museum. Miss Thompson came in and was very annoyed to find me there. She said she was 'not accustomed to this sort of thing' – 'Sunday work being not at all necessary.' However, stayed in the office all morning, then went down to Warby's at Elm. His collection is really excellent. Had a long talk about Fen archaeology. The quantity of pottery found is enormous. Warby has at least 50 complete or nearly complete vessels and boxes of fragments. He has no scientific training but the highest credit is due to him for what he has done in saving material under the most difficult circumstances. This will at least provide something for others to work on.

Came back through the Park with Italians singing melodiously as they made their way to Bowthorpe Hall, where their hostel is.

January 16 Tuesday

Two very charming women came in this morning from London. They said things were very bad there and the damage becoming serious. Further attempts are being made to evacuate more people but so many, even now, believe that the war is almost over.

January 17 Wednesday

Letter from Poulter to say that there is to be an American photographic exhibition in the Castle and that the American ambassador will probably come down to open it next month. *[See Images 31 and 32]*

Wish there were not so many 'planes going out from Lincolnshire. Noise today is almost as bad as at Colchester.

January 20 Saturday

About midday Miss Ellis came in with a delightful little boy named Woolley, about 8 years old and a most enthusiastic museum man, just as I was at his age. Talked about his collections and promised to go and see them.

January 25 Thursday

This afternoon old Mr Warby came in from Elm with a box full of sherds from Stags Holt, at the boundary between Elm and March, including several repairable vessels, all 2nd century stuff. Brought his granddaughter with him. Said she was not interested in his researches but he said, 'My daughter was wonderful keen on the old relics, but there, a year ago she took and died. Ah well.'

Am delighted to have this pottery, which makes a fine accession for the next meeting. Apparently all this stuff is found when ploughing.

Heard the 6pm news. Russian offensive dying out but there is no doubt the Germans have lost important towns and territory and must be seriously worried. Another big Russian attack may carry them to Berlin. And then what?

January 27 Saturday

Feel excited at the prospect of going home. Caught the Colchester train. Very late in leaving because there was no engine. A railway guard got in. We got talking about the present decay of the railways which he blamed upon 'the higher-ups' and the enormous amount of troop trains going through with men on leave from Europe. Prophesised that things would be much better when the railways are nationalised, which will, he thinks, be done after the war, as he is sure a Labour Government will get in.

Colchester at last at 5pm. How very strange to be home again. At once felt that Wisbech was only a dream and that I had simply been away on a tour somewhere. Home to tea, which might have been one of a hundred Saturday teas except that Mother was not there. Father seemed very well. Miss Payne glad to see me.

Then went to Holly Trees and saw Poulter. Went straight into a long discussion on the Museum. He is due to retire in April and should he leave? The Committee will obviously urge him to stay on, particularly as the war now shows little sign of ending this year. He assures me that my passing from the Museum is quite unnoticed.

January 28 Sunday

Cycled over to Sherbourne Mill. Joy was most kind and asked me to stay for a delightful lunch. Afterwards walked round the farm, looking down from the hill across the snow filled valley, the muck heaps by the stable steaming and Fisher, wrapped in sacks, coming down the path with the milk-pails. A good many 'planes went over while every now and then a rocket fell far away.

Went on into Colchester by Ardleigh and called to see Bob, at Lyon's place. There he was, his great thick coat ruffled in the wind and his magnificent crest as firm and high as ever. He greeted me without the slightest enthusiasm and backed away snorting but crept up to take bread from my hands. Left him sadly, for I shall never ride or drive him again.

January 30 Tuesday

Called at WAC Office. Capt Folkard goes next week and Maidstone is taking over. A lot of new girls but nobody as nice as my dear little Daphne.

To the Repertory workshop and talked to Diana, then took her out for a meal at Last's. Diana says she misses me.

[Left Colchester and] got to March just before 9pm. In the waiting-room was a Welsh soldier, waiting for the Wisbech train. He has been 18 years in the South Wales Borderers and ran away from home to join the Army owing to a quarrel with his father. Spoke of the bad times in Wales in the 1930s. He was in Malta then and the regiment were 'asked' to contribute 2/6 each man per week to help starving children in Wales. He is of a Welsh speaking family from Llanelli but said he had forgotten almost all of it. He got out at Coldham, on his way to the Italian PoW Camp near Friday Bridge.

February 2 Friday

Busy at office chores and letters all day. Am beginning to watch for the postman every afternoon, so anxious am I to receive any letter at all which forms a link with the outside world.

Decided to call on Miss Ellis at Old Market but as I knocked at the door, which was partly open, a most charming, tall, dark woman came hurrying down the dingy staircase towards me and said, 'Are you Mr –?' (something or other). I said no, I wasn't, I was the Curator. 'Oh are you? Well, do come upstairs and meet the Arts Club, I'm sure you'd like it.' Only too delighted I went up the stairs. We went into a large room which apparently serves as a studio and workshop. There were about half a dozen people there including the delightful woman who captured me, whose name is Charlotte Osborne. Everything was very jolly and we had a mug of strong sugarless tea and a bun. This is the best evening I have had since I came to this town.

February 4 Sunday

Russians still advancing but a curious air of caution in some papers. There is a brief report that both Britain and America have refused to give Russia the big credits asked for.

February 6 Tuesday

'Planes going over in great flocks. Prepared notes on the Roman Fens for a lecture I am to give to Lever's Latin class tomorrow.

In High Street today passed two Americans talking in Italian to two of the Italians.

February 7 Wednesday

Set to work to arrange a special exhibit for Lever's Grammar School class in the Library this afternoon. Lecture went very well, a class of 20. Have never talked to children before. Lever seemed very pleased.

Quite a crowd in today, lovely sunny afternoon. Took 7/6 in coppers in the donation box.

February 14 Wednesday

My birthday, 35 years old, now definitely middle-aged, with youth far behind.

February 15 Thursday

Last week's 'Standard' and 'Colchester Gazette' came today. Fire watching has now been ended after a lot of heart-searching on the part of the Civil Defence Committee and the Council. By second post came a most delightful surprise – a large box from Colchester, full of the most unimagined luxuries: an orange, shaving cream, razor blades, a lamp battery, half a pound of chocolate and a dashing silk neck-tie, all from dear Father and Miss Payne, lovely childish gifts to mark my entry into middle age. How extraordinarily kind of them to think of sending these unobtainable things.

February 18 Sunday

Cycled to Friday Bridge to old Warby's and saw his collection again. After going through everything, the old man spontaneously offered to give the whole lot to the Museum now that it is in my care. A most wonderful accession.

February 21 Wednesday

Went out to Bank House to see Miss Peckover. Went into a wide, high hall, paved with black and white pamments, through a small anteroom, very full of furniture and pictures, into the library and there was the tiny old lady, wearing a long black shawl, her hands trembling, standing by a desk. She tottered towards me, saying in a quavering voice, 'Mr Rudsdale, I believe. How kind of you to come and see me!' Alas, it was almost useless to answer, as she is so deaf. Spoke very slowly and rather loudly but she heard only occasional words.

The furniture was all good, solid, early Victorian stuff, with the exception of a magnificent 18th century mahogany desk, near the south window. Here Lord Peckover used to sit and write. The desk has stood there so long that the side nearest the window has bleached almost white. The sides of the Library are lined with high bookcases, stacked with thousands of volumes, ancient and modern, rare and worthless, their gilded backs glinting in the sun. Everything is spotlessly clean. Wonder how it is done, as there is now only the companion, Miss Simpkin, the cook and a maid.

Talked a bit about Lionel Penrose, who is obviously her favourite nephew, and then thought I ought to go. She stood up, smiling sweetly, her parchment-like face wonderfully kind and said she hoped I could find my way out as she thought it too cold to come to the door.

Came away wondering whatever is to be done with this house. The National Trust own it since she made it a gift last year but what is to happen to it? What use can be made? A museum? But how could it be supported?

This evening went round to Clarkson Avenue and saw Mrs Burnett, a very pleasant woman, who was most willing to let me have a room. Arranged to go there the week after next. She charges £3.3, all in.

'Colchester Gazette' came today. The Colchester WEA have been discussing Town Planning. When asked in a questionnaire – what building to do you consider to be the most beautiful in Colchester? – most of the pupils answered, 'The Regal Cinema!'

February 22 Thursday

Saw in 'Daily Telegraph' today that Edinburgh is now preparing for flying bombs and the ARP (almost disbanded) is to be mobilised next month. Yet we are supposed to be waiting for the war to end at any time!

February 24 Saturday

Worked in the Library and was highly diverted by a wedding just below the windows, apparently of some persons of great local popularity, judging by the size of the crowd and the screams and catcalls when the happy couple emerged to be photographed. The bride was accompanied by her father in a tailcoat, spats and a cloth cap. The wedding group were taken by an elderly photographer with one of those old-fashioned stand-cameras.

While the wedding was going on, three small boys in the Museum (Londoners) were looking out of a window. One, aged about 9, said with firm conviction, 'When a man gets married he don't have to buy nothing – the woman brings everything'. We hear that some more children have been sent up from London as the divers and rockets become worse. One rocket fell at Romford a little time ago and did tremendous damage. Some of the Romford people are now in Wisbech.

February 27 Tuesday

Caught the 11.15 to Colchester. Went up town, called for Diana and took her to tea. She was delighted to see me. Went to Holly Trees to see Poulter. How bitterly I regret that I ever left my home.

Walked through the moonlit streets, through the crowds of Americans, soldiers and girls to Winnock Road. Father very well and very glad to see me. They have had several alarms lately. Father still religiously records the time and duration of each alarm in his little pocket-diary.

February 28 Wednesday

Called on Mr and Mrs Rose and stayed talking until 10.30pm then walked home. Thought about Fox One, not a mile away, and would like to have called but they would not want me.

March 1 Thursday

Woke at about 3am. All was quite silent. Suddenly there was a tremendous explosion, the house shook, the windows and doors rattling, and a rocket fell somewhere a few miles away. A few seconds pause and there came the weird, prolonged rumble as the air closed up behind its passage through the stratosphere. Dozed off again and woke at dawn to the sound of 'planes warming up at Wormingford.

[At Colchester] five or six lorry loads of German prisoners came up North Hill and behind them two lorries full of conscripts. Hard to tell which looked the more miserable but the Germans looked considerably healthier than the conscripts.

Beautiful afternoon, brilliant cold winter sunshine. The view of the town from the railway was wonderfully clear and I have never seen it look better, all the dear familiar landmarks standing out, the towers and spires, Barrack Street School, the smoke of a train running into St Botolph's Station, cars on the Bypass Road. Deep, deep, regrets.

Got to March at 4.20pm and found no train to Wisbech until 5.40. Our engine ran through, in the last stages of decay and written on the tender in chalk 'Any old iron? Yes, take me away.'

March 3 Saturday

The usual practice siren this morning. The ARP crowd are disappointed that nothing happens and now go round with long faces saying 'Ah! But you don't know what he'll do next!' Then in a mysterious whisper, 'Gas!'

March 4 Sunday

Asleep last night before midnight only to be awakened soon after by the sirens. Heard the sound of 'planes coming in fairly low. Went down to see what was happening. The clocks struck 1am and there was a distant explosion. Felt despair – if this sort of thing is to begin all over again, what chance is there to oust the ARP people at the Museum?

Walked round the Crescent and went through the churchyard. A policeman stood at the back door of the Museum, guarding the precious lives of the ARP crew. Walked through the Market and saw two wardens unlocking the doors of the surface shelters there.

Flashes in the eastern sky and a curious sound of stuttering, as if a bomber's engine was cutting out. A pause, three sharp explosions and then a long continuous roar for 2 or 3 seconds. Suddenly at 2.25am the sirens screamed 'all clear'. This is the first alarm in Wisbech for two months.

March 7 Wednesday

Prepared to move to 43 Clarkson Avenue tonight. [It is] a very pleasant house. Had it all to myself this evening, so settled in and started writing letters and journal.

March 10 Saturday

A most unexpected visit from Miss Margaret Sherry, daughter of Sherry the chemist in Crouch Street, [Colchester]. Have never met her before but she is extremely lively and beautifully dressed. She is a sergeant in the ATS but in civil life is a journalist on a Bedford paper. Apparently she is a great admirer of Byron and Dr Penry Rowland, knowing we had Byron material in the Museum here, advised her to come along.

Took her to lunch, showed her over the church and the town and sent her back on the 5.10 train. Most delightful girl.

March 13 Tuesday

Old Edwards wandered into the office soon after 10am and a little later, to everybody's amazement, Miss Peckover came in, with her companion, Miss Simpkin. She looked very frail and tottering. She stayed about a quarter of an hour, chatted brightly about the Museum and asked me to go to Bank House on Thursday morning, when she will show me her manuscripts and library.

March 14 Wednesday

At about 2pm a big searchlight battery came through the town and crossed over the bridge in the direction of Wisbech St Mary. This looks ominous as there have been no searchlights in this district for two years now.

March 15 Thursday

Went to Bank House and was shown into the great Library. The old lady [Miss Peckover] was most charming but tottered about in an alarming manner, bringing first one and then another manuscript for me to see. There were two magnificent Greek codices, 10th or 11th century and a 'Chronicle of the World', French, about 1400. Went out into the gardens. There are five gardeners and the two greenhouses and the Orangery are kept going, with the heat on, war or no war. In the gardens is a fine maidenhair and several other rarities. Although not covering a very large area, the odd, straggling shape of the place gives an atmosphere of lonely seclusion.

Miss Simpkin showed me round and coming back through the stable yard, opened a door in the brick wall and led me into the Quaker Burial Ground, a tiny garden with two or three rows of simple tombstones, nearly all of the Peckovers. Here, in the course of time, the little deaf old lady will come to rest among her family.

March 17 Saturday

[Tonight] somewhat alarmed to see searchlights springing up on all sides of the Fens, waving pale gold like inverted moonbeams. Felt sure that this meant nothing good.

Had just had cocoa and biscuits when the siren sounded. Went out. All the street lights were on, burning merrily. Most of them are gas-lights and so can't be put out in any case. A few minutes later a very low flying 'plane came rushing in, right over the town, and then the whizz and shriek of bombs and flashes and explosions. A man came along, in a great hurry and I asked him where the bombs had fallen. He said, 'Either Norwich Road or Clarkson Avenue. I'm going back to my wife – I'll bet she's scared!' and he trotted out of sight.

Got my cycle and hurried down Norwich Road. To my delight the lamplighter was just beginning his round, an hour late, putting out the gas-lamps!

Glad to see the Museum safe and sound. Went inside to find the place full of chattering women and hurrying, busy little men. Continual noise of doors slamming and general uproar. Found Penny [a Warden in the ARP Control Room] and showed him my official pass to see bomb damage but he was very offhand and did not say exactly where the bombs were, insisting though that there had been no damage to historic buildings. It was clear, however, from the conversation all around that they had fallen somewhere on the other side of the church.

Went upstairs to the office, to be met with an almost hysterical Miss Thompson, crying in a cracking voice, 'I can't have you here this time of night! I can't do with it!' I said very mildly that I intended to see if there was any damage to windows but she still screamed 'Go away! And tell these good-for-nothing fools to go home!'

I walked into the Museum. As far as I could see our windows and skylights were safe but as we have no blackout it seemed unwise to put lights on. Went home leaving the ARP gang still in possession.

March 18 Sunday

Went out to see what had happened. What had fallen appears to be a large container, about 4 feet long, containing some half dozen small 'anti-personnel' bombs. The container fell near William Road and the explosives in the Vicarage garden. Several houses in Alexandra Road have smashed windows [including] the Mayor's house. They think there are one or two small bombs unexploded in the Vicarage paddock – the number of explosions did not agree with the number of bombs usually carried in these containers. Saw the Mayor come trotting out of his house, looking very pleased and important – obviously a direct attack had been made against the Chief Citizen!

March 21 Wednesday

Yesterday morning and again today, two RAF men drove to the Museum and spent several hours in the Control Room drawing the parts of the bombs picked up in the Vicarage garden. Our misery last night is summed up in five lines in the papers – 'A few enemy 'planes' 'Southern England' 'met with strong AA fire' – (what a lie!) 'a few bombs were dropped'. No mention of casualties or damage.

March 24 Saturday

News on the radio that the Allies are over the Rhine.

March 25 Sunday

Looked at the 'Sunday Despatch', which adopts an amazingly optimistic attitude [about the war] but another article suggests that the advance over the Rhine may have prevented another Blitz, as it is known that the Germans had recently 2,000 bombers ready. In January we were told by the press that 1,500 bombers were waiting. Are we to believe that during the last two months of intensive bombing, the enemy have been able to increase the striking force by a third? If so, this wicked bombing is obviously useless and must be stopped at once, as it has no effect on the enemy's power and is capable only of destroying non-combatants and their homes.

March 26 Monday

Went below to tackle Penny about our tables and chairs. He was very off-hand and would not give any hint of the ARP organisation closing down. 'Germans aren't done yet, you know,' he said with gloomy relish.

Shortly before midnight was wakened by the siren. Went outside into a horrid grey world, lit with a few glimmering lamps here and there. Heard a 'plane come across from the south-west but the 'all clear' came within four minutes so it was probably a false alarm. Had a sudden feeling that this may be the last alarm of the war. Surely the Germans cannot bother to send out any more raids?

March 27 Tuesday

News in the paper, Lloyd George has died. Long obituary in 'The Times'. I can remember seeing him, his long white hair flowing, as he stood on the balcony at the Town Hall and addressed the crowd after the Colchester Oyster Feast. This must have been 1922 or 1923. We boys leaned out of the windows, above the densely packed crowd, to see the little figure on the balcony and catch a few phrases of the great Welsh oratory.

The news tells us that the Allies are 50 miles over the Rhine but there is no sign of a general collapse. The papers begin to give little hints of a war between America and Russia.

March 30 Friday

News coming over the radio all day about the Allied advances into Germany.

March 31 Saturday

Town was packed today, everybody buying in stores in case 'peace breaks out', when all shops will instantly shut and thereby deprive the population of food and drink.

Bombers were going over all day and the news tells us that the Allies are far into Germany. For the last two days the newspapers have not mentioned either rockets or divers. Eleven generals have been released from prison camps. Perhaps Parrington's brother is amongst them.

Can it really be that we have heard the sirens for the last time?

April 3 Tuesday

This morning a Mr H S Willatt of Elm Road brought in the remains of a skeleton. This was found near Crooked Bank, Begdale, about 18 inches deep. Roman sherds were found in the same field. Arranged to go there tomorrow.

April 4 Wednesday

Went down to Begdale to see where the skeleton was found. The site is in a small field on the north side of Crooked Bank, which was recently ploughed out of old grass. The skeleton was found at a depth of about a foot, smashed to pieces by ploughing. Dug for an hour and found both legs and arms and a few vertebrae. [Later] found I had lost my pen in the field, the one which Rose gave to me years ago.

April 5 Thursday

Tonight went down to the Control Room to hear the radio. The Deputy Controller, Muntzer, came in and looked rather annoyed at finding me there. Tackled him on the matter of the Museum's furniture but he denied all knowledge of the chairs being ours. Showed him the broken table in the ambulance room but he expressed no regret at the damage and rudely said, 'If it's yours you can have it mended and charge it up, but it may be Mr Ollard's [the ARP Controller].' When I hinted at the possible vacation of the basement in the near future, he could hold out no hope at all and pointed out that a full staff would probably be maintained after the end of the war – 'I can tell you, we're pretty worried about what the Russians are going to do.' He then said very rudely: 'I suppose you know we had a lot of bother to get this place? Questions in Parliament and all that sort of thing. Old Rothschild [Wisbech's MP] asked one or two and got his arse kicked for it. I advise you not to stir up trouble.'

April 8 Sunday

A lot of aircraft were out during the night, probably troop-carriers back from Holland, as we heard on the news that paratroops were dropped in North Holland last night.

It seems that the Mosquitoes are now to operate from continental aerodromes, so there may be some chance that the bombers may move over as well. What a wonderful relief if they did.

April 12 Thursday

Have just heard on the midnight news that President Roosevelt is dead of a cerebral haemorrhage. The effects of this may be far reaching – a new President, perhaps an American election – no one can say what may happen. How strange that this man, who held in his hand the fates of half the people in the world, should die from the breaking of a little blood vessel, the same mechanical disaster which killed my dear Mother.

It was also announced on the news that no more men over 31 will be called up after this month.

Had a letter from Poulter. He has now been re-appointed at Colchester indefinitely.

April 13 Friday

There is a very strong hint that Churchill will announce the 'end' of the war next Thursday.

April 15 Sunday

News is taking a rather curious turn today – the Americans are retreating back across the Elbe in some places.

April 17 Tuesday

The 6pm news announced that Churchill had 'postponed' his end-of-the-war statement. No reasons given but this morning's papers say that Eisenhower has made a statement that he will say when the war ceases and nobody else. Must be some serious trouble somewhere. The Russians are getting very near Berlin.

April 18 Wednesday

Two very pleasant Italians came into the Library today and spent a couple of hours there, working through the books with great interest. One, a young man, was an interpreter at the Bowsthorpe Hall hostel.

April 20 Friday

Today's paper reports that Churchill has now said that he cannot understand why there is all this talk about 'V-Day', that he doesn't know when it will be and that he deplores all this idle speculation about it. It seems now that it is unlikely that anything will be done until Denmark and Norway are occupied. However, end of the war or not, all blackout restrictions are to be lifted next week, except for a 10 mile belt round the coast, where lights might help submarines to take a bearing or to shell a town.

April 21 Saturday

Found a letter in the office in Mary Ralling's writing and at once anticipated bad news. It was – Miss Payne is ill and has been in bed for a week. Mary Ralling says that Father is well and happy and that 'everybody' (meaning herself) is running in and out of the house but it is obviously very difficult. Must go down next week.

April 23 Monday

Tonight windows streaming with light, curtains flung back, blinds raised. Some people talk enthusiastically about burning their blackout curtains and shutters. Others are being more cautious and keeping them carefully. The war is not yet over.

April 24 Tuesday

The nights are growing shorter now but still the bombers come and go all the time. Some people consider that the war is over and say openly that they cannot understand why peace is not declared but the Germans still fight on, gradually retreating. War news is very odd – no sign of any link between the Americans and the Russians, which has been expected for the past week. Suppose they attack each other when they meet?

April 25 Wednesday

At 9pm, on the radio, came news of a very serious split with Russia over Poland. Berlin is surrounded but still no linking of the American and Russian forces.

April 26 Thursday

This evening went down to the Control Room and heard the ITMA [radio] show. Still no sign of the ARP people going.

Churchill firmly announces the last of the rockets. Hope he is right for once.

April 28 Saturday

Got to Colchester. Went home and found Father very well and Miss Payne much better. The old man was obviously very proud and pleased at the way in which he had coped with the situation and had looked after her. He was in great form.

April 30 Monday

During the night I dreamt of trees covered with snow and that I was standing on a leaded roof, looking at the scene. Amazed to wake up and find that there was snow, falling thick and heavy, driven by a strong north-west wind, a most extraordinary sight.

Strange to see the early corn, in some places 9 inches high, peeping through the snow. The branches were bowed almost to the ground under the great weight. Snow was still falling fast and boys on the bus were saying 'Let's go tobogganing tonight instead of cricket!' and people were talking about their young lettuces being completely buried.

Went up to the WAC office. Maidstone very pleased to see me and soon had me hard at it settling queries of one sort or another. The old place is quite changed now that Folkard is no longer there.

Had lunch with Diana, then to the Holly Trees. Poulter still on the theme: 'It's a pity you ever left – what a fool you were!'

The sun came out at lunchtime and the snow vanished as mysteriously as it came. Caught the 5.25. A huge ambulance train was in the bay at the back of the up platform, the upside approach blocked by police, with buses, ambulances and lorries standing about. This is the only ambulance train I have seen during this war but I can remember them arriving at St Botolph's Station more than 25 years ago and the wounded men, often caked in Flanders mud, going up to the hospitals in open private cars, amidst the cheers of the large crowds which always used to gather.

May 1 Tuesday

Sent out the notices for the Museum's Annual Meeting. The papers are full of gloating accounts of the murder of Mussolini and his woman.

Listening to the radio tonight at 10.30, there came the sudden news that Hitler is dead. So both the leaders are gone, two men in large part responsible for the most appalling misery known in the world. Hitler is thought to have committed suicide but the facts are still obscure. At 11pm came the news that Admiral Donitz has declared himself Führer.

May 2 Wednesday

In the papers that the Civil Defence Corps 'stands down' today. It was true – Penny was below, packing up papers. I demanded the return of our table. He asked me to leave the chairs down below a little longer otherwise they would have nothing to sit on!

Tonight bombers were going out en masse, perhaps carrying food for the Dutch. The 9pm news reported a general surrender in Italy and the capitulation of an Army of over a million men.

Jones, the Deputy Surveyor, called and was talking about 'peace celebrations'. Apparently there are rifts in the lute – the schools are not going to any parades and some sections of the Civil Defence won't go either because they loathe the Controller, Ollard. All people want to do is to forget about the whole affair.

Air raid alarms are now ended. How very, very strange that is. So the alarm on 26 March really was the last.

May 3 Thursday

Got Miss Thompson to wash the plaster busts in the Library, ready to put them back on the tops of the bookcases, from which they had been removed as an air raid precaution.

The ARP men in the basement all day, definitely moving. Almost impossible to believe.

May 4 Friday

ARP still packing but Penny cannot give any date when they are likely to be clear.

There was news of a big German surrender in the north yet tonight the bombers still stream out in the dark. They may be taking out food.

May 5 Saturday

Still no news of 'peace' but an air of expectancy in the market, with everybody anxiously buying in stocks of food as if for a siege rather than to celebrate a victory. There was no practice siren today.

May 7 Monday

Heard a cuckoo this morning about 6am. Busy day. Committee meeting at 11.30am, only six members came, with dear old Guy Pearson in the chair. I presented the 109th Annual Report, which was accepted. Among the gifts was the metal canister which contained the bombs dropped on 17 March. The ARP people apparently don't want this, so we've taken it. Miss Peckover was made President once more, although it is hardly likely that she will ever again attend a meeting. Then they made a presentation to poor old Edwards – a cheque for £25, as a token of their regard for his 22 years service. The old fellow was most moved, while I sat gazing down the corridors of time at 1967.

And now it is nearly midnight and the war is over. All day there was an air of expectancy, with the press yelling 'any moment now'. Then at last the announcement came on the radio at 8pm. Tomorrow and Wednesday are to be holidays, all shops shut. There is a total German surrender to all the Allies but the Russian attitude is still not clear. By this evening there were flags all over the streets, people standing in little groups, people carrying flags (even quite small Jacks on sticks cost 10/-). Went into Porper's bookshop and a woman came in and said, 'I think I'll buy a book, just to celebrate.'

And so ends this long and disastrous war and I find myself alive and well, with a home and my books intact.

[See Image 33]

Afterword

E.J. Rudsdale continued to serve as Curator and Librarian at Wisbech Museum up to the late 1940s. His father, John Rudsdale, died in 1946. In 1949 Rudsdale was appointed Consultant Archaeologist at Scarborough Museum for nine months but was hampered by poor health and subsequently resumed his post at Wisbech. Throughout the rest of his life Rudsdale continued to maintain his journal on a regular basis. He also kept in close contact with events in Colchester through friends such as Hervey Benham and Harold Poulter (Poulter continued to live at Hollytrees Museum until his death in 1962). Rudsdale published articles on the history of Colchester in the *Essex Review* in the postwar years and became a founder member of the Friends of Colchester Museums in 1949. In November 1951 he underwent an emergency operation for appendicitis but died of kidney failure on 14 November, at the early age of forty-one. The inscription on his tombstone in Wisbech Cemetery states: 'He studied and preserved antiquities.'

Shocked by the news of his death, his friends in Colchester raised sufficient funds for a museum display case to be purchased in his memory and his name is commemorated in the naming of a road, Rudsdale Way, in the Prettygate district of the town. Rudsdale himself, however, had more modest ideas of a memorial. Lying ill with bronchitis in 1949, he rewrote his will and, with thoughts of Colchester Castle, stated that after his debts had been settled:

Any residue to Colchester Corporation with the request that they shall place a small tablet in the Castle Tower, as follows:

In Memory
Of
E.J. Rudsdale, 1910-49??
Who loved Colchester
Here he liked to stand on a
Summer afternoon

It is hoped that his wishes for such a memorial may one day be realised.

Main People Referred to in E.J. Rudsdale's Journals

Baldwin, Charlie, District Chief Foreman, EWAC.

Belfield, Mrs, lived at Birchetts Wood, Dedham.

Belfield, Penelope, daughter of Mrs Belfield.

Bentley, Miss, Rudsdale's landlady in 1944, lived at Woodside, Boxted, near Colchester.

Benham, Hervey, son of Sir W. Gurney Benham.

Benham, Mauna, daughter of Sir W. Gurney Benham.

Benham, Sir W. Gurney, the proprietor and editor of the *Essex County Standard* and the *Colchester Gazette* and Chairman of Colchester Museum Committee.

Blomfield, Joan, daughter of Sam Blomfield.

Blomfield, Molly, daughter of Sam Blomfield.

Blomfield, Sam, a member of Colchester Museum Committee.

Browne, Rose, Rudsdale's girlfriend, ran a café in Church Walk, Colchester.

Butcher, Museum Attendant at Colchester Castle Museum.

Carter, Douglas, served at ROC Post, Great Horkesley.

Chapman, Museum Attendant at Colchester Castle Museum.

Conran, Jacqueline, lived at Valley Cottage, Higham, married to the art curator, G.L. Conran.

Craig, Alec, District Committee member, EWAC.

Cutting, District Foreman, EWAC.

Davis, Diana, Stage Manager, Colchester Repertory Co.

Diaper, served at ROC Post, Great Horkesley.

Edwards, L.A. Curtis, retired Curator, Wisbech Museum and Literary Institution.

Farmer, George, Rudsdale's schoolfriend.

Folkard, Captain F.T.F., District Officer, EWAC.

Hall, Heather, District Accounts Clerk, EWAC.

Hampshire, a friend of Rudsdale's who kept horses at Port Lane Stables.

Harding, Museum Attendant at Colchester Castle Museum.

Hughes-Stanton, Blair, artist, lived at Stratford St Mary.

Hughes-Stanton, Ida (née Graves), Blair Hughes-Stanton's partner.

Hull, M.R., Curator of Colchester Castle Museum from 1926-1963.

Laver, Dr Philip Guyon, Honorary Curator at Colchester Castle Museum.

Leslie, J.C., Executive Officer of the Essex War Agricultural Executive Committee, Writtle.

Maidstone, Assistant District Officer, EWAC.

Minter, served at ROC Post, Great Horkesley.

Nott, Stanley, District Cultivation Officer, EWAC.

Page, Alec, District Committee Member, EWAC.

Page, John, served at ROC Post, Great Horkesley.

Parrington 'Parry', farmer at Sherbourne Mill, Lawford.

Parrington, Joy, his wife.

Pawsey, served at ROC Post, Great Horkesley.

Payne, Miss, housekeeper to John Rudsdale.

Peckover, Alexandrina, owner of Peckover House, Wisbech.

Penrose, Professor Lionel, Secretary of Colchester Civic Society and a renowned psychiatrist, medical geneticist and mathematician. Penrose had taken up a medical appointment in Canada in 1939 and had previously lived at Thorington Hall.

Poulter, Harold, Assistant Curator and technician with responsibility for Hollytrees Museum.

Ralling, Annie and Mary, sisters who were neighbours of the Rudsdales and lived at Winnock Lodge, Colchester.

Rudsdale, 'Dot' Agnes (née Webb), Rudsdale's mother.

Rudsdale, John, Rudsdale's father.

Rose, Dodo, wife of Stuart Rose.

Rose, Stuart, artist and agricultural worker, lived at Little Rivers, Boxted.

Round, Captain (later Major, then Lt-Col) Charles James, Chairman, Lexden & Winstree District EWAC, lived at Birch Hall, Birch, near Colchester.

Round, Joanna, daughter of Captain Round.

Rowland, Dr Penry, the Rudsdales' GP.

Sadler, Ralph, Deputy Executive Officer of the Essex War Agricultural Executive Committee.

Saunders, Jeffrey, a schoolfriend of Rudsdale's.

Seymour, a teacher at Rudsdale's old school, Colchester Royal Grammar School.

Sisson, Marjorie, wife of Marshall Sisson.

Sisson, Marshall R.A., architect and historic buildings adviser, lived at Sherman's, Dedham.

Spencer, District Labour Officer, EWAC.

Tovell, Mary, bookshop assistant at Colchester Castle Museum, trained as a nurse at Erith Hospital, Kent.

Underhill, 'Het' Beatrice, Rudsdale's aunt and mother to F.M. Underhill, lived in Maidenhead, Berkshire.

Underhill, Frederick Maitland, Rudsdale's cousin. He worked as a bank manager and was also Honorary Curator of Hambleden Museum in Buckinghamshire.

Warby, an amateur archaeologist from Elm, near Wisbech.

Warren, Frank, District Committee Member, EWAC.

Waters*, Museum Attendant at Colchester Castle Museum.

Young, Daphne, District Clerk, EWAC.

*Name has been changed

Animals mentioned in E.J. Rudsdale's Journals:

Bob, Rudsdale's horse, a Welsh cob. He was stabled at Bourne Mill in Colchester.

Robin, Rudsdale's horse from 1942-1944

Abbreviations

AA	Anti-aircraft guns
AFS	Auxiliary Fire Service
ARP	Air Raid Precautions
ATS	Auxiliary Territorial Service
ATC	Air Training Corps
BEF	British Expeditionary Force
CO	Conscientious objector/conchie (slang)
EWAC	Essex War Agricultural Committee
HE	High Explosive
HG	Home Guard
NBR	National Buildings Record
NFS	National Fire Service
PoW	Prisoner of War
RAF	Royal Air Force
RAI	Royal Archaeological Institute
RDC	Rural District Council
ROC	Royal Observer Corps
USAAF	United States Army Air Forces
WAC	War Agricultural Committee/War Ag (slang)
WEA	Workers' Educational Association
WLA	Women's Land Army
WRNS	Women's Royal Naval Service, known as 'Wrens'

Places Associated with these Journals that are Open to the Public

Abbotts Hall Farm, Essex Wildlife Trust Nature Reserve
(www.essexwt.org.uk)

Bourne Mill, National Trust
(www.nationaltrust.org.uk)

Colchester Castle Museum and Castle Park
(www.colchestermuseums.org.uk)

Fingringhoe Wick, Essex Wildlife Trust Visitor Centre
(www.essexwt.org.uk)

Hollytrees Social History Museum
(www.colchestermuseums.org.uk)

National Buildings Record, National Monuments Record Centre
(www.english-heritage.org.uk)

Peckover House, National Trust
(www.nationaltrust.org.uk)

Wisbech & Fenland Museum
(www.wisbechmuseum.org.uk)

Dedham Vale Area of Outstanding Natural Beauty and Stour Valley Project
(www.dedhamvalestourvalley.org)

Money and Wages

Rudsdale refers to money in his journals in pounds, shillings and pence (£.s.d). There were 12d to the shilling and 20s to the pound. Shillings are also indicated by a '/' in the text. The sale of horses was conducted in guineas and there were 21s to a guinea.

A Ministry of Labour census of the weekly earnings of skilled and unskilled manual workers in 56,000 establishments, conducted in July 1941, found that average wages for men were £4.19s.3d and £2.4s.4d for women. Rudsdale's wages at the Essex War Agricultural Committee of £4.10s.0d in 1943, therefore, fall within the bracket of the average wage of the majority of the male working population.

Bibliography

Primary sources

Rudsdale, E.J., 'The Colchester Journals 1920-1944', 'The Wisbech Journals 1945-1951', 'The Scarborough Journal 1949' and accompanying notes. Essex Record Office, ERO D/DU 888 (A2308)

Essex Record Office in Chelmsford is an excellent starting point for local history research on the county of Essex. The range of archive holdings is searchable via the Record Office's online catalogue SEAX (www.essexcc.gov.uk/ero). The archives can be used to trace Essex ancestors and uncover the history of buildings, villages and towns. There is also a vast range of resources available to show how events, such as the Second World War, were experienced in Essex.

Printed sources

Benham, H., *Essex at War* (Benham & Co: Colchester, 1945)

Benham, H., Editorial: 'A Man Who Loved Colchester' (*Essex County Standard*, 16 November 1951)

Benham, H., *Life with the Locals* (Hervey Benham Charitable Trust: Colchester, 1996)

Berridge, P. and Hodgson, T., *Guide to Colchester Castle Museum* (Jarrold & Co: Norwich, 1997)

Blythe, R., (Ed.) Private Words: Letters and Diaries from the Second World War (Penguin Books: London, 1993)

Broad, R. and Fleming, S., (Eds), *Nella Last's War: The Second World War Diaries of Housewife, 49* (Profile Books: London, 2006)

Brown, A.F.J. (Ed.), *Essex People, 1750-1900: From their Diaries, Memoirs and Letters* (Essex Record Office: Chelmsford, 1972)

Cannadine, D.N., 'The Transformation of Civic Ritual in Modern Britain: The Colchester Oyster Feast' *Past & Present*, Vol. 94 (1), pp. 107-130 (1982)

Carter, D., *Boxted: Portrait of an English Village* (CLW Publishing: Colchester, 2006)

Clacton VCH Group, *Clacton at War 1939-1945* (VCH Essex: Colchester, 2003)

Clarke, G., The Women's Land Army: A Portrait (Sansom and Co: Bristol, 2008)

Cooper, J. (Ed.), *The Victoria History of the County of Essex: The Borough of Colchester, Vol. IX* (Oxford University Press: London, 1994)

Denney, P., *Colchester: History and Guide* (The History Press: Stroud, 2004)

Foley, M., *Essex: Ready for Anything* (Sutton Publishing: Stroud, 2006)

Gardiner, J., *Wartime Britain 1939-1945* (Review: London, 2004)

Grimwood, I., Land Girls at the Old Rectory (Old Pond Publishing: Ipswich, 2000)

Hull, M.R., *Roman Colchester* (Oxford University Press: London, 1958)

Hull, M.R., *The Victoria History of the County of Essex: Roman Essex, Vol. III* (Oxford University Press: London, 1963)

Parris, L., and Fleming-Williams, I., Constable (Tate Gallery: London, 1991)

Pearson, C., 'Curators, Culture and Conflict: The Effects of the Second World War on Museums in Britain, 1926-1965' (Unpublished PhD thesis: University of London, 2008)

Pearson, C., 'A Man Who Loved Colchester: The Journals of E.J. Rudsdale, 1920-1951', *Essex Journal for History and Archaeology*, Vol. 32/2, pp. 42-48 (2000)

Phillips, A., *Colchester: A History* (Phillimore & Co. Ltd: Stroud, 2004)

Rickword, G.O., E.J. Rudsdale Obituary 'Notes of the Quarter', *Essex Review*, V?ol. LXI p53

Rudsdale, E.J., 'Colchester Museum, 1846-1946', *Essex Review*, Vol. LVI, pp. 1-8; 58-63; 141-147; 189-193

Rudsdale, E.J., 'Morant's 'Colchester, 1748-1948', *Essex Review*, Vol. LVIII, pp. 90-95

Rudsdale, E.J., 'Some Notes on the Siege of Colchester', *Essex Review*, Vol. LVII, pp. 161-172

Sherry Podgorska, M., *The Way of My World: An East Anglian Autobiography* (Courtworth Publications: Colchester, 1996)

Sadler, R.N., *Sunshine and Showers: One Hundred Years in the Life of an Essex Farming Family* (Ingoldesthorpe Publishing: Chelmsford, 1988)

Short, B., 'War in the Fields and Villages: The County War Agricultural Committees in England, 1939-1945', *Rural History*, Vol. 18, pp. 217-244 (2007)

Summerson, J., *50 Years of the National Buildings Record, 1941-1991* (Royal Commission on the Historical Monuments of England: London, 1991)

Thornton, C., Bourne Mill, Colchester: Historical Report (National Trust, 2007)

Wentworth Day, J., *Farming Adventure: A Thousand Miles Through England on a Horse* (George G. Harrap & Co. Ltd: London, 1943)

Wentworth Day, J., *Harvest Adventure* (George G. Harrap & Co. Ltd: London, 1946)

Other titles published by The History Press

A Schoolboy's War in Essex
DAVID F. WOOD

In this charming book, David F. Wood recalls his days as a schoolboy in Essex, where family moved when the Luftwaffe threatened his native London. He describes watc airmen parachute to safety during the Battle of Britain and witnessing a Messersch dramatically crash-landing close to his home. The accounts of his days spent pla with his new friends in the nearby countryside provide a stark contrast to the ra of a war that was going on all around them.

978 0 7524 5517 4

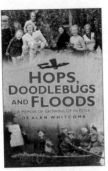

Hops, Doodlebugs and Floods: A Memoir of Growing up in Es
ALAN WITCOMB

This is the tale of a boy born into a typical East End family in the Second World War, beginning with his early memories of hop picking and having little money, moving on to his life in the 1950s and his experience of the devastating east coas floods of 1953. This is an entertaining, humorous and nostalgic read for anyone v remembers Essex in the Second World War and beyond.

978 0 7524 5181 7

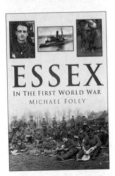

Essex in the First World War
MICHAEL FOLEY

Before the First World War, Essex's economy was largely based on agriculture, and it people rarely travelled beyond its borders, or even out of their towns or villages. Th war opened up a whole new world for the people of Essex. This well-illustrated an informative book sets out the experiences of the county and its inhabitants against was happening in the broader theatre of war. It offers a valuable insight into life for folk in the First World War and will appeal to anyone interested in the county's hist

978 0 7524 5178 7

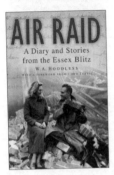

Air Raid: A Diary and Stories from the Essex Blitz
W.A. HOODLESS

This gripping account of the impact of the Blitz upon an Upminster couple wa recently unearthed by the diarist's son. The Blitz diary began less than a year aft Mary Hoodless had married, just three days before the Declaration of War in 19 Such a personal record running through the Blitz period is unique. The entries light on the minutiae of trying to continue everyday life with a sense of norma against the backdrop of fear and uncertainty.

978 0 7524 4813 8

Visit our website and discover thousands of other History Press books.

www.thehistorypress.co.uk

The
Hist
Pres